GW00391060

TOUCHED BY THUNDER

Thank you Kimmage Manor, Dublin, Saint Patrick's College, Wicklow, and Gerry, Marie, Brídeena and Natalie for giving me space and time to finish the writing.

Touched by Thunder

Waylon Gary White Deer

CURRACH PRESS

CURRACH PRESS
55A Spruce Avenue,
Stillorgan Industrial Park,
Blackrock,
Co. Dublin

Cover by Bill Bolger
Cover Illustration: Waylon Gary White Deer

Origination by Currach Press
Printed by SPRINT-print, Dublin

ISBN 978 1 85607 855 9

Author's Note

Because each chapter has a different life theme, some of the dates and events you'll read about in one chapter will repeat in others. This is OK. It only means that the same periods of time are being revisited through other perspectives.

List of Illustrations: Titles, Credits, and Descriptions

Front cover title: 'Choctaw Dancers'
Credit: Gooddog Films

Frontispiece title for foreword: 'An Arrow Through Time'
Description: This painting depicts the story of the 1847 Choctaw donation to the Famine in Ireland, travelling as an arrow through time.
Credit: Courtesy of Action from Ireland (Afri)

CHAPTER ONE: SONGS AND STORIES

Frontispiece title: 'Spirit of the Earth'
Description: This painting was commissioned for *Feast or Famine* by Emmett McCourt and published by Guildhall Press.
Credit: Courtesy of Emmett McCourt

Interior image #1: 'Choctaw Drink Water Songs'
Description: Once the people were on a long journey, and began perishing from thirst. Flocks of birds led them to water, and then gave the people songs.

Interior image #2: 'The Wine Singers'
Description: A '49' is a Plains Indian after-hours social dance where things can get hazy.

Cartoon: 'Otto Von Wieghorst'
Description: Dr Von Wieghorst has some interesting ideas about time.

CHAPTER TWO: FAMILY AND FRIENDS

Frontispiece title: 'Holy Family'
Description: This painting was completed at Kimmage Manor, Dublin.

Interior image #1: 'Red, White and Blue'
Description: Indian boarding school.

Interior image #2: 'Stickball Spirits'
Description: Old-time stickball players with medicine man and drummer.

Cartoon: 'Otto and Oo-tah, Xmas 1988 (again)'
Description: Since Otto thinks that time may flow backwards, Xmas 1988 may well be a repeat for the Von Wieghorsts.

CHAPTER THREE: PAINTINGS

Frontispiece title: 'Rez Boys'
Description: Reservation guys down at the casino.

Interior Image #1: 'Choctaw Stickball'
Description: This painting is typical of my early work, and is in the old two-dimensional style of traditional Indian painting once referred to as 'Bambi Art'.

Interior image #2: 'Gallup Inter-Tribal Ceremonial'
Description: Depiction of an annual event which features fourteen tribal groups.
Credit: Courtesy of Irial Mac Murchú

Cartoon: 'Visually Incorrect'
Description: This kind of cartoon sometimes got me in trouble with school instructors.

CHAPTER FOUR: POLITICS AND PERFORMANCES

Frontispiece title: 'Big Time Contest Pow Wow'
Description: When there's money to win, contest dancers can sometimes get crafty.

Interior image #1: 'At the Edge'
Description: At the edge of the neon are the faces of Yeis that were in the first paintings I can remember.
Credit: Courtesy of Michael Powell

Interior image #2: 'Little Brother of War'
Description: Stickball has always been more than a game.

Cartoon: 'Bunny on the Cross'
Description: Commercialism and religion often merge.

CHAPTER FIVE: IRELAND

Frontispiece: 'Intertwined'
Description: Depicts the Choctaw donation to Ireland, with a Choctaw mother holding an Irish child.
Credit: Courtesy of Irial Mac Murchú

Interior image #1: 'Choctaw Trail of Tears'
Description: At the time of the 1847 Choctaw donation to Famine Ireland the Choctaw people were still being driven out of Mississippi.

Interior image #2: 'Solidarity in Green and Red'
Description: Choctaws at the beginning of the 20th Century. The painting depicts solidarity with the Irish North and freedom for all indigenous peoples.
Credit: Courtesy of Irial Mac Murchú

Cartoon: 'The Prophet Bubba'
Description: In Oklahoma, Christianity and Cowboy culture often merge.

Foreword

Foreword

Waylon Gary White Deer has, since 1995, been a frequently invited and popular visitor to Ireland and my hometown of Derry in particular. Like many Irish people who know him, I have a deep affection for Gary, not just because he is a likeable and engaging friend, but also because he is Choctaw – the American First Nation who helped Ireland during the Great Hunger – An Gorta Mór. I am, therefore, especially honoured to have been asked to write this foreword to his memoir.

Over the past two decades I have travelled on many occasions to the United States of America for meetings on Capitol Hill, The White House and in cities throughout its vast land. The United States is a great country and I have many friends there. Indeed, the Peace Process in Ireland would not have been the success it has been without the support of the United States. For that I will be eternally grateful. Throughout my travels, however, I have been conscious of the plight of America's diverse and myriad First Nations who suffered horrendously as a result of European colonisation.

Some years ago I was honoured by my sadly departed good friend Floyd Red Crow Westerman, a wonderful actor and musician who notably played the role of Chief Ten Bears in the movie *Dances with Wolves*. Floyd travelled to Derry City to meet me and he blessed me in his own private spiritual ceremony.

Since I was a boy I have had an unbounded admiration for the First Nations of America. I have a great empathy for their struggles and an even greater disgust at how they were betrayed throughout history. Not only are they among the noblest people on the planet, their sustainable and environmentally friendly way of life placed them ahead of all others in their respect for Mother Earth. Yet they were described by those who murdered them and stole their land as 'savages'. In 1832, during the height of the Choctaw removals, President Andrew Jackson said of the First Nations, 'these tribes cannot exist surrounded by our settlements and in continual contact with our citizens. They have neither the intelligence, the industry, the moral habits, nor the desire of improvement. They must necessarily yield to the force of circumstance and before long disappear.' Such racism would appal us today; it should have appalled people then.

Just sixteen years later, the ancestors of Waylon Gary White Deer exposed the falsity of Jackson's opinion. *The Arkansas Intelligencer*, reporting the

Choctaw donation of US$170 in March 1847, described it as 'the poor Indian giving his mite to the poor Irish'. What makes the Choctaw donation so remarkable is the fact that just sixteen years earlier, in 1831, President Jackson, through the Indian Removal Act, began the forcible removal of the Choctaw from their ancestral homelands in Mississippi to Oklahoma – removals that continued until the early 20th Century. During their removal, in what was historically the first 'Trail of Tears', it is estimated the Choctaw lost half their people to hunger, exhaustion, exposure and broken hearts.

That the Choctaw would identify with the suffering Irish and respond with compassion and humanity is astounding and humbling. Ever since the arrival of Christopher Columbus on the island of Hispaniola in 1492, the European white man had introduced upheaval and havoc to the native people of the Americas. The Choctaw, therefore, had every reason to turn their backs on a European country that, despite its own colonisation, was contributing to the colonisation of North America. But they didn't.

Stories of the starving Irish awakened memories of the Choctaw's own recent trauma and, from their meagre resources, they contributed what little they had towards Irish famine relief. For that we shall never forget them.

Waylon Gary White Deer is the embodiment of a friendship between the Choctaw Nation and the Irish that was started in the early 1990s by fellow Derry man Don Mullan, and which culminated in a visit to Oklahoma by President Mary Robinson in 1995, during which she thanked the Choctaw people for their humanity towards Ireland. Those who are fortunate enough to know Gary have encountered a highly intelligent and talented Choctaw who, despite the incessant pressures of modernity, has managed to walk the delicate line between old and new, always sensitive to, and respectful of, the traditions and ways of his ancestors. In many respects, this makes Waylon Gary White Deer unique in that he has refused to sell his soul to the insatiable drive of western culture towards increased materialism.

Gary lives a simple life, conscious, like his Choctaw ancestors, that the Earth's resources are to be shared with fairness and justice for all humanity, especially the most vulnerable. It did not surprise me to learn that the commissioning fee of £10,000 offered to Gary in 1997 by the Irish Government for a painting commemorating the 150th anniversary of the Choctaw donation was donated by him to Concern Worldwide for famine relief today. For Gary it is all part of the process of 'Completing the Circle', of reminding us that we share a common humanity and a shared future.

Waylon Gary White Deer will always be welcome in Ireland. And I encourage you to read this memoir which is full of wisdom, insight and no small measure of Gary's boundless sense of humour, as well as examples of his wonderful artistic genius. This is a memoir that will make you think, as well as laugh and cry.

The Choctaw–Ireland connection has enabled Gary to see his Choctaw nationhood with a broader common humanity and human identity. This memoir challenges Ireland, and European civilisation generally, to wrestle with its own identity and history; as well as how both have impacted on America's First Nations. Ultimately, the dialogue that ensues will encourage us to deepen our commitment to building a future for our children; a future founded upon the health of the planet and the just sharing of its resources – the bedrock of future peace and stability.

Martin McGuinness, MLA
Deputy First Minister
September 2012
Derry, Ireland

CHAPTER I

Songs and Stories

FRYBREAD JESUS

Leona sat alone in their small kitchen gazing into her bowl of hominy and pork. She was thinking that he shouldn't drink so much, that he always made trouble when he drank. Well, she missed him, she admitted. She was about to pick up her frybread when she saw it. There, on the brown surface of the bread between two grease bubbles was the image of a bearded man wearing a crown of thorns.

She took the bread, carefully wrapped, to a priest. 'Amazing,' Father Bob said. A mystery. Then she took the mystery home and invited her sisters over. Their responses were the same. Amazing. Mysterious. They placed the frybread on a lamp table with a hand-lettered sign which read: 'Blessed art they who feed upon Me.'

Soon, others came to see the mystery, Indians at first but then Mexicans, Blacks, and finally, white people, parking in the barren yard. A woman squinted at the image, threw down her crutches and tottered back outside. A man said his rash vanished upon viewing it, and another woman claimed her dead son had appeared.

To the little shrine Leona added a donation jar. Within a week she had enough money to pay her husband's fines. Following his release from jail he stayed in town. She went home to wait for him but at midnight she grew tired.

Later Leona heard him stumbling in the kitchen and she rose and shouted from their bed that there was food behind the pitcher in the icebox. Drunk again. Why couldn't he have come home with her? Those who have eyes but will not see, she told herself.

And then when he beheld it he stumbled from the kitchen to feed upon the Body of Christ.

SONGS AND STORIES: 1954 –

Ein zooger aus zooger
(Otto Von Wieghorst)

I didn't find my tribal identity in Ireland, but an Associated Press article once claimed I did. The same article also claimed that I roamed the country visiting tribal elders to soak up old stories and songs. As Von Wieghorst fans already know, to zooger is to spin someone's profile to fit an entertaining news angle, like 'Giant Elk Devoted to Homeless Ministries' or 'Giant Elvis Found Lurking in Jungle Room'. Sure, I'd been zoogered, but how had I really learned songs and stories? And what had really happened to me that time in Ireland?

The first story I remember hearing was told to me at bedtime, maybe in 1954. You might know the way you sometimes only recall things that shine. The details of the room, who the storyteller was and the tone of the words are grey and hazed; but I do recall faint light coming through a window. The story was about my grandparents. They lived in a double-room cabin, a 'dog-trot' house, one cabin used for sleeping and the other for cooking.

> Your grandfather rode to town, leaving your grandmother at home. She was sitting inside watching a dog lying by the fire. 'That dog looks like it could almost talk,' your grandmother said aloud. Suddenly the dog sat up. 'I can talk,' it said. 'If you don't go to the fork of the road by noon tomorrow your husband will die' Then the dog lay down again.
>
> The next morning your grandmother left for the fork in the road, reaching the place about noontime when she heard your grandfather's horse coming up the trail. As he rode into view his horse threw him. It was a lonely area and your grandfather was badly injured, but your grandmother was there. If she hadn't listened to the dog her husband would have died.
>
> *Unremembered relative, possibly an aunt*

With stories there are two kinds that matter; those we feel, and those we know because they happened to us. We carry both kinds beneath our skin, like hidden tattoos. Most of my stories happened to me so I know them pretty well. Those songs or stories I thought that I was meant to feel or know I tried to remember, or else they made places within me. In Indian Country we don't chase after stories or songs. They come around to where we are.

When missionaries took firm hold of the Oklahoma Choctaw they banned tribal stories and songs. Over time almost everyone stopped singing and telling, fearing a pagan hell. When I was growing up, tribal stories were fading and our songs were mostly from the *Chahta, Uba Isht Taloa Holisso*, a missionary hymnal with English subtitles like 'Sinner Can You Hate the Saviour?' It was a stunned and ringing silence, like after a whirlwind.

> The Lord don't like sinners. They piss him off.
>
> The Book of Bubba; *summary of Chapter 13*

Sounds that travelled behind and ahead of us to make an arc of clear remembering were stilled. The whirlwind that scattered the stories and songs had gathered unseen beyond the pine hills. We had once crossed the Mississippi River to leave the wind, to keep the arc of remembering clear and alive but we were overtaken. The whirlwind came strong again above the hills we believed would hold it back, and as it swept the remembering away it also blew something strange in. Shame settled down over the people like clouds of blinding dust.

When I was born, older female relatives were just putting aside their *kiteh*, wooden mortars used for pounding corn, along with their fanner and winnower baskets. Family members were seeing Choctaw *alikchi*, Indian doctors, for ailments. Missionary Christianity had forbidden telling children's stories but they were told anyway. I liked *shukhata anumpa* or 'possum talk' tales. My favourite is about crow and June bug, but there are others.

> Crow once had the most beautiful voice in the forest, but the problem was he knew it. He would fly up on his branch before sunrise and sing all day long and into the night. This got on the other animals' nerves. 'We don't want to hurt crow, but he really needs to stop!' they agreed. 'You're powerful, bear,' the animals reasoned. 'You can make crow stop singing!'
>
> 'I'm too powerful. And you said you didn't want to hurt crow,' bear reminded them. And so it was with panther, wolf, and eagle, all saying they were too powerful to do anything. Then a small voice squeaked, 'I can do it!' The animals peered down and saw June bug. 'I'm powerful too! I can make that crow stop singing!' the bug declared. The animals smiled sadly and walked away as crow droned on above them.
>
> Very early the next morning crow glided to his favourite branch, cleared his throat and opened his mouth wide to sing, but could only make an awful choking sound. 'Caw! Caw!' he sputtered. June bug had flown down crow's throat and got stuck there. That's why crow can't sing. And so it is to this very day.
>
> *My paternal great-grandmother*

There were family stories of witchcraft, little people, and beings in the woods but like many others we moved around a lot, blown restless, and some of the stories moved with us. When I turned sixteen I hitch-hiked from my grandparents' house in the hills to help an old man make *kapucha*, stickball racquets. The game of stickball is old and similar to lacrosse except two racquets are used. Missionaries called stickball a pagan sport.

As far as I knew, the old man was the only ball stick maker left in the world. New racquets hung on a rope stretched across the old man's porch, dangling like charms from a giant pagan necklace. My father once played on one of the old man's teams, but Jesus had all but ended Choctaw stickball in Oklahoma. Sidney White showed me what wood to cut, how to shape the handles and shave down the cups thin to bend into a loop.

> They had a big stickball game with a lot of betting; horses and saddles, money, rifles, blankets. The women wagered everything, down to their handkerchiefs. A champion player was scoring most of the points. One woman had wagered a lot, and was in danger of forfeiting all her bets. She walked on to the ball field carrying a white handkerchief. When the champion player stopped to catch his breath the woman came up and touched his back with the handkerchief. The player fell dead. Her handkerchief had been hiding a knife.
>
> *Sidney White, Choctaw*

Stickball, *kapucha ishtaboli*, is rough poetry. The east goal shines yellow, the colour of the young sun in morning and the west goal, where spirits go, is the red of sunset. Like the sun, the ball travels between east and west, chased by surges of upraised ball sticks or by shouting clusters struggling over tall green grass. But the ball really resides against the heart of the sky, between sunrise and sunset. And medicine is used to win.

Much later there was the time when east played against west at Greenleaf, a Creek tribal town, where we followed in a long line around a ceremonial fire carrying our ball sticks and breechcloths in early morning light as the dance leader sang. We of the east went into the woods behind our goal, and west left for the woods behind theirs. We put on red paint and breechcloths and then we crouched, holding ball sticks, listening to a war talk.

We left the woods and circled our goal as, down the field, west did the same, their shouts echoing back. Then we gathered in the middle of it all, two lines facing, east and west, and we laid our ball sticks down on the earth to touch the ball sticks of west. Our medicine man and theirs walked the narrow space between, stepping over each touching of sticks before we all shouted and grabbed our ball sticks again as the sun was thrown into the sky.

When I was a teenager I started to notice traditional tribal songs. I was at Indian boarding school in Santa Fe, New Mexico. For over 125 years the Bureau of Indian Affairs has used boarding schools to try and turn Indian children into anyone or everyone else, and my family has a history of being in them. The Institute of American Indian Arts was a fine arts high school for Indian students from almost everywhere in Indian Country.

> Let your art be a transition from the old tribal world into the new, modern world. Become part of modern society but take images from your tribal world with you.
> *Lloyd New, Cherokee. Director, Institute of American Indian Arts*

In 1968 a colony of real hippies lived in Santa Fe out on Canyon Road. Postcard adobe buildings had earned the town the nickname Fanta Say. The area was dotted with Indian pueblos, high and purple mesas and Penitentes or 'Penitents' a Christian sect that flogged themselves. In their season, tourists flooded Santa Fe, streaming into shops and restaurants, buying kachinas, silver and turquoise jewellery, camera film, enchiladas, ristras and pinon nuts and sampling the native chilli, either red or green.

On the face of it, our school was exotic, too. Students were Aleut, Seminole, Choctaw, Iroquois, Apache, Muscogee Creek, Hopi, Crow, Comanche, Navajo, Pueblo, Cherokee, Meskwaki, Cheyenne, Pawnee, Assiniboine, Lakota, and from many other nations; teenagers dropped into a high desert landscape of light and energy that ran like gypsy karma through a mix of Spanish food, Indian arts, and American plumbing; enough of a bright feel to provoke the urge to sport sunglasses. For it was that kind of place, and time. Out among the tourists and adobes wafted a big, fat, hand-rolled, late-sixties psychedelic, anti-war, long-haired, free love sort of rebellion. From the Indian school we watched it pass like a hip parade. We began echoing pop phrases like 'right on' and except for our rodeo club members, we enjoyed the parade's rock music scene. And we sort of liked it that beads and feathers were thought of as cool.

> Jimi Hendrix: Purple haze all in my brain, man.
> Otto Von Wieghorst: Vass?
> Jimi Hendrix: Yeah, lately things just don't seem the same.
> Otto Von Wieghorst: This iss because you are dead.
> Jimi Hendrix: Actin' funny but I don't know why …
> Otto Von Wieghorst: Because you are dead, Chimmie.
> Jimi Hendrix: Say what?
> Otto Von Wieghorst: Ja you are dead, und so iss the 1960s.
> Jimi Hendrix: No man, we ain't dead. It just smells that way.

Songs were coming around. I'd been sent away to hear my own stories, to feel with everyone else the kind of place we were in. Some of us seemed to change into wolves; a dormitory attendant said they saw human footprints turning to wolf tracks. And the girl's dorm was haunted by ghosts of long-ago flu victims from when the basement had been a makeshift morgue. There were stories of ice caves inside Taos Blue Mountain. The caves held the burials of Indian babies, it was said.

We heard stories of healing pilgrimages to the church at Chimayo, and tales of Penitente crucifixions. Beyond the city, grey and red and ochre hills flanked rural villages where only colonial Spanish was spoken. Past the school fence the traffic ran like energy lines down into an old Spanish plaza where the City Different kept a war monument dedicated to fighting the 'savage Indians'.

Mainstream Anglos held most of the money, power, and influence. White colonial Spanish clung to the middle social rung, their parish schools staffed with teachers from Spain, and they were followed on lower rungs by Spanish with Moorish blood, Chicanos, Mexicans, and descendants of Spanish–Indian slaves. The lowest rung was for Indians, although we were the people tourists most wanted to see. But we didn't talk about the town's social ladder.

We had our friends, work details, romances, school clubs, trips to town and art classes and we were being moulded into good Americans; as we turned eighteen, male students were taken from their rooms to register for the Vietnam draft. We were left to ourselves, and hung around each other. Our separateness dulled the changes that kept cruising by in the America just beyond the school fence, changes that would some day find us all.

Out in California Indian activists had seized Alcatraz Island and Roger Mudd of *CBS Evening News* came to campus to check the political pulse of Indian Youth. Unfortunately, the school's director fingered me to be the CBS interviewee. But before the school term started my friend Dominic had talked me into trying the bleached-blond surfer look that was trendy. Dominic thought an all-American look would impress his sister Consuela, who I liked. Besides being a bad idea the dye only turned my hair red, and Consuela went back to Mexico.

> In the woods are many kinds of trees and plants. They are the medicines for most of the illnesses we have, even for a broken heart.
>
> *My mother*

Fellow students took note of my dyed hair and began calling me a race traitor. I didn't want to be seen on the *CBS Evening News* as traitorous. I was also clueless about Indian activism, as most of us were. I'd heard of Reyes Tijerina and the shoot-out at Tierra Amarilla, not far from Santa Fe. I'd heard of the Black

Panthers. I didn't know anything about Indians taking over Alcatraz. What I did know was that after school we could all go to town.

On weekends this meant that my friends and I would find someone over eighteen to buy us cheap booze. We would walk the railroad tracks to avoid carloads of white Spanish boys who didn't like having an Indian school in their town. Every so often one or two of us would forget this fact and wander off to get caught, knocked down, stomped, and whipped by belts tipped with filed metal buckles, or flailed by chains.

So it was regrettable when two friends and I went to a Spanish high school dance to try and pick up girls. When we got there we ducked into their bathroom to guzzle down our half-pints of rum and steady our nerves. Soon I was seeing double. I remember lurching towards a girl and pulling her onto the dance floor. It was a slow song and I wrapped my arms around her mostly to steady myself.

She responded by holding me very tightly. There was a tap on my shoulder. It was the girl's boyfriend. I held the girl tighter and ignored him. Squinting with one eye shut I saw the boyfriend waving and pointing, along with several of his excited friends. After the music ended there was a pause. Something was about to happen, but I tried to talk to the girl anyway.

> Hey Chollie. I'm drunk goddamit. I'm drunk. Well I'm drunk you know, but I'm OK. Chish na to?
>
> *My father*

Suddenly my friends hustled me across the dance floor and through the front door. Half the dance piled outside as they shoved me into a waiting car and ran. Five carloads began chasing us. My get-away driver was a friend of a friend and he was stressed, zooming down side streets while glumly checking his rearview mirror. I drunkenly flipped off our pursuers, which upset the driver even more. After a nervous run he slowed in front of my school and yelled at me to jump. I rolled out, hit concrete and banged my knee just as our pursuers pulled up.

I rose and hobbled towards the bare length of stretched chain separating the school driveway from the boulevard while footsteps thudded behind me. As I dove under the chain the footsteps stopped; my pursuers possibly fearing hoards of redskins lying in ambush. On the other side of the chain from me the Spanish boys shouted and waved their belts. It was like an old movie scene where a hunchback taunts an angry mob from a church bell tower.

Otto Von Wieghorst: Listen to zee bells, Chimmie. They are beautiful, Ja?

Jimi Hendrix: You're trippin', Otto.

Otto Von Wieghorst: So many colours uff sounds.

Jimi Hendrix: I'm hip.

Otto Von Wieghorst: Look, Chimmie, far up in zee dark tower. See zee bell ringer? Who iss this mysterious creature?

My knee was starting to throb. I flipped them all the finger again and then like Quasimodo, limped unsteadily towards the beckoning lights, saved by the senseless grace of the hammered. It wasn't long before such behaviour landed me before the student tribunal; high achievers, scholars, and athletic types appointed by the school. At first I was happy to merely stand accused of skipping kitchen detail, a minor offence. But my punishment was expulsion and the tribunal seemed to want to order up a public flogging as well.

Skipping detail was the only provable complaint against me, but the tribunal seemed to have been given orders to make the most of it. For unknown reasons the school director interceded. Each day after class I was to report to his office, where he became consumed with talking about his own misspent youth, often calling my work detail to say I'd be late again, which made the kitchen staff mad. I was such a good listener the director decided that I was bright.

He shared this idea with my instructor, who said that I was pretending to be bright to avoid work. To demonstrate, she hauled me down to the local Mensa club. The chat that night was over an art film the club had viewed; *Christ on the cross, pigs slaughtered*. I hadn't seen the film but was asked for an opinion. It was a big moment. I was to be exposed as an imposter. The geniuses stroked their chins. My instructor smiled knowingly. 'Well,' I said, 'it sounds like the film sucks.' The geniuses liked my answer; they thought the film had sucked, too.

We left after that and probably missed seeing them burn holes through objects using their giant brains. Besides carloads of Spanish guys hoping to catch me walking to town, the student tribunal, kitchen staff, and my instructor were all upset, with only the director holding them at bay. When he asked if I would do the CBS interview I didn't think I had much choice. The next week I went to face a camera crew beneath the school's big cottonwood trees. I was about to be zoogered for the first time, but didn't know it.

I thought I had a better comment ready about the Indian takeover of Alcatraz than the one I'd given the geniuses, something like, 'America should give

Alcatraz back.' My answer miffed the reporter. 'Not enough passion and you're speaking too softly,' he said. Again the camera stopped. 'No,' the reporter said,' show more passion and talk louder.' I began again, and again the camera stopped. 'Talk louder,' the reporter ordered. 'Show more passion.' Several failed takes later he began to glower and grit his teeth.

My next try was loud and passionate because I was annoyed. Finally, the reporter smiled and nodded. I went away feeling that I'd been asked for an acting audition instead of an interview. The next day I was striding by the television room when the segment appeared on the screen, which startled the dorm's couch potatoes. They turned to stare at me, turned back to the TV and then turned to stare again, their heads swiveling in unison.

Later a friend told me that he had watched the segment. 'It was OK,' he said, 'except for the red hair.' Millions of viewers now knew that out on Alcatraz Island trouble was brewing and Indian Youth seemed suitably annoyed. Looking back, there was a clever angle to the little segment that read like a headline: 'Indian Youth Share Passion of Alcatraz Insurgency.' My comments had been zoogered loud enough to fit a news angle.

Our school had an Indian Foods Day. We were to build traditional houses. We Southeastern Indians had to make a Cherokee seven-sided cabin with mud chinking, and we were issued what the school said was our traditional food, which we were supposed to cook. They gave us water chestnuts to fix and a used deer leg that the Northwest students had already scorched. Being from the South, I think we were expecting a hog fry. We also had to play against the Iroquois; our stickball against their lacrosse. On that day stickball won.

> Your grandfather drilled holes through the ends of his ball stick handles with a wood auger. He melted bullet lead and poured it into the holes. Whenever an opposing player would get too successful your grandfather would run by, whack him with his sticks, and knock him out.
>
> *My father*

One weekend my friend Beatle, a Lakota, talked me into going to a peyote meeting. I'd never been to a peyote prayer meeting. We hitch-hiked from the Indian school towards Taos Pueblo and were let out in front of a tipi that glowed orange with firelight. We went through the tipi door and I looked around, surprised. The place was full of hippies. There were hippie women in long dresses and granny glasses; hippie men in beards and sandals.

The ceremony was led by three Taos elders in long braids with folded white sheets around their waists, old-school Southern Plains style, and there was a

Navajo couple from Shiprock. Otherwise it was wall-to-wall hippies. They began to pass the gourd rattle, staff, and water drum around the tipi again, each man singing four songs accompanied by a drummer. The Navajo guy kept dozing, his wife constantly elbowing him. The three old Taos men sang with a pure flow, but then the hippies would start in, nasal and out of tune.

> Ke' na ma hey, Gishi Manitou
> Ke' ma ma toh weh na keh Gishi Manitou
> Ke' na ma hey, Gishi Manitou
>
> > *'Is that you, God? We're praying to you'*
> > Sac and Fox peyote song

That hippie singing was hard to sit through. I shot Beatle a mean look for inviting me and he began to stare blankly away. The tipi was flanked by adobe ruins, houses missing a roof or a wall; a hippie commune. The next morning after everything was over I walked away alone, heading for the road, passing a hippie holding a baby goat. 'You shall return,' he said.

'No, I won't,' I vowed, eager to hitch-hike back to school.

At the highway another hippie offered me a ride, his Volkswagen bus filled with ancient Pueblo pottery. It occurred to me much later that he probably made a living looting Indian graves. My host cranked up the radio and shouted that he wanted to stop at Taos Hot Springs, the crumbling ruins of an old health spa seen in the movie *Easy Rider*. As we arrived we saw several naked hippie girls doing backstrokes beneath a line of Spanish guys perched on a retainer wall, clothed and quiet and motionless and staring, an unusually tense scene I thought.

A Taos girl I knew wanted me to go wading with her, so we stepped into the warm, clear waters but kept our clothes on. I forget what our uninhibited but repressed point was, since my host threw off all his clothes and swam towards the hippie girls like a torpedo. The fast drumbeats from the tipi had stayed inside me despite trying to hit on the Taos girl while pretending to ignore the giggling, glistening, naked splashing nearby.

The singing made me think of other songs; round dances I'd heard at Taos Pueblo, another hitch-hike weekend with friends up from the Indian school into a circle of night dancers and drumbeats out among moonlit sagebrush and chamisa. There had been stomp dance songs at the school and also Oklahoma 49 singing, faster round dance style songs with English words that the Pawnee, Kiowa, Cheyenne and Comanche students knew. *Goo-daw-gyeh* or 49 songs were once old Kiowa war expedition songs, and they're now sung intertribally at after-hours social dances.

Oh my Blackjack Daisy
She got mad at me because I said hello to my old-timer
But that's just OK with me, ya ho! Ay ya hey ay ya hey yay …

'Blackjack Daisy', a 49 song

'49s' are often held in dark fields with romance and drinking a big part of the attraction. The dancers face the singers and their drum, slowly circling with arms joined in a rhythmic side-step as they sing along. They say in the 1920s a carnival barker was advertising a girlie show shouting, 'See the dancing girls of 49'. Later that night at the Indian social dances someone began teasing the women dancers, shouting 'See the dancing girls of 49' and the name '49' stuck.

Although I hadn't paid much attention, there had been other songs. Further back were Plains powwow songs I had heard. I thought of Creek hymns I must have heard at Bowen Indian Mission when I was younger still, and Choctaw hymns at funerals. And there was the time when I looked down on the tops of the big hats of Indians drinking and singing just below my window; my first clear memory of anything. Meanwhile, even long talks with the director couldn't keep me in school at Santa Fe.

It started with three of us getting drunk, a Crow friend and a Ute, and my Crow friend wanted to see a girl he liked. There was a ground floor classroom inside the girl's dorm which we broke into, and then we climbed the stairs to the second floor. I remember we were walking down a brightly-lit hallway carrying beer when a girl came out of her room, smiled, and pulled the fire alarm. We ran out the way we came in.

Behind the girl's dorm was an outdoor amphitheatre under construction and we hid there. Soon police cars were searching for us. We thought we were safe crouching below ground in an unfinished concrete bunker, but then we got cold so we built a fire. The flames rose too high and blackened the concrete, so we left. There were several large, round outdoor lighting globes lying around and I took one. I found my way back to my room, lay down, and went to sleep. My hand was still stuck inside the globe when the dormitory attendant came by.

I don't understand you boys sometimes.

Dormitory attendant, Institute of American Indian Arts

My two friends were sent home. Because the director still somehow thought I was bright I was allowed to finish out the year, but couldn't graduate. That spring I watched from my dorm window as diplomas were issued beneath the cottonwoods. I had been left behind. After the ceremony the graduates marched off to the sound of a Pueblo drum. As they passed I noticed that some of their expressions seemed a bit dramatic, like they were feeling very Indian. After all, I thought, they were merely transitioning into the 'new, modern world'.

> And Bubba spake unto the multitude upon this wise: Reckon I don't need no fancy book learnin'.
>
> The Book of Bubba, Chapter 17, verse 6

Right after that my Crow friend showed up, driving in from Montana. It was good to see him. We hadn't managed to graduate but we crashed a graduation party anyway and again got very drunk. Because he had a car we were asked to make a beer run. My friend drove carefully and seemed to be observant. I had just complimented his driving when we were caught going the wrong way on Cerrillos Road, Santa Fe's main thoroughfare. 'What did we do wrong, officer?' I remember my friend saying. Then we were taken to jail.

> Sunday morning when I go to church honey, hi-ya
> I don't see you 'cause you're in the county jailhouse hi-ya
> Sunday morning when I go to church honey, hi-ya
> Breaks my heart to see you drunk every Saturday hi-ya
>
> Oklahoma 49 song

That fall they enrolled me at Carter Seminary, another Bureau of Indian Affairs school but in Oklahoma, where I was assigned a social worker. It was 1969. Gone were weekends in Taos and cruising town. At the new school we lived behind a fence topped by barbed wire, and we were transported in grey buses with metal bars across the windows. Students were Chickasaw or Creek, Choctaw or Seminole, male and female, ages six through eighteen. We were on the fringes of Southern America, thirty minutes from the Texas State line.

All of us spoke English but with tribal words mixed in. Our Creek–Seminole vocabulary mainly consisted of *likwi* (sour), *doksi* (rotten), *kumuksi* (smelly), *chebo* (ass), and *fumbi* (stink); Choctaw–Chickasaw words were *showa* (stink), *holabi* (a lie), *kosoma* (smelly), *ishkish* (sphincter), and *hobuk* (neutered), allowing us to insult each other in three languages, including English. During my first week I was challenged by a Seminole who liked to flash a knife.

We were led inside a small basement bathroom by other students who held the doors shut while they turned a radio up loud. The fear of being knifed distracted me, and my challenger landed the first punch, which bloodied my nose. Before I could hit him back he grabbed me. As I struggled to break free he did an odd thing; he began crying and hugging me, saying he was sorry. I shoved him away but didn't hit him. When they let us out there was enough blood from my nose on both of us to satisfy everyone. No one knew what had really happened.

Male students were issued clip-on ties for required church attendance. We sometimes performed at civic clubs, so we practiced stomp dance songs with a girl leading the dances because none of us guys knew how. As a prop, the school bought a fake eagle feather headdress and one student wore it each chance he got. We usually had to chase him to get the headdress back, his glasses fogged from sprinting but also from some cinematic inner fire.

Many students were on CCF, the Christian Children's Fund, and had sponsors who sent them money for clothes and school supplies, well-meaning people whom the sponsored children would never meet. Each month thank-you letters had to be written for sponsor support describing activities, hobbies, ambitions, and reporting school grades. It was a struggle for the CCF students to think of interesting things to write, as our days were fairly much the same.

Carter Seminary was on the outskirts of Ardmore, a small town populated by folks who drove pick-up trucks, ate biscuits and gravy and spoke with a 'Howdy y'all' twang. School food was US government surplus commodities. It wasn't inspiring cuisine, but us older boys never seemed to get full. During mealtime each table would finish eating as fast as possible and then send their swiftest runner straight through the dining hall with serving bowls; the first runner to reach the kitchen came back with second helpings for their table.

> One time a cattle truck wrecked outside Carnegie, Oklahoma. There were dead cows everywhere. Some Kiowas noticed the accident. They were hungry for meat. Each family hurriedly picked out a cow and specially marked it so no one else could claim ownership. Then they went home to get their butcher knives. So there were still dead cows everywhere but now they were wearing scarves and sunglasses.
>
> *My friend Donnie Beartrack, Kiowa and Cheyenne*

I was assigned to sort out the little boys, who lived below us older ones down on the first floor. I showed them how to make their beds and brush their teeth, and I introduced a couple of them to the mysteries of flush toilets. As well as I could, I kept them from getting picked on by the older ones, who liked to try and make them fight. I was also assigned early morning kitchen detail, reporting to the cooks by 6.00 a.m.

Part of my job each morning was to climb the basement steps and open the double doors leading down to the dining hall. On the other side there was shouting and door pounding from the older boys. I'd ease open the doors, quickly flatten myself against the wall, and then let the crowd shoot down past me, a little kid or two tumbling down the steps in front of everyone. But if mealtimes were exciting, being in the dorms wasn't.

We lived four to a room in very old buildings that were soon to be replaced. We slept on iron frame bunk beds and shared a toilet and a shower with the next adjoining room. In the daytime we could play basketball or walk around, but kept inside at night there was nothing to do. At times a restless student gang of sorts entered rooms to pick on weaker students, forcing them to choke themselves with towels, or shoving them around. In quieter moments we sometimes talked about girls, our homes, or we told stories.

> There was this Indian boy who ran away from boarding school. He was hitch-hiking and got killed by a car. Sometimes late at night a car will be coming down that same road and they'll see an Indian boy hitch-hiking. If they stop for him he always gets in the back. They ask him where he's going and he always says he's going home. When they ask him something else they don't get an answer. Then they turn around and see that there's no one there.
>
> *My friend Tommy Sam, Choctaw, Carter Seminary*

Southeastern tribes believe people can change into owls for bad intent. Whenever we got too bored we'd call down the dormitory stairs yelling '*Sti-ginni! Sti-ginni!*' Which is Creek–Seminole for an owl-person. The little boy's attendant, a middle-aged Choctaw lady would panic and pull the fire alarm. We'd open the top door which led to a two-storey fire slide and have a good time sliding down, laughing and yelling as we evacuated the dorm, talking and joking outside while the dorm attendant nervously searched the sky for owls.

> Witches can change into owls but they have to remove their intestines first in order to fly. Once a witch took out his guts and placed them in a wash tub. While he was away another Choctaw came by, saw the witch's intestines and sprinkled salt on them. That killed the witch.
>
> *My friend Truman Bell, Choctaw*

The school provided guitars and a drum set, and for a while some of the older boys tried to have a rock band, although no one knew how to play an instrument. No one could sing either, and eventually the band would ask me to sing at practice, not because I was any good, but because everyone else was worse. Sometimes the older girls would come to watch us, staying until our off-key chords and bad vocals finally drove them away.

The older girls joined a social club in town and invited some of us older boys on a hayride. None of us boys had heard of hayrides. The white chaperones put all the Indian kids in a separate flat-bed truck filled with hay and then climbed in with the white kids into another truck. We spent our unsupervised time trying to burn the hay or threw it around, embarrassing the girls, who huddled in a corner. We also pocketed most of the hot dogs from the cookout, since we were usually hungry. We didn't know we were having a romantic evening.

> Have you noticed how some Indians have a hard time being romantic? One evening when your aunts were teenagers and lived at High Hill, they were sitting outside. It was summertime, and both of them had gotten very dark. Your aunt Emma began thinking about her boyfriend in town. She looked up at the moon, sighed, and in English she said, 'Sure are lonesome!' Your aunt Bessie misheard and got mad. 'Losa!' she said. 'Why ... you more losa (dark) den me!'
>
> *My Uncle John*

They bussed us into town to go to school, and at lunchtime us older boarding school boys expected one another to hang out together in a hotel parking lot across from the school. After lunch, the lot was our territory, and white kids avoided it. Someone would produce a cigarette and we'd take turns passing it around while staring and looking tough. Anyone caught socialising with white kids came under severe criticism from the group, or else they were ostracised. Only Indian students from town were allowed to join our lunchtime circle.

Carter Seminary issued us school lunch coupons, good for sixty-five cents. Sometimes us older boys sold ours to the white kids for fifty cents, and then we'd go play pinball with the money. When our pinball money was spent we'd go back to school to try and find the girls, who always had extra lunch coupons. Most of the time they felt sorry for us and gave us enough coupons for something to eat, although they would make us ask nicely, or even plead.

We seldom had family visits but my father came down from Tulsa to see me twice, once to take me out to eat fried chicken and another time for my Aunt Lizzie's funeral. My father was drinking that day as we drove along, saying how Aunt Lizzie's death had hit him hard. Her burial was at High Hill Indian Church, up in the hills. Everyone sang Choctaw hymns, and on the way to the cemetery the procession of cars grew to over a mile long. Aunt Lizzie had many friends; black, white, Indian. Although she was poor she was well respected.

My father explained how Aunt Lizzie's daughters couldn't get her to Talihina Indian Hospital in time, so they tried to have her admitted to the white hospital in town. Because she didn't have medical insurance, the hospital required a thousand dollars cash deposit before they would treat her. She died in the waiting room, slipping into a diabetic coma while her relatives tried to pool together enough money so she could be seen.

Older Indian ladies used to carry their money tied up in handkerchiefs. When they came to town they would place their handkerchiefs on the store counter. After they finished shopping they would open the handkerchiefs and the store owner would count out the money for them.

My maternal grandmother

Our boarding school held student council elections, and I was chosen as school president. To celebrate, I went to town and got drunk. They say the police pulled me out of a watery ditch and took me to jail. I woke up in a cell with two older Indians, who asked me who I was. 'I'm president of Carter Seminary,' I told them, feeling important. The first one looked at me strange and said, 'Yeah, I used to be student council president there, too.'

At boarding school they had what they called lyceums. Certain Choctaws would come and talk to us. We were told how wonderful it was that we didn't have to be Indians anymore because we were getting educations. At Jones Academy we were told not to speak Choctaw, to speak only English. They taught us many things, but I don't think they should have ever taught us to be ashamed of who we were.

My father

By then I had reached legal age and didn't like living behind barbed wire. I didn't like the idea of stomp dancing for civic clubs or sitting through church in a clip-on tie. I didn't like ducking in my bus seat to avoid being seen behind metal bars, and I didn't like how homesick little boys ran away from the school, sometimes through fields of snow. Right after Christmas the boy's advisor gathered up us older boys to announce that since neither our families nor society wanted us, our only opportunity in life would be to join the army.

The next day I quit school and went to my grandmother's house in Tulsa where I found work, passed an equivalency exam and applied for college. Then my father started showing up, taking me to military recruiters. The Vietnam War was still on and it seemed that my father's plans for my future involved shipping me off to the front. I promised him that if I didn't hear back from a school within a week I'd enlist. Five days later I had a school acceptance letter. That fall I was attending Haskell Indian Junior College in Lawrence, Kansas.

Do you want to be a baker?

My father

Lawrence, Kansas was a medium-sized Midwestern town. You could tell by the way the people spoke that you'd left the South. My father had gone to the same BIA school right after the Second World War, when it was known as

Haskell Institute. I enrolled in 1970 when Haskell started offering a two-year college degree but still taught trade courses. 'Your father took baking here,' the dean said briskly while riffling through a pile of old records. 'Would you like to be a baker?' he asked.

'I want to go to college,' I said. Dean Bowman frowned.

Haskell had a secret Choctaw club. You had to know which room at the student union to quickly slide into, and when. Once inside, older Choctaw ladies who worked at the college fed us. There weren't any club officers, official activities or speeches, but in that windowless room Mississippi Choctaw students led tribal dances several years before they would reappear in Oklahoma. Those were small moments but the sounds and steps and spirit stayed within me as a tribal energy I belonged to, though it all came as bits and pieces.

Ohoyo pisa chukma
Felima cha, talowa.

'When you see the good looking woman turn around and sing'
Choctaw Sunrise Walk Dance song

Students weren't allowed to have cars, so going on dates was limited to places we could walk to. After dinner at the chow hall we'd trek to a nearby pizza parlour which had a player piano, showed silent films, but most importantly, sold beer. As we entered the pizza parlour the all-white patrons would quickly grab their children and flee, leaving half-eaten pizzas, tips, and pitchers of beer which we would finish for them.

We would turn what was intended to be a quiet family restaurant into a full-blown bar, sometimes standing five deep to order, ignoring the player piano and the Charlie Chaplin movies, filling up the long tables, talking, laughing, drinking, but never buying pizza. One night I strolled down to the pizza parlour to see a Cherokee girl and met my future wife instead. Lori was Kiowa, Comanche, and Apache and from Oklahoma.

Does anybody think these people were just sitting around drinking tea?
Condoleezza Rice

Lori was quiet and shy, but easy to get along with. She said she had ten brothers and sisters and Jeffrey, her oldest brother, was going to Haskell. Jeffrey was tall and tough, and he hung around another Kiowa who was short and tough. Between them they terrorised several local bars. But Lori was nice, and it was good to have someone to talk to. We all need someone like that sometimes. Soon, Lori and I had started a small campus newsletter.

Our biggest story was about a local bar that refused to serve Indians, including me, which led to the involvement of the American Indian Movement, the Native American Rights Fund, and the Kansas Civil Rights Commission. I had recorded the bar owner, in an interview, as saying that he'd never serve an Indian unless they had a Kansas University identification card, which, like most Indians, Haskell students didn't have – a lot of trouble to go to for a beer.

As we walked to town we were sometimes harassed from cars by Kansas University students. Town residents also complained about us being drunk and loud or passing out on lawns. This kind of tension produced resentments. Waiting in front of the chow hall, my room-mate began making negative comments about white people in town who claimed to be Indian. Then a Navajo friend of mine, also waiting in line, told us a story.

> One time on the Navajo reservation a white couple got caught in a blizzard. Their car hit a snow drift and broke down, and the couple froze to death. A Navajo came by and found their baby still alive. He wrapped the baby in a blanket and took it home. The man's family lived in a very remote part of the reservation. It was a severe winter so they decided to keep the baby until spring, when they planned to go to the trading post, report the accident, and hand over the child.
>
> But by the following spring the family had become attached to the baby. They raised the child as their own. The baby was given a Navajo clan, a Navajo name, and its first language was Navajo. Now … are you going to tell me that baby wasn't Navajo?
>
> *Lester Babbitt, Navajo*

Lori and I married in the summer of 1971, and a newspaper reporter from the *Yuma Sun* interviewed us. We shared our biggest newsletter story, and she thrilled over Lori's Apache bloodlines. She posed us at her desk for a photo as if we had our own office. The reporter seemed friendly but her article's headline made us wince: 'Ink Paint on Their Faces They Go to War; Geronimo is Battle Cry' – We'd been zoogered into crusading savages.

My first marriage placed me at the edge of another tribe's culture. Lori was from a community of peyote meetings, powwows, dance societies, sweat lodges, medicine bundles and hand games, each tradition with its own songs. Her family was one of a handful who hadn't given up tribal ways to go to church or to work in distant cities. For my new in-laws, staying put and following tribal traditions sometimes carried penalties. Indian churchgoers sneered as they passed my in-law's house, calling their dance ground 'the devil's half-acre'.

Area Indians leased their lands to white farmers since local jobs were scarce

or only seasonal – like hay baling. For women there were brief weeks of sacking peanuts at Albert Kelly's warehouse, and as they worked they joked that they were 'over-sack-xed'. Kiowa social dance lyrics commented on how the local Indian women were replaced by immigrant Mexican men, 'peanut boys', who earned the minimum hourly wage of the time:

Peanut boys, peanut boys, hey hey ya hey yo,
Gonna stack those sacks so high
Albert Kelly pay us dollar sixty-five

Kiowa 49 song from Carnegie, Oklahoma

So in 1973 there were trips to the water tower to fill up the two metal cream cans in the bed of my father-in-law's truck because his well had too much sand. A wood stove provided winter heat along with the chore of splitting logs. At times kerosene lamps were used. I couldn't address my mother-in-law, nor could she talk to me. She would turn to someone else and say, 'Tell my son-in-law I want him to …' My new wife's ten brothers and sisters, parents, and grandfather all lived together at the end of a long dirt road. Going to town was a big deal.

Despite beat-up vehicles that didn't run right, suicidal alcoholics, a chronic lack of money and small frame houses overflowing with bodies, Hollywood was still making Indians appear cool provided we were the right kind; colourful tipi-and-horse tribes, preferably from the 1870s. It was also becoming cool to attend powwows even if you were a churchgoer. Powwows filled weekend halls and arenas with buckskin, sound, and feathers. My father-in-law was in demand as a head powwow singer, both in big cities and at small community dances.

And mostly I observed, hearing songs rise and shiver, seeing the sheen of silverwork and satin, the sway of shawl and buckskin fringe, the sparkle of cut beads, dyed porcupine hair roaches, eagle feathers, saddle hackles, grease paint and moccasins, the dancers flowing around the drum. Standing or sitting with my in-laws for hours close to the singing I couldn't help but catch a few songs. I also began observing how eastern Indians, who didn't come from colourful, cinematic horse cultures, were being attracted to all the buckskin and feathers.

Haway chani Wakon'da hey tah way

'God this is your day'
Lyrics from an Otoe war dance composed by Sidney Moore, Sr

These eastern tribal people mimicked Plains dress and dances, becoming the 'right kind' of Indians, deliberately or otherwise. I didn't want to be one of them for snide remarks were made by real Plains Indians about 'off tribes' grab-bing their dance ways. But when my older in-laws told stories I listened so I could help my children remember family accounts of chiefs and medicine people, old songs, and wars with the US army that I overheard on car rides or at my in-law's kitchen table. All this was good, for my own family also had stories.

> At High Hill there are little people, kanokasha. They used to have a big bell that would be rung when someone in the community needed help, and each family had a certain number of rings. To play tricks, the little people would sometimes ring that bell at night, making everyone think there was an emergency. The kanokasha would take the horses, too, and ride them all night long. Those horses would come back tired and lathered, and you could see their manes would be tangled from where the little people had held on to them.
>
> *Lizzie Jones, my great-aunt*

My wife's people were descendants of Chief Set'tyday, Satanta or White Bear, the Kiowa patriot who belonged to the On-day or Ten Bravest Men Society. The On-day wore long black buckskin sashes. During battle they would symbolically stake themselves to the ground with their sashes using arrows, as they couldn't retreat or be captured. After Satanta was tricked and taken captive by the Americans he was imprisoned at Fort Richardson, Texas.

Because he was a member of the On-day, Satanta placed a blanket over his head and plunged three stories head-first from his third-tier prison cell down to a stone courtyard, satisfying the requirements of his society. During his lifetime he had many exploits and was known by the whites as The Orator of the Plains. Satanta once captured a bugler from the American military. He made the soldier teach him bugles calls, and afterwards when the Kiowa had encounters with the US Cavalry Satanta would play counter calls to confuse them.

> The sun took a wife, and she had a child. She became lonesome for her home on the earth and would look longingly down through the clouds as the sun travelled the sky every day. She decided to made a long rope, and when she finished she placed her baby in a cradleboard upon her back and slid down the rope towards earth. But the rope was too short and she wasn't strong enough to climb back up. Eventually the wife of the sun had to let go. She fell to earth and died. Because he was in a cradleboard, her baby lived.
>
> In those days there were remarkable beings, and the child of the sun was adopted by an old woman named Spider Grandmother. As the boy grew the old woman warned him about playing a certain game that involved throwing a hoop in the air and trying to shoot an arrow through it. The arrow might come down

and hit you, he was told. Being a little boy he didn't listen to Spider Grandmother and played the game anyway. One day the arrow came down and hit his head, splitting him in two.

The accident created twin boys. After they grew up they were given a mission to fight evil upon the earth. When their lives were finished they divided themselves into ten medicine bundles, nine of which exist today. The bundles are so sacred that the names of the twins are spoken only when necessary.

My former father-in-law

About 1975 a relative sent me to an Indian doctor for help. Maybe you know someone like Fixico Tulsa. He was elderly, old-school, and very kind. Soon he began asking me to start learning what he knew. He had a thick book with hand-written pages in the Creek language which he wanted to teach me to read. The book contained dozens of medicine songs. I knew that if you begin that kind of work you have to stay home most of the time, in case someone needs you. I was young and wanted to see the world, so I declined the offer.

Yellow butterflies circle
Red butterflies circle
White butterflies circle
Black butterflies circle

Fixico Tulsa, Muscogee Creek medicine man.
Song to make something look pretty (English translation)

Then in 1976 another circle opened up again. The hippie's prophesy came true and I was back in a peyote tipi, invited by a Pawnee friend. The ceremonies were conducted by my friend's father-in-law, a Delaware, and they attracted eastern tribes, some Plains people, and even a Hebrew. There weren't any Choctaws at those prayer meetings. Cut off by remote hill country and missionary Christianity, Choctaws have had few sustained cultural contacts with the state's other thirty-eight tribes. Yet it's not like Oklahoma is that big a place anymore.

You can drive from the pine hills of Choctaw Country in the southeast corner of the state to Cheyenne Country in the northwest in less than four hours while passing through several Indian nations, as Oklahoma was once a tribal dumping ground for American expansionism. Some eastern tribes were force-settled by the US army near the Plains people where they learned the Peyote Way from them. I found comfortable familiarity sitting among fellow eastern tribesmen in ceremony, which was more tuneful than a tipi full of hippies.

And there were many songs fast like bright horses that ran through the corn shuck prayers, red-and-blue blankets, firelight, water drum sounds and burning cedar. The white world calls peyote a drug. For those who use it within authentic prayer ceremony, peyote is a grandfather creation, a sacrament believed to contain God's spirit. I never saw anyone hallucinate from taking it. Once I heard of a priest who warned against Grandpa Peyote.

'Peyote is not a sacrament. It will make you crazy,' the priest insisted.
'Tell you what,' an old Indian answered, thinking of peyote tea. 'You drink a gallon of your sacrament and I'll drink a gallon of mine. Then we'll see who goes crazy and who can get up and walk away.'

If you attend peyote meetings and you're a guy, you're expected to sing. My Pawnee friend and I were driving to a meeting at Duck Creek, and four short songs kept running through my mind, fast as horses and as hard to catch. We were passing through Tulsa, and all the lights and neon signs seemed to fuse into the songs I was trying to remember. At Duck Creek after their midnight water ceremony those little songs came trotting out, my first time to sing in a meeting. Whenever I think of those songs now, they glow with car light and neon.

Ni ha ni hih ni ha na ni heh
Ni ha ni hih ni ha na ni hih
Ni ha na yana hey ya na hey nay yo wah.

Pawnee peyote song, one of the first four I learned;
referring to a white bird that once appeared in the tipi

Peyote people often make relatives with each other. Soon I had several moms and dads, brothers, sisters, aunts and uncles from many different tribes. One old Shawnee man took me for a grandson. He used a home respirator and sometimes asked me to come sit with him because he was afraid he might fall asleep, lose his oxygen mask and suffocate. We would stay up all night together and in his small living room he told me old Shawnee stories.

Shawnee warriors encountered a white trader, who gave them something to drink. Eventually the warriors fell down and became motionless. Another Shawnee passed by, saw them all lying on the ground, and reported that the Whites had poisoned them. The Shawnee sent a big war party to retaliate but when they got to the place where the warriors had fallen they found them alive and holding their heads, moaning. It was our first experience with alcohol.

Bill Panther, Shawnee

There were reasons why my Shawnee relative wanted to tell me his stories, and maybe one day I'll know why, too. I listened when he sang or talked on those late nights as he sat next to a green, metal oxygen tank whose long clear hose snaked over the lace doilies pinned firmly to the sofa arms by his late wife. Those were good songs and stories and I remember some of them, but I was really there to make sure my Grandpa Bear Man was safe.

Bear Man tried to teach me good behaviour, mainly how to stay out of trouble. Indians can get jealous, he said. Should someone ask if you can paint, tell them you wish you could. Should they ask if you fix feathers say maybe, just a little. Should they ask if you know any songs, tell them you're still learning. Don't buy anything new if you can help it. Stay low to the ground like a little child, he said. In the mornings he made me go outside, face the sun, hold up my hand, pray, turn clockwise and then come back in to wash my face.

> Our old folks used to say that a time would come when there would be a 'big eye.' One day there would be a big eye in the middle of our houses they said, but the big eye wouldn't watch us, we would watch it. 'Grandson, listen. You watch too much television.'
>
> *Bill Panther*

In 1976 within a five-minute walk of where Lori and I lived there were peyote relatives who liked to sing. They would tie up a practice drum and invite me over. On Friday nights we'd sit on the floor in someone's bedroom, several of us, taking turns drumming and singing. Sometimes we caught songs from one another, and sometimes we told stories. Saturday nights we'd go to prayer ceremonials and Sundays we'd come back tired.

If we remembered any songs or stories it was because we had helped each other sing the night before and whenever older people had talked, we had listened. I met my friend Willie in a peyote tipi. Willie is Yuchi, and like the Choctaw, the Yuchi were force-marched from ancestral homes in the southeast to Oklahoma. After the meeting was over Willie invited me to his ceremonial ground. Kellyville is located on a flat hilltop, their camps ranged around three clan arbours. So the following weekend I was there at Kellyville with Willie.

> A long time ago the sun lightly cut his arms, like they do during green corn ceremonial. The sun's blood formed a rainbow and all the Yuchi travelled upon it. That's how they say we came to earth.
>
> *Willie George*

Stomp dance songs I'd heard at boarding schools were being sung on that hill. We sat under Kellyville's north clan arbour, joining the dances and then taking our seats, listening to talks from the chief's arbour, telling jokes, rising to dance again through the long summertime dark until the sky showed blue and the coals were ash white. We walked back to the camps to eat before we all went home, which for me wasn't that far away. Lori and I had moved again, to nearby Sapulpa where I had found work. We were now in our mid-twenties.

Willie and his brothers were our new neighbours, fluent in the song cultures of three seemingly separate traditions, powwow, peyote, and stomp dance – not unusual in a small state with thirty-nine tribal circles that at times overlap. Hang out in tribal circles and you'll eventually absorb tribal songs. By invitation I went to Yuchi green corn ceremonies for several years, sitting under the same clan arbour. Once towards morning when their crowd had thinned Kellyville asked me to lead a dance. Without realising, I'd filtered in enough songs to pull it off.

> Pretty girl, pretty girl
> Way down in Kellyville
> I don't give a god damn
> Way down in Kellyville.
>
> *Stomp dance song with English words*

Almost all southeastern tribes stomp dance. Choctaw dances are different. Otherwise, Cherokees or Shawnees or Seminoles or Yuchis or Caddos who are visiting say that a Muscogee Creek tribal town dance can easily join in. Willie and I liked Stoke Smith's in Cherokee country. If you're a good stomp dance leader lots of people come out to dance behind you including many shell shakers, those women who wear metal can or turtle shell anklets filled with river pebbles and who, with a quick double-step produce a fast, rhythmic, in sync sound.

Together, lots of shell shakers can sound like a freight train circling in the firelight, the men also in line, chanting and maybe whooping. Back at Kellyville, Willie and I were old news. Sometimes when we walked out to lead we had to wait until we heard one or two shell shakers out in the dark rise reluctantly, their turtle shells swishing as they slowly made their way towards the firelight. At Stoke Smith's everyone came out for us right away.

> One night at a certain tribe's ceremonial dance a naked woman staggered from the camps waving a bottle of whiskey. People were shocked. The woman began laughing and whooping, finishing off the whiskey before she fell backward, passing out. This shocked everyone more.
>
> A crowd gathered around the woman, and one of the men took off his cowboy hat and placed it over her exposed vagina. 'What should we do?' someone asked aloud. 'What should we do?' someone else wondered aloud, and another person also exclaimed, 'What should we do?'

An old man walked by, squinted down at the woman and said, 'The first thing you should do is get that cowboy out of there.'

Yuchi story

Maybe when we were at Stokes we were like Elvis leading stomp dance. Well, maybe and just a little. Then in 1982 Lori and I moved to Ada, a place with no traditional Indian activities for miles. Indians in the area were Choctaw and Chickasaw and dedicated to fast pitch softball or drinking, church, or work. Soon I made Creek friends while attending the local college and we began visiting some of the nearby Muscogee Creek tribal town grounds

When I speak for my ceremonial ground I look out across the fire and pick out a tree. I begin at the top branch, which represents the first thing I need to say or announce. Then my talk descends with the tree limbs, each of my remarks represented by another branch; talking from the left side of the tree, then going to the right side downward, then back again to another branch on the left side. Doing this puts my thoughts in order. When I reach the ground I know my talk is finished.

Spencer Frank, Muscogee Creek, Speaker for Cedar Creek Tulsa Tribal Town

We went to Hillubee, Weogufkee, Arbeika, Green Leaf, Nuyaka, New Tulsa, Fish Pond. We sometimes led at the all-night stomp dances or in the mornings we played stickball, going home in the afternoons. My new friends spent hours pondering whether a tribal town we were visiting still had their original ceremonial fire, an old-school Creek pastime and a bit esoteric for me. But there were beautiful songs, and strong circles of dancers.

My friend's father was a Creek medicine man who took care of a ceremonial fire, feeding it when no one was around. He knew songs that went with that fire, and other songs as well. One song had words that talked about a 'big eye' which was used for bullet medicine. The bullets would pass a person by without striking them like corn kernels passing through the big openings of a sifter basket. And he told stories about the Tukabatchee fire:

People in flying canoes came to us from the sky and brought powers with them. One gift they had was the ability to make seasons change in good order. Later, some of them married with the Tukabatchee people, and so the Tukabatchee have the power beneath their ceremonial fire to order the seasons; to cause snow, rain, and sunshine in their proper times and amounts. If the fire isn't fed it will get hungry and start to feed on the people, causing cancers. The weather will become unbalanced as well, and seasons will collide.

Joe Cook, Muscogee Creek doctor or medicine man

Tukabatchee, the ancient mother town of the Upper Creek Confederacy occupied land that had fallen into the hands of a family of missionised Creeks. The family of Christian Indians banned all ceremonial activities on the property and treated my friends as pagan trespassers. On Saturday afternoons what remained of the ceremonial membership had a meal and played stickball close to the forbidden fence line, and I was invited to join in.

On the following day after their church services were over the family upholding the ban would hop the fence with deer rifles and blast the cow skull goal off the stickball pole. My friends resorted to tying their third replacement goal to a rope, raising the cow skull like a flag, then lowering it, taking it with us until the next Saturday when we would again face the unsettling prospect of armed churchgoers piously lurking in the woods.

It was the whirlwind, blinding and scattering, sweeping people away, blowing in shame and bibles. The great wind billows and curls along the sandy reaches of the South Canadian where bright lime willows sprout from sandbars and there are echoes along the banks from revival shouts, gospel choirs, Sunday sermons, altar calls, and the wind picks up speed there and unfurls strong when it shifts south at the bridge and shoots above the four-lane highway, blowing past lonely farms, fields of dark cattle, and tumbling straight down into Ada.

Down in Ada, Lori and I grew tired of the religious repression and organised a powwow at the Chickasaw tribal gym, the first in the area. The intertribal community overwhelmed the gym, parking up to a quarter-mile away. The dance was open to the public and began and ended with Christian prayers, but local Indian churches ordered re-baptisms for all who had dared to attend. At least the clergy hadn't sent in snipers armed with deer rifles.

Christianity is a wonderful faith with great teachings and most of us have a religion or our spirituality. When the human heart is fooled by religion, when an idea or a doctrine or a policy or a feeling is taught as divine vision but is misused to conquer and disrupt, to tear apart and take away, to cheat, lie, and disrespect, to gouge out the spiritual eyes of a people in the name of a truer light and then to further diminish their spirits for the greater interests of others, then that isn't divine vision; it's religious colonialism.

Later I introduced my Creek friends to Adam Walker, an elderly Chickasaw who hosted stickball games at his place. We helped Adam put on a few intertribal stomp dances. A small Seminole contingent of dance leaders and shell shakers would show up along with Johnson Fatisha, who knew the sole surviving dance of his tribe, the Chickasaw Gar Fish Dance. It had been an almost inevitable glide through intertribal Oklahoma for me that may have began with marriage into another tribal nation, or maybe it had started at intertribal boarding schools.

Or it may have begun with a grandmother who had spoken Choctaw and Creek and was sometimes thought to have been both. Missing were Choctaw formal traditions. When I'd leave intertribal circles there were only Choctaw softball games, or church. Under missionary pressure Choctaw traditions had gone dormant. Besides hymns, my family only had my grandfather's drinking song left that they say was also banned, but by my grandmother.

Hoksobishfalaya oom bilili li,
Texas 'hoyo tohili la chi

'I'm going to ride a mule to go chase Texas women'
My paternal grandfather

Ten years earlier in a camp house my aunts had heard old dance songs coming down the road. The songs had returned after two generations. They were like lost children suddenly grown up, hardly anyone recognised them. While most of Choctaw Country had traded tribal traditions for church, drinking, and softball, two hours south of Ada was the Yellow Hill Choctaw community and the songs my aunts had heard coming down the road.

I still felt a pull from the Mississippi Choctaw songs and dances I'd been taughte around fifteen years earlier. In my early thirties, I'd held back a bit from intertribal circles, saving a clear space within me for my own tribal songs and dances. In 1983 I decided to drive down to the Yellow Hill community, a place where there is a flat-topped hill that the springtime covers with yellow flowers. On that even rise a group of Six-Town Choctaw once made a ceremonial ground.

The Six-Towns were the last Choctaws out of Mississippi; loaded onto cattle cars in the early 1900s and shipped to Oklahoma. From ceremonies upon their yellow-flowered hilltop they again saw the world through Choctaw eyes. And from the crest of Yellow Hill came a prophesy. In 1937 a meteor shower interrupted their ceremonies. An elder named Loksi, or Logan Parker, made a prediction. It would be their last dance for a long time. Soon, Choctaw boys would be going to war again, the old man told them on that night.

Then fire would travel under the road leading to Yellow Hill, he said. After that the dances would return. The people of Yellow Hill quit dancing. Shortly afterwards, the Second World War began and many Choctaw men left to fight overseas. In the 1960s an electric cable was laid beneath the road leading to Yellow Hill, like a line of fire that travelled underground. And as Logan Parker had also predicted, a decade later the Six-Towns gathered to dance again.

> All our ceremonial songs come from God. That's why Choctaws don't compose those kind of songs.
>
> *Buster Ned, Choctaw dance leader, Yellow Hill*

Buster Ned was the leader of the Yellow Hill revival, an ex-marine in his sixties whose white wife spoke with an Okie accent. Buster wore braids, a Choctaw shirt, and factory-made moccasins. For its time Buster's Choctaw revival was courageous enough. Missionary Christianity had a death grip on Oklahoma Choctaw communities. Sermons were often laced with fear and guilt. Many Choctaws fled to Tulsa or to Dallas, or into white bloodlines.

Or they stayed safely in church. Choctaw preachers seemed more eager than their white counterparts to condemn those who flirted with tribal traditions. Although he had married a white woman and had been away a long while, Buster had come back to revive the Six-Town songs and dances. Buster seemed fairly friendly, and he invited me to attend sings at his double-wide trailer, old Six-Town songs sung by his two aged uncles.

I caught some of those songs and listened as Buster spoke of the meanings of the dances. He explained how Yellow Hill had 'put the dances to sleep' because of missionary pressure. He talked of tribal designs and old stickball games and spoke reverently of the late Billy Washington, Yellow Hill's renowned medicine man. He told me that when your voice ascends as you're singing you are touching the spirits of your ancestors. That you can feel it.

> Ohoyo ut kania kosh
> Nan iksa kanimo, nan iksa kanimo
>
> *'I lost my woman but it doesn't matter'*
> *Six-Town Falata or Mourning Dance song*

Sometimes others from his community would be there, and then Buster would pass around photos of himself dancing with spots of light at his feet that he said were kanokasha, little people. Once he passed around cassette tapes of over two hundred Choctaw songs recorded by his uncles. We couldn't listen to them; they were for a reporter who wrote stories about Buster. In time he asked me who my folks were and when I answered he became sullen.

I was suspicious and asked my father if he had heard of Buster Ned. 'Knew him in boarding school,' pop replied laconically. 'Beat the crap outta him ... almost every week.' I tried to think of more positive links between myself and

Buster. Billy Washington had been good friends with my grandmother and used to stay with her family. And Nanih Chaha or High Hill, my grandmother's community, had often played stickball against Yellow Hill.

> Billy Washington would come stay with us. He would doctor our yard, and his medicine would burn the feet of those who wanted to do us harm. One time there were two dogs that would sit in front of the house, off a ways, and they watched us come and go. Everyone knew that the dogs were spies. Billy Washington fixed medicine and made the dogs leave. An owl would fly around to bother us, and it was thought to be a person. Billy Washington captured the owl and placed it inside a cage. Once he built a fire in front of our house and sang songs into it as protection.
>
> *My father*

Mentioning Billy Washington to Buster was a stretch, although Billy had been my grandmother's doctor. But Choctaws can be clannish, and the Six-Towns were called Yowani, a corn weevil. Because their dialect was once shaped by refugees from other tribes they were sometimes thought of as not quite Choctaw enough. Buster in turn insisted that the Six-Towns were the only true Choctaws, their versions of songs and dances the correct ones.

> The Six-Towns had a big iron cook pot which they would roll in front of them when they went to visit other Choctaws. They would stand outside a town and demand that their pot be filled with food. It would be impolite to turn down visiting Choctaws who claimed they were hungry, and the Yowani counted on this. After they emptied their big black kettle the Six-Towns would visit another Choctaw town and make the same demand. That's why they're called Yowani, corn weevils, because they eat up all the food.
>
> *My friend Claude Medford Jr, Choctaw*

One evening Buster asked me to chant for the war dances, my first time to sing. All the dancers lined up, women in long dresses and beadwork, men in flat-brimmed black hats, beaded sashes and Choctaw shirts. The singing went well, but afterwards Buster became sullen again. The next time I went to visit him a single cloud filled with thunder seemed to follow me; appearing in a clear late afternoon sky, and rumbling as I travelled.

When I turned west the cloud turned with me. Night came and the cloud exploded with lightning flashes as I came to Buster's double-wide trailer. Inside, Buster and his wife were bedding down on sofas. Their bedroom had been given over to a university musicologist, Buster told me proudly. He was excited. The musicologist in their bedroom was writing a book about him and was going to record an album for him. If I wanted to know anything

I could wait and buy his book, Buster said, or buy the album. His wife yawned impatiently.

I congratulated Buster and headed for the door. Unlike other gatherings and ceremonies I'd been part of, Buster's revival had mainly consisted of school and store performances, public bookings. And his revival hadn't been all Choctaw; there were non-Indians among Buster's dancers. It was his own personal revival, and I'd been there through slim invitation. I looked up into the night sky. The thunder cloud was gone.

There wasn't much more to do but drive away, and I never went to see Buster again. Eight years passed while my family grew. I painted and travelled to support everyone, and didn't take time to see about my tribal songs and dances anymore. Then one spring in 1992, a Choctaw community in Tennessee invited me to do a summer arts residency with their youth. They had seen one of my paintings.

Choctaws had been living north of Memphis since the 1950s when families from the Bok Cito community migrated up from Mississippi to sharecrop for white farmers. They found that crops grew better in Tennessee. They could use the front door of white-owned businesses and not have to wait in an alley at the back door. They could eat in restaurants, their children could go to public schools, they could use public facilities, they were safe in their homes, they had escaped Mississippi's crushing apartheid system.

Theirs were small, close-knit communities that had kept up with their songs and dances but they didn't have a dance ground. An old Choctaw chanter named Wood Bell asked me to dance with their communities. In preparation, an elderly woman made me a traditional shirt. Wood knew many songs and I absorbed a few. Wood, like Buster, had long hair and wore a Choctaw shirt every day along with a flat-brimmed black hat. Wood Bell was a traditional community patriarch. If Wood approved of you, nearly everyone did.

If you want to become a good Choctaw chanter swallow several live crickets.
Wilson T., Choctaw doctor or medicine man

Later that summer I was asked to make a ceremonial ground for the Tennessee Choctaw. I had absorbed an older pattern over the years not thinking I'd have to remember any details, mislaid parts of a cultural blueprint tucked between layers of other things that we were able to put back together. A remote field next to a high bluff presented itself and suddenly they were all there; songs, stories and dances leading like bright pathways back to the centre of things again. We called the place Ittibachafa, which means United.

In our old village black slaves showed up. They escaped the white people and had been running for days, and they were dirty and hungry. The people fed them and said they would hide them from the whites. Before the runaways had a chance to clean up they heard singing. The people were having a dance, and the runaways went over to watch.

A Choctaw who knew English began talking to them. The runaways told him they liked the singing very much and wished they knew a song so they could lead a dance. 'We have easy songs,' the Choctaw told them. 'Just sing "*kosoma li yeh!*" and we'll sing back.' One of the runaways was announced as a dance leader and he walked out by the fire and began to dance.

Everyone fell in line behind him. '*Kosoma li yeh!*' ('I stink!') the runaway sang, and everyone sang back '*Kosoma toh'ba!*' ('You sure do!')

My Uncle John

It was an honour to make a dance ground, to see women cooking, children playing and laughing and, at night, the light of a ceremonial fire. As the circle filled I was pulled into it. Mississippi Choctaws came to join us, making long lines of dancers between the arbours. Then the Indian church in town began to preach against Ittibachafa, and many families listened to threats from the pulpit and stayed away. Many others did not. On a bluff above the Mississippi River the old Choctaw world had come together again.

An old and simple song is remembered in Mississippi from a time when there was a temple on top of Nanih Waiya mound. In those days we had sun priests who ascended Nanih Waiya to pray for the people. The song is about an epic journey led by a sacred pole. The pole was buried inside Nanih Waiya, and the people settled the area, becoming a large nation. They say that when this song was sung 'the sun would dance'.

Aba itti chin 'ke ya li

'*May the heaven-pole stand for you*'
Nanih Waiya song

In the days of the sun priests, babies were placed in cradleboards with a weight on the front of their heads. Children would then grow up with high foreheads, a process said to heighten intelligence. Thunder and lightning were also associated with intelligence, and sun priests who had their foreheads heightened were said to be heloha is-soh or touched by thunder. It's a very old reference. A Mississippi Choctaw elder once explained all this; and how those words fit me.

In the world I've been born into everyone works for money. From 1993 through 1995 I worked for the Chickasaw Nation as their cultural resources director. Job survival was tricky; my staff was riddled with political appointees. At the beginning were days of small wonder, enhanced by the novelties of wearing a tie and having an office, a secretary, and access to a tribal vehicle. But before my directorship began I'd been asked to put together a Chickasaw dance troupe.

The Chickasaw tribal administration had requested a cultural makeover; their tribe had a single surviving dance left, the Gar Fish Dance. My job was to teach a group of volunteer employees enough songs and dances to create official cultural performances. A few Chickasaw elders remembered stomp dancing though they couldn't recall any songs, but Choctaw elders could remember Chickasaws visiting and dancing with them at Choctaw dance grounds. On these two slender premises, I hung a Chickasaw dance troupe repertoire.

It was a time of war, and a foreign people were invading an old homeland. Tribal prophets foresaw new lands where the people could go to and be safe, so they gathered up their belongings, even taking with them the bones of their dead and they left, beginning a long journey. There were two brothers, Chahta and Chikashah, who led the people from distant lands to the west, and there was also a sacred pole that the people followed. They say the pole was made of cane.

At night in the centre of their great encampment the pole would be placed upright, but in the morning the pole would be found leaning in the direction they were to travel. Also leading the people during the day was a small white dog. Both the pole and the dog went before the people as they travelled. One day the pole not only stood upright, but it also danced. Chikashah and his followers claimed that the pole was unreliable, while Chahta and the majority of the people said the pole had emphasised that they had come to the end of their long journey. Chikashah and his followers were unsatisfied and so they continued to travel, while Chahta and the rest of the people settled where the pole had remained upright. Chahta and his people built a mound over the sacred pole with earth carried in baskets. This mound still exists, and is called Nanih Waiya, or 'Leaning Hill'. They built a temple atop Nanih Waiya, and then raised three more earthen mounds near Nanih Waiya to form a square, with a space for a plaza in the middle.

One of the newer mounds served as a burial for the bones the people had carried with them. It is said that in wartime the people would gather in the centre plaza of these four mounds. White farmers and gold seekers destroyed three of the mounds, leaving only Nanih Waiya. Today, the people of Chahta are known in the English language as Choctaw, while Chikashah's people are called the Chickasaw. The Choctaw and Chickasaw still share a common language.

Ken York and Truman Bell, Choctaw

For our relatives, the Chickasaws, I combined Choctaw social dances with the southeastern intertribal stomp dance style I also knew. I had to come up with a traditional look for them as well. I used a Creek–Seminole stomp dance clothing model for the men, and to the women's long plain apron dresses I added Choctaw-style beadwork. I recruited two Seminole friends to help, a stomp dance leader and a shell shaker. Soon my little troupe were performing simple dances, looking well turned out and making for a credible public effect.

The Chickasaw administration was pleased. But at the core of the troupe were songs I remembered and stories that went with them. So that's how I really learned stories. I knew and felt them as a child or later they came through other relatives or friends, or I was at ceremonies or in boarding schools or in other places, or else something became a story because it happened to me. That's how I learned songs. I was there with everyone else whenever they came around. Sometimes the sounds stayed inside me and sometimes they didn't.

Want to know why everyone says that boy sings like our most famous chanter? His medicine man went to that old chanter's grave and captured his voice. The medicine man figured out how to do that so he could give the old man's voice to that boy.

My friend J.C., Choctaw

My trips to Ireland began in 1995 when Don Mullan brought me over to represent the Choctaw donation to Irish Famine relief. In 1847 ordinary Choctaw people had donated $170, a 'widow's mite' to the starving people of Ireland. In 1997 Don arranged for me to paint a mural in the Irish North, in Derry, on the side of the Creggan Neighbourhood Centre. The British Army was on the road every day then, and the RUC, the Royal Ulster Constabulary, were often in the streets dressed in black with flak jackets and automatic weapons.

A Catholic was driving his car and was stopped at a British army checkpoint. 'Where are you going?' a soldier demanded. 'I'm going to Killamon,' the driver answered. 'You're going to kill a man!' the soldier exclaimed. 'Then what are you going to do?' he asked. 'I'm going to Kilmore,' the driver replied.

Joke overheard in Derry City, Ireland

The mural work was done on a rickety painter's scaffold one story up, which local kids would shake after waiting for me to become absorbed with the painting. While working, my back was exposed to the avenue they said was sometimes used by Loyalists for drive-by shootings. At two o'clock each afternoon a British army helicopter would hover as if to observe the progress. To date, the Corned Beef Tin has been my most unusual art commission.

> I used to wake from dreams where I saw paintings. I would paint what I dreamed about. Kanokasha, the little people, would help me mix my colours. That's how ideas came to me and that's how I painted them. Someday Chollie you'll have dreams like that. And then the kanokasha will come to you and show you all the colours to use.
>
> *My father*

One afternoon I walked down to buy more paint at the Diamond in Derry, a small town square set in the middle of massive 17th century stone fort walls that surround shops and residences. A war memorial rises out of the Diamond, and from somewhere beyond it I heard faint music. It was the Siege of Derry Parade, an annual march of Protestant Loyalists that glorifies an old victory over Catholic forces, and it was heading for the Diamond.

I turned to leave but found I couldn't; the space behind me had slowly filled up with a crowd of Catholic Nationalists tightly packed back to Butcher's Gate, standing silent and wary. The parade was ten feet in front of me. There was nothing else I could do but watch as the dull, overcast day grew thick with tension. A Loyalist crowd had gathered on the other side of the Diamond, some of them in hard hats painted with the Union Jack.

> Different tribes have different ways.
>
> *Lena Noah, my great-aunt*

At one point, a fife and drum band from Belfast marched by and their drum major, a boy of about sixteen, started taunting our side of the Diamond. This prompted shouts from the Butcher's Gate crowd as band members began holding up seven fingers while grinning and jeering, a sign meant to signify the Greysteel Seven; Catholics massacred by Loyalists. The band pointed their flutes at us as if they were rifles, and then they attacked the crowd.

Swiftly the RUC lined up facing us as if we were the cause of the attack while the band was allowed to march away. Bottles and full cans of beer began flying over the heads of the marchers, launched by the Loyalist crowd, sailing past the war memorial and landing among us. Then the British army parked armoured vehicles behind the police line. The Loyalists had come prepared with lethal objects to throw, while our crowd could only manage a couple of odd things to lob; an empty plastic soft drink bottle, and an umbrella thrown by a woman.

Once an enemy war party crossed a river to attack a Choctaw town. Between the river and the town were Choctaw women working in the cornfields. The enemy was sure they could capture the women and then sweep into the town. But when they attacked, the women didn't run away; they stood their ground. The women began throwing rocks from the field, killing some of their attackers. The rest of the enemy fled back across the river. Those women saved their town.

Danny Miller, Choctaw

A man next to me was hit in the head with an unopened can of beer. He opened the can and with blood streaming, gave a defiant toast. I noticed an old woman holding a blood-soaked handkerchief, and children were getting hit by flying glass. A British army photographer knelt in front of me with his camera, for which I paused. Everyone else was busy watching the sky, dodging bottles. Then the RUC donned helmets and prepared to charge.

After a few minutes the RUC mysteriously marched off, leaving the army and their armoured vehicles between us and the parade. Maybe you've felt this way at times, when it seems like you're the only one being targeted. You think you're imagining it, so you shrug the feeling off. But when I finally glanced behind me I discovered that I really was the only target; everyone else had sensibly melted away as soon as the police had put on helmets.

And then the army vehicles pulled out and I was alone with the parade again. I made a decision; I would stand my ground. Besides, it would have looked bad if it seemed that I'd been left and hadn't realised it. Gradually the Loyalists grew tired of throwing things at me, or maybe they just ran out of ammunition, but I stayed until there were no more marchers or flying bottles, until the dull grey had been abandoned to a hush of broken glass.

Óró, sé do bheatha 'bhaile
Anois ar theacht an tsamhraidh

'Oh welcome home, now that summer is coming'
Óró, Sé Do Bheatha 'Bhaile
Sung to welcome home from prison Irish Volunteers of the 1916 Easter Rising

On my way back up to Creggan, I passed a squadron of RUC armed with helmets, clubs, and transparent riot shields marching down through Butcher's Gate. A group of small boys with stones met them and unleashed an accurate barrage, sending the RUC men scurrying back inside the Derry Walls. That night there would be Molotov cocktails thrown and more rioting. The paint shop near the Diamond had long since closed for the day.

Later, during the long flight home, I reflected that despite foreign invasion, Nationalist communities still maintained Irish political identity. I'd been taught to think of myself as Native American and in many ways I had been socialised as American. But the Creator had placed the Choctaw upon the earth as a free sovereign nation. Could any other power sign away or remove that right? I saw the smoldering embers of my nation as a bright flame again.

> Grandson, listen. I'm going to tell you about that American flag. Each star represents a piece of land they stole. And that flag has red and white stripes on it. The red is for the Indian, and the white is for the American. The stripes all begin and end with red. That means we were here when they came, and we'll still be here when they leave.
>
> *Bill Panther, Shawnee*

And that's what really happened to me in Ireland. I've always had a tribal identity, as most Indians do. But my political identity changed from who America said I was to being a Choctaw national. Our old folks were never Americans. The whirlwind has made most of us forget our original nationhood. And although most Indians in the country they now call America say they are Native American as I once did, certain songs and stories keep remembering who we really are.

> One of these days, they said, another people will invade America. These people will be either from Asia or the Middle East, and they will fight with the people who came among us the first time. The new invaders will win, and they will go from house to house searching for Americans. If you hang a Choctaw shirt in front of your house, they said, then the new invaders will pass you by.
>
> *Choctaw elders*

Certain songs and stories you know because you are part of them. They are old within your blood, and you feel them there. The best way to hear such stories and songs is through an immediate voice; living resonance. For each generation the sounds begin anew like a baby's cry, as the sense of who we are must be heard and reheard to bring forward the ethos of a people. Such songs and stories are often communal property, understandings relied upon like tribal elders, sung and spoken bloodlines of ancient national sensibilities.

> There is no substitute for the human voice.
>
> *Br Jack Driscoll, former president, Iona College*

If you want to see how Choctaws think traditionally and how old songs and stories affect everyone, watch the dances. See how everyone is moving? It's an interplay; agreement and cooperation. Everyone is travelling to the same domain together, entering an unseen but familiar place on a pathway made of sound. And sometimes those sounds are most holy, original from the time of creation, and so they remain bright and new.

They also come as familiar beings clothed in night air. And you see the people stirring, filled with such sounds. And we know and hear that in each nation songs and stories are different. Choctaw elders say every nation dances, each nation sings. Let's go out among them and we'll enter the circle and be where there is a locking of arms, a holding of wrists, entwined voices, same-step harmony within a cycle of telling and retelling, travelling and arcing and remembering behind and ahead until all the songs become smoothed and rounded.

Sounds that have shape and travel have colours; swirling night blues moving through sunrise glimmers, curving and flowing out from within us and then back into us again. Their resonance shakes with each living breath and you know them inside you that way, alive and shivering. It's why a certain song or story makes a place within you; it is a touching of spirit, sounds spun and re-spun returning through living air, and time.

CHAPTER 2
Family and Friends

THE BEAUTIFUL DANCE

I want to tell you something about my death. After a Choctaw dies their relatives will dream of what we call The Beautiful Dance. It's the last tribute for the deceased. After I die you will have this sort of dream yourself. At The Beautiful Dance you'll see your relatives and friends who have gone on, and they'll notice you and talk to you. Some may ask you to go with them. Be careful not to do that because if you do, the next beautiful dance will be for you.

My father

FAMILY AND FRIENDS: 1066 –

'Tis Better to Have Loved and Lost than Never to Have Lost A-Tall
(Lester 'Road Hog' Moran)

I once heard of a small town in England which had a Protestant church whose members, without knowing why, turned to the right after entering it. Later workmen tore down the old interior right wall and uncovered an even older Catholic altar. Although the building's earlier history had been forgotten, behaviours survived over time. We're all like that. We have sensibilities we carry forward, often without knowing where they came from. Somewhere through distant family lines, events we never knew of echo down into all of us.

> Every person from your past lives as a shadow in your mind. Good or bad, they all helped you write the story of your life, and shaped the person you are today.
>
> *Doc Zantamata*

My maternal grandmother's half-sister once researched a few shared family ties going back to 1066, and then she went to the Butler family reunion in Carlow, Ireland. In her documents Norman–Irish names changed into French through time, leading to a guy named Sir Guy de Perce. Almost everything else I know about my maternal side is from what my grandmother told me. Her maternal grandmother, Luisa Belle Lilly, had family stories. Luisa was a 'Cherokee midwife', and is listed as such on an old document. She was said to be from the Paint Clan.

> Grandma Luisa was North Carolina Cherokee. She was a midwife, but also a healer. She made sick babies well through touch and prayer, but she could also move things without touching them, and could make chairs dance around the room. She knew plants, and would go out into the woods to pick them to fix medicine for people. Grandma Luisa could also see the future.
>
> *My maternal grandmother*

Those kitchen table stories still echo in me. The last house Luisa lived in is haunted by her; renters flee after hearing her calling for her dead grandbaby. Her family, the Lillys and the Butlers were mixed-blood Cherokee plantation owners in the 1860s. Luisa and her sisters hid the corncob dolls their black 'mammies' had made because they feared invading Yankee soldiers would knock the heads off them. When the enemy did arrive they ransacked the family's plantation, slashing featherbeds open and emptying them into molasses barrels.

The family fled North Carolina and the invading Union forces west to Texas, which was relatively Yankee free. The men joined up with Hood's Rangers, a Confederate unit. While the men were away at war Luisa's sister ended her evening prayers with 'God bless Uncle Pierce, God bless Uncle Asbury, and God damn the Yankees.' Damning Yankees wasn't enough to stop Asbury from dying from a 'mini-ball in his head', however. After the American Civil War the family didn't return to war-torn North Carolina and instead stayed briefly in Texas.

> My great-uncle was killed in the Buckhorn Saloon in San Antonio, knifed by a man named Harry Morris over a gambling debt. My cousin spent years trying to track the man down but could never find him.
>
> *My maternal grandmother*

Another relative, Pierce Denton Butler, became president of Grayson College. Other family members crossed the Red River north into Indian Territory to settle. Belle Starr, the notorious woman outlaw, rode up to their new digs with her hand on her pistol demanding a breakfast of fried chicken, biscuits, and gravy, which was promptly provided. Marrying too statutorily young even for such turbulent times, my grandma's mother and the rest of the wedding party swam their horses out to the middle of the Red River to avert civil jurisdiction.

So it was that in 1897 my maternal grandmother was born near the community of Dixie, Chickasaw Nation, before Oklahoma Statehood. The family soon moved to the Choctaw Nation, where as a small girl my grandmother lost her father to food poisoning. She grew up, graduated from college, taught Choctaw schoolchildren and attend tribal encampments, stickball games, and dances. She described some of the Choctaw men in those days as wearing red and blue neck scarves, cowhide vests, and large black hats with wild peacock feathers.

> My father used to hunt with Choctaws, and was best friends with some of them. He was very sad when one of his friends had too much to drink and froze to death in a snowstorm. They found the man sitting on his horse, leaning against a tree.
>
> *My maternal grandmother*

She spoke admiringly of the Choctaw tribal police, famous for pursuing white outlaws. There were Indian outlaws too, and she witnessed one of the last Wild West shoot-outs in early Oklahoma; two Choctaws, Parker Thompson and George England, engaged in a gun duel on the main street of Coalgate, blazing away while bystanders dove for cover. Eventually, my grandmother picked a local boy to marry whose family was from eastern Tennessee. His family seemed to be white southern hill folk except that their older women weren't white.

> Rebecca, my mother-in-law, was approached by a census taker about her looks. He rode into her yard one day saying he was thirsty. She brought him a cup of well water and then he said, excuse me ma'am, but you appear to be Indian. Would it be alright if I signed you up for a tribal land allotment? Unlike my grandmother Luisa, Rebecca didn't claim to be Indian. Rebecca got mad and ordered the man away.
>
> *My grandmother*

It was the early 1900s. Like her sister Molly, Rebecca Higgins was dark with black, straight hair. The sisters claimed to be 'Black Dutch', a term used in the American South to deny Indian racial identity and avoid persecution. They were from the Eastern Cherokee border area, raised without a knowledge of money. But by all reckoning Rebecca's in-laws really were white southern hill folk. I have their family Bible.

Inside its handmade cowhide covers are recordings of births, marriages, and deaths, the oldest entry dated 1801. Rebecca's son, my grandfather, a former heir to that Bible, was drafted in 1917 to serve in World War I as he rode a hay wagon from town. I was told at my grandfather's funeral that at his going-away-to-war party guests danced to Old Joe Clark and Shoot the Buffalo. Once overseas a concussion from an artillery round threw my grandfather into a shell hole, burying him alive beneath the explosion of earth that fell on top of him.

He dug himself out with his mess kit, my grandmother said. He told her that while in France he saw 'bodies stacked like cordwood' and from France he brought back an artillery shell carved into a vase that read 'Meuse–Argonne Drive' and a packet of Flanders Field poppy seeds for my grandmother. He was also treated for shell shock and didn't work for fifteen years. When the Great Depression hit, my grandmother eked out a living as a sales clerk to feed her family. It was a struggle until my grandfather finally got a job driving a truck.

Years of uncertainty left a kind of nagging worry in my grandmother, a mark she carried with her even when life became good. During Depression times she had to be careful not to lose her job. There were two children; my mother and her younger brother. There were also neighbourhood children to feed, hungry and surviving on flour cakes. Though her resources were often stretched, my grandmother never turned any of them away from the family table. And as those years ground slowly by, Flanders Field poppies would sprout up red in her garden.

> In Flanders Fields the poppies blow
> Between the crosses, row on row,
> That mark our place, and in the sky
> The larks, still bravely singing, fly
> Scarce heard amid the guns below.
>
> In Flanders Fields, *John McCrae, May 1915*

My mother was born in 1918 and grew up in McAlester, a small town not too far away from my father's High Hill community. She went to work in the same store as her mother to help support her family. After the Second World War began, her father found work guarding German prisoners at a munitions depot, a good job for the times. Luisa was living with the family then, and my mother had inherited the same gifts of healing and prediction it was said.

> Grandma Luisa would take your mother into the woods to show her which kinds of plants to use for different ailments. Your mother was born with a veil over her face, which is a sign of having second-sight. Luisa was teaching your mother healing so she could help people.
>
> *My grandmother*

In her day, they say my mother was a good looking woman and judging by her early photos I believe she was. There is an old photograph of her when she was a teenager posing against someone's car wearing a summer dress, one foot propped on the running board, smiling, young and pretty. Her ambition was to be a writer. She resented her younger brother whom she would complain was her parent's favourite, something she never quite got over. During the war my mother enlisted in the Women's Air Corps and was stationed in Washington, DC.

Her brother became a night fighter pilot flying P-38s, the 'Black Widow'. His plane crashed, his death reportedly caused by a German–American saboteur who worked on the squadron's fighter planes. In the early morning hours when her brother's plane went down my mother was home on leave, sleeping in her parent's house when she felt herself being lifted into the body of an aircraft. The plane fell in fast descent, the air around her cold and damp.

> I felt myself falling as if dropped from a great height. I awoke with bedsprings bouncing, my nightgown cold and wet. At breakfast I told my parents that their son was dead. They didn't believe me. Later that day the War Department officially confirmed my brother's death.
>
> *My mother*

Although my mother had similar experiences throughout her life she didn't become a healer like her great-grandmother Luisa. Christianity conflicted in her and she abandoned her spiritual gifts, fearing they were of the devil. After the war she graduated college and married a man whose name she didn't care to recall. He would sometimes beat her and she would run to her parent's home, crying. They soon divorced. In 1949 she began teaching at Wheelock Academy, a boarding school for Choctaw girls where my father also worked.

> At Wheelock Academy the girls were forbidden to speak Choctaw. If they did, one of the dormitory staff would make them brush their teeth with soap.
>
> *My mother*

So my future parents went on dates, riding horses across the hills of southeastern Oklahoma. They saw each other at work. Everyone they knew said they made a good-looking couple. She introduced my father to her parents, and they approved. Their 1949 wedding picture shows my father cutting a simple cake, looking up with knife in hand wearing a slight, polite smile. My mother is also seen smiling, but her smile is forced, her eyes uncertain.

I know most of my paternal family history through my father, through stories told by his maternal grandmother, Pokini Rebecca Leflore, who was from Mississippi. Through the 1800s many Choctaw families resisted the death marches to Indian Territory, staying in a homeland overrun by white vigilantes who often shot Indians and burned down their houses. Pokini's family were among those who stayed. They were mostly Nashoba Iksah; Wolf Clan.

> The family was driven to live in hill caves where they couldn't light fires; the smoke would have given them away. Cloth stretched between trees caught rainwater for them to drink, they said. They left the caves only at night to avoid the 'big guns'.
>
> *My father*

When they finally came down from the hills they found their home in ashes, along with their crop seeds. Without another planting season, they no longer had a future in Mississippi. Some time in the 1880s they walked 500 miles to the west where thousands of other Choctaw had already gone, to a place now called Oklahoma. Pokini would end the telling with a warning in the Choctaw language: 'Stay away from white people. They're no good.'

> Five bands lived in their new area near a sacred spring where weapons weren't allowed. Band chiefs would meet together at the spring to hold councils. My grandmother said that afterwards 'the drums would sound and the people would dance. And they were happy'.
>
> *My father*

Rebecca Leflore also spoke of weddings that required the groom's relatives to furnish a house complete with a well. She told of divorce, too. Following a year of marriage, divorce was a wife's choice, she said, consisting of splitting her red wedding blanket, each spouse taking their half in parting. If after the first year of marriage the wife chose to stay with her husband the couple was expected to remain together for life.

In 1920 her son, my paternal grandfather, would also marry. His given name was Sampson, his surname was White, derived from *Issi Tohibi* or White Deer. He was enrolled at Jones Academy, a Choctaw boarding school, and met my paternal grandmother there. After the wedding Sampson and his mother moved to High Hill, my paternal grandmother's community, where my father was born in 1921 or 1922; no one is sure. Missionaries had made inroads; otherwise it was a small Choctaw-speaking settlement that shared labour and resources.

> My grandmother said that our last name came from a man called Issi Tohbi, White Deer. It was the only name he had. In those days they only had one name, not like today.
>
> *My father*

An old tribal teaching was followed at High Hill called *eeyi kowa*, or 'broken foot'. The idea was that if a person needed help with a major undertaking like building a house, everyone joined in to help with work, or food, or whatever else was needed, as if the person had a broken foot and couldn't help themselves. In the fall the men gathered wood for widows and the elderly. They fished and hunted, raised chickens and hogs, and everyone kept a garden.

Travel to the nearest town was made on horseback or in wagons. The local streams held different kinds of fish. Deer, quail, and wild turkey were plentiful. The community had natural rock springs for drinking water and there were tall pine hills, meadows for horses and in the woods many plants for medicines. Corn was prepared by pounding the shucked kernels with a wooden mortar and pestle. When my aunt Emma was a little girl she used a *kiteh* and *kitosh*, a mortar and pestle to beat hickory nuts into the corn meal to surprise her family.

> Emma really did surprise her family with that meal. She had forgotten to shell the hickory nuts first, so right after they started eating everyone began coughing and choking.
>
> *My Uncle John*

But there was always enough to eat they said, and for the times the people did well. It is remembered about the High Hill community that they didn't know there was a Great Depression until some of them went to town and saw soup lines. High Hill also supported a class of Indian doctors or medicine people. The people preferred the Choctaw doctors, although there was a white doctor in town who would sometimes come out to see them.

> Once there was a flu epidemic and many people in the area were dying. A Choctaw doctor at High Hill gathered a plant with a red stem and made medicine for everyone. No one at High Hill ever got sick during that epidemic.
>
> *My cousin Margaret*

The corn they grew was purple and speckled with white kernels; my Aunt Emma calls the yellow hybrid corn sold in stores 'white man's corn'. High Hill hosted dances, and would put up a yellow pole at its dance ground to announce them. They also played stickball against other communities. My father remembered the Choctaw doctors of High Hill making medicine at stickball contests shirtless and with wild turkey tail headdresses standing straight up from their foreheads. Sampson was said to have been a rough but not talented player.

> You know how some guys are natural athletes and can run and jump real fast? Well, that wasn't your grandpa. But if some of them natural players on the other side started running and jumping around too good, your grandpa would hit them with his sticks and take them out of the game.
>
> *Willie Byars, Choctaw elder*

Under missionary influences, traditional lines of authority were breaking down. A council of elders replaced the civil and war chiefs, making decisions for a range of issues that included settling family disputes by holding court each Sunday on the church grounds. The role of *moshi* or special maternal uncle continued. As boys reached the age of twelve they were sent to live with their *moshi* for a year, where they were taught how to work and hunt and to make things, and how to conduct themselves properly once they became men.

Rebecca Leflore donated a vacant cabin to a homeless white widower and his sons whose house had burned down. The man was allowed to grow and sell cotton and he gave one-third of his profit to her. Far from Mississippi, where her family's own home had been burned by white vigilantes, my great-grandmother found compassion for another family who was white, giving them a place to stay, letting them earn a living. Because of her white sharecroppers, Pokini's family always had a little money, though there was still an abiding mistrust.

Nahullo chi holabi ho'n

> *'That white man is lying to you'*
> *My grandmother Minnie;*
> *her remark to any Choctaw she saw talking to a white man*

In the late 1920s a shadow fell over High Hill. People started dying, and the Choctaw doctor, Billy Washington, was sent for. *Na losa falaya*, a long black being, walked a 'dark trail' down from the hills through the churchyard, Billy said. The being took lives. More would die, Billy warned, and he advised everyone to move away. Soon there was another flu epidemic but this time the Choctaw doctors couldn't save anyone. Sampson developed a fever and began to hallucinate, saying he saw a bull jump over the wood stove in his cabin.

In the older Choctaw way of reckoning, the unseen world is populated. Choctaws speak of na losa chitto, a large black being that hunters sometimes see at night. The hunter will feel a presence behind them or they may hear heavy breathing. When they turn around there will be a black void looming as high as ten feet. The *na losa falaya* or 'long black being' that the Choctaw doctor, Billy Washington, saw at High Hill seemed similar, but as it walked its dark trail down from the hills it brought death. And there were many deaths.

My grandfather died of influenza in a wagon bed while being taken to another Choctaw doctor. After her mourning period my grandmother Minnie quickly remarried a Chickasaw with a reputation for marrying Choctaw women to get their tribal land allotments. During her brief second marriage she lost a baby girl and then a little boy. She became ill herself, dying of tuberculosis while still in her twenties. Abandoned at the funeral by his step-father, my father went to live with his grandmother, Pokini. But she also soon died.

So he was sent to his *moshi*, who was a bachelor. Charged with raising a seven-year-old, my father's uncle Ben enrolled him at Jones Academy. The school had a strict English-only language policy but my father only spoke Choctaw. His first English words were 'kick me', the result of a joke played on him by an older pupil. He was issued a military uniform and with other students my father lined up each morning to march and drill. The school was largely self-sufficient. Students milked cows, raised livestock and tended crops.

My father learned English but his school nickname was Choola, or 'Fox'. Of his close relatives, he alone had survived. Years went by. Then a lawyer came to see him at the school with papers to sign. He was given 200 dollars for 100 acres of his father's land allotment. His step-father had sold his own undivided interest in the land to a county sheriff who petitioned to buy the whole parcel.

The land was rich in oil and gas deposits. The Bureau of Indian Affairs, responsible for protecting tribal allotments, had turned a blind eye to the sale.

In his teens my father joined the school's stickball team, playing for Sidney White, the same man I would learn to make ball sticks from. The team played exhibition games and competed against other Indian boarding schools, including Goodland Orphanage. My father also joined the boxing club, and on the eve of the Second World War he was a member of the school's National Guard unit. In 1941 that unit would be called into active service.

> We loved our Choctaw language but we were told to forget Choctaw and learn English. So I forgot my Choctaw but I didn't learn English too good, either.
>
> *The Reverend Bertram Bobb, school friend of my father;*
> *delivering my father's eulogy*

At seventeen my father went to war, part of the 45th Infantry Division's Choctaw Platoon, comprised solely of Jones Academy boys. They trained together and were deployed to fight in the invasion of North Africa, and then Sicily. They fought at Anzio, and helped to capture Rome. The Platoon participated in the eastern invasion of France and were at the forefront of their battalion's attack on the Siegfried Line. But the boys hadn't forgotten the Choctaw language. They used their tribal tongue to transmit coded messages during combat.

> I was on reconnaissance patrol in a jeep with three other guys. I was standing on the seat looking through my binoculars when I saw the helmet of a German sniper. I didn't have time to react; he shot me too quickly. The bullet entered the base of my neck next to my collar bone. The other guys ran off thinking I was dead. When they came back to check on me I was lying across the seat of the jeep. It was a long time before I was taken to a field hospital, and by then the wound had closed up. So the medics left the bullet in me. It's still there.
>
> *My father*

In 1946 my father went home to High Hill. Only his uncle John's family remained. My father looked out on the hills and down the dirt road and asked where everyone had gone. A munitions depot south of McAlester had opened during the war and began to hire Indians. The families that were left had all moved into town to work making explosives. His uncle John told him, 'Seems like one day they all went to town and never came back.' So my father enrolled at Haskell Institute up in Kansas, then an Indian vocational training school.

He took baking, and was hired by the Bureau of Indian Affairs as a baker for Wheelock Academy, the Choctaw girls school. Following their 1949 wedding at Wheelock my parents settled in Idabel. Then my mother became pregnant with me and went to stay with her parents in Tulsa to be near Claremore Indian Hospital. Despite her somewhat mixed heritage she, like her grandmother Rebecca, didn't claim to be Indian. It helped that she was light skinned.

An Indian nurse at Claremore didn't like her attitude. There was an argument, and a last-minute change of plans resulted in her being admitted to the White hospital in Tulsa. During her labour my mother complained that her anaesthetic wasn't working and that she was in severe pain. The doctor ignored her. My mother sat up and punched him in the face. I came into the world a short time later on 17 December 1950 at 2.03 a.m.

That old doctor wouldn't listen to me.

My mother

I was born with jaundice, kept in a critical care ward. On one of my father's visits he infected me with the flu, and they say I almost died. Indian hospitals weren't reliable then, and maybe I wouldn't have lived long if my mother had gone to Claremore. I recovered and was taken to Idabel. Shortly afterwards, I was baptised at Wheelock Mission, a Choctaw church founded by the missionary Alfred Wright. But, like many others of their generation, my parents had seen the world or distant parts of it during the war. They had come to like new places.

They worked at Wheelock for over two years, until they grew tired of the place and quit. My father left to find work with his friend, Konzi Big Head, a Yuchi Indian and an older relative of my future friend, Willie. My mother went to her parent's home in Tulsa to wait. It was a rough neighbourhood. My grandmother had recently shot an intruder with a revolver kept under her pillow, while her husband slept. The man fled, leaving behind a trail of blood.

Intermountain Indian School in Utah hired my father. He sent money so my mother and I could join him. My grandparents were reluctant about it. Their daughter was going off to live in a strange place, and they were afraid they wouldn't see their only grandchild again. Just before the train left for Utah my grandparents grabbed me from my mother's arms, walked to their car and drove away. I don't think I've been quite as popular since.

Your grandparents snatched … snatched you right out of my arms! And I still had one foot on the train platform. I cried all the way to Brigham City.

My mother

Eventually, my parents drove in from Utah to get me. Our new home was in Brigham City, a Mormon town that had an Indian boarding school with an all-Navajo enrolment, where both my parents had found jobs. Once again my mother taught class and my father worked as a baker. My first memory is there, of Navajos drinking and singing on a street corner just below my window. It must have been early 1954. I could see the tops of their hats, high crowns and wide brims. As best as I remember, the song they sang was 'On Top of Old Smokey'.

> On top of Old Smokey
> All covered with snow
> I lost my true lover
> From courting to slow
>
> *'On Top of Old Smokey', a traditional American folk ballad*

From what I can recall, Utah was an interesting place. When the school term ended my parents returned to Oklahoma. They had become restless again. My next memories are of staying with various relatives while my parents looked for work. During this time I picked up a very limited Choctaw vocabulary, my primary language being the English that my parents spoke to me. I recall going to Choctaw churches and to Bowen Indian Mission in Tulsa where they sang Creek hymns. Then my father decided to join the Navy.

They stationed him in California, and my mother and I moved there. To prepare me for school my mother taught me how to read. She used the *Dick and Jane* books, and a small yellow primer about a monkey named Winky. Somewhere I'd heard of Hawaiians. It was 1956. On my first day of school I was taken to a classroom filled with children who looked like me. They can't be Indians, I reasoned; they must be Hawaiians.

> See the boy in the book? His name is 'Bill'. What is Bill doing? Can you see what Bill is doing? Why he's jumping! Yes, he's jumping. Can you say 'JUMP'? Very good. Bill can jump. Say the word 'jump'. The word is 'JUMP'. Let me hear you say 'JUMP'. Very good. Now watch me jump. See? I can jump. And Bill can jump. 'JUMP BILL JUMP'.
>
> *My first grade teacher*

Our teacher would show us pictures from a book about children playing, make us repeat a word or phrase and pick one of us to act out the activity. At the time I didn't think that was strange. 'Jump Bill jump' was followed by our teacher picking someone to jump. We were quiet in class, absorbed in our pantomimes. One day the teacher asked me a direct question, and I answered in fairly good English. And I could read English. I'd been mistakenly placed in a class for Mexican children being taught English as a second language.

Later I tried to teach my baby brother, Joshua, English. 'JUMP JOSH JUMP', I'd shout. It was around this time that I remember our parents began to fight. My mother would go to look for my father in bars, taking me with her, or he would come home drunk and threaten us. After a while my mother anticipated his drinking sprees and we would leave before he arrived, staying at a cheap motel for the night. The next morning we would come silent and careful back into the house, walking softly by my father who would be passed out on the sofa.

When he sobered up I'd check under the sofa cushions for loose change. After his binges my father's pockets bulged and jingled with nickels, dimes, and quarters. Those cushions were like slot machines that always paid out. Then my father started hitting my mother while he was drunk, which was scary. It's odd how scary situations can gradually seem normal. We didn't have a television but the motels did. I began to look forward to my father's drinking sprees. They meant that we could run off to a motel room to watch television.

Around this period I made my first prayer. I'd been having nightmares so I prayed for a happy dream. That night my dream was a cartoon in blacks and whites and greys of two little monkeys playing checkers. Their antics were lively and crazy and I laughed all the way through the dream. I've had a simple faith since, free of any religion, that there is a Creator who loves us and who will always help us. After that I prayed to the god of little monkeys who play checkers who I knew watched over my mother, my baby brother, and me.

> The most minute transformation is like a pebble dropped into a still lake. The ripples spread out endlessly.
>
> *Emmanuel Levinas*

We moved back to Oklahoma, where our parents seemed to be stuck in a strange but familiar play. First, our father would come home drunk. Then our mother would object. Her voice would become high and whiny, his voice deep and loud. This would be followed by higher, more persistent whining, the responses coming deeper and louder. Their voices would crescendo. There would be a crash or a thud and after that, sobbing.

> Everything has rhythm. Everything dances.
>
> *Maya Angelou*

Our little family would drop into what was left of the High Hill community for funerals, or sometimes to see older relatives. By then most of the Indian land allotments at High Hill had been sold to outsiders. We had relatives scattered among other rural tribal communities, but it was High Hill that held my father's memories and affection. On that stretch of dirt road the small, white frame church remained along with the camp house and a cemetery. People came to sing Choctaw hymns, or to gather in the camp house for dinners.

Kanokasha, little people, still lived at High Hill although the Choctaw doctors there had long since died. The dances had long been put away, the stickball games almost forgotten. The sifter and fanner baskets were stolen along with the church bell that kanokasha sometimes rang. In time the camp house fell down and was rebuilt, but when it collapsed again all final traces of it were hauled off. Then the Corps of Engineers flooded thousands of nearby acres, forever changing the look and feel of the land. But missionaries still came around.

One by one the missionaries got to us kids, but I avoided them. I wanted to stay Indian.

My cousin Bobby

Relatives in town had begun to go to Creek medicine people and above their front doorways hung owl feathers, which would twitch and turn whenever visitors approached. It was how you knew who was seeing a Creek doctor. Older relatives still spoke Choctaw, younger ones didn't. There was an abiding fear of *shillup* or ghosts, and of white people as well. Families were clannish, insular. Yet many of the next generation would move even further away. The munitions plant jobs had ended, and being Indian was not a great asset.

In the 1950s and 1960s I saw the aftermath of the long black being, the dark trail, funerals, survivors and their swift exodus into town. The people had resettled on the social fringes of a white southern town where they were often thought of as drunks, or as unintelligent. There didn't seem to be much surface racism, just a general notion that Indians weren't as good as white people. Many Indians stayed silent and began to forget who they were.

After everyone moved into town they didn't need to work together anymore. They had their own jobs and houses, and their own families. I guess the old tribal spirit went away.

My father

There were false songs and stories as well; John Ford type westerns that showed how Indians were supposed to look and behave. My older relatives would laugh or shake their heads at the grunting, whooping screen images, but they were too powerful to simply be ignored. Hollywood westerns spawned a generation of American television shows; *Gunsmoke, Bonanza, Cheyenne, Bat Masterson, The Rifleman, Wagon Train, Wyatt Earp, The Virginians, The Big Valley, Davey Crockett, Have Gun – Will Travel.* All over America, people were being programmed.

It was pervasive stuff, especially for Indian children. Looking back I can't really say how imbedded those images became or precisely how they coloured the way we looked at ourselves. Like Coca-Cola and donuts they were part of a uniquely American diet that wasn't good for anyone. Many years later I was asked to give a paper about Hollywood westerns at a John Ford Ireland Film Symposium in Dublin, and for the first time I seriously reflected on decades of seeing Indians portrayed as two-dimensional savages:

'Leni Riefenstahl Goes Hollywood: Cowboys, Cavalry, and Colonialist Cinema'

I don't think Indians were the primary intended audiences for Hollywood westerns, because we laughed at them. Our impersonators amused us; Mexicans, Italians and Germans in bad wigs, fake eagle feathers and grease paint whooping, grunting, and dying their way through whatever shoot-em-up happened to be playing. But although we laughed at westerns, we couldn't escape their effects.

We disappointed by appearing in public without cinematic grease paint or feathers. When riding horses my friends sometimes sensed something missing; the dramatic underpinnings of a full orchestra soundtrack. And on the schoolyard and in public places we heard John Ford dialogue. We were called 'murderin' redskins', 'savages' and 'wagon burners'; insults and misperceptions which persist.

Last week in Dublin I was called 'chief' and asked if I had a 'squaw'. Someone else wanted to know if I had brought my tomahawk. Seeing me with a cigarette, a priest asked if I were sending smoke signals. And I disillusioned an Irish journalist when I showed up featherless. She was amazed to hear that my relatives live in houses, and that there are over 350 tribal nations in what they now call America, all with different languages and cultures, but not all of them residents of Monument Valley.

The Hollywood western, America's longest running cultural export, perpetuates the now global notion that Indians are colourful, mythical creatures forever stuck in the 19th Century. Such hardwiring requires willing audiences. Like John Ford, Leni Riefenstahl, who was Hitler's star director, also had willing theaters to play to, and her acclaimed centrepiece docudrama *Triumph of the Will* remains both masterful, visual storytelling and fascist art.

In her essay 'Fascinating Fascism' Susan Sontag explains the elements of fascist art: 'The fascist dramaturgy centres on the orgiastic transactions between mighty forces and their puppets. Its choreography alternates between ceaseless motion and a congealed, static, 'virile' posing. Fascist art glorifies surrender; it exalts mindlessness: it glamorises death.'

Sontag could have been describing the Hollywood western.

As colonialist cinema, the western carries another core element, dehumani-sation through romantic myth. An immigrant nation, America has an ongoing need for a common and epic origin account with which to bind its disparate groups. Two overarching cultural icons, the cowboy and the Indian, have historically been used to help stitch together an otherwise divergent American social fabric.

The Indian icon has a dual persona; the drunken murdering savage and the noble spiritual savage, alternating according to popular trends. Both manifestations are suitably painted and feathered, for to be outside the proscribed narrative is to cease to exist. Tribes designated by the media as being the most colourful have a resulting magic resonance; Sioux, Cheyenne, Comanche, Apache, Hopi, and somewhat inexplicably, Cherokee; perhaps because the phonetics of 'Cherokee' seem pleasing to English speakers.

Well outside the iconic narrative are tribal nations like the Penobscot, Musco-gee Creek, Walapai, Miccosuki, or my people, the Choctaw. The American army once drove the Choctaw 500 miles from our ancestral homes. Yet, in 1847 after extreme loss of life from starvation, exhaustion, and the elements, the Choctaw raised $170 from 'meager resources' to buy food for the victims of An Gorta Mór, the Great Irish Famine. I don't think John Ford ever made a Hollywood western about that.

Ford's westerns were mostly concerned with the interplay between his white protagonists. Admittedly film-making is a collaborative craft, and Ford's job was to render wilfully believable the scripts he was paid to interpret. Masterpieces of visual storytelling often dehumanise all the more credibly, however. In *Stagecoach* the Apaches show up rather late but as a menacing force of nature, like a tidal wave or an avalanche or a forest fire, but not as real human beings.

The film's stagecoach journey is literally a moving vehicle for the film's main characters; a social snob, an embezzler, a drunk, a homicidal gambler, an escaped convict, a whiskey peddler, and a prostitute, all restrained by questionable authority. From an Indian view, this assortment nicely sums up our experiences with frontier America. The Indians are ritually slaughtered; the ratio is one white fatality to fifteen presumably dead Indians. That's some mighty fancy shootin' there, pilgrim.

Again, comparisons with fascist art are inescapable: 'National Socialism – or, more broadly, fascism – also stands for an ideal, and one that is also persistent today, under other banners: the ideal of life as art, the cult of beauty, the fetishism of courage, the dissolution of alienation in ecstatic feelings of community; the repudiation of the intellect; the family of man (under the parenthood of leaders)' (Susan Sontag, 'Fascinating Fascism', 1974)

Stagecoach was a star vehicle for John Wayne, status that would become inseparably more transcendent; the cowboy icon of American origin mythology finally had a face and a name. The Duke came to personify America's iconic cowboy, materialising larger than life on the big screen. The role of culture hero personified had been there all along, like a frontier prophecy lurking in the American psyche awaiting cinematic fulfillment.

John Ford's *Fort Apache* also follows a familiar frontier narrative. The Duke is a cavalry officer pitted against the inflexible Colonel Thursday, played by Henry Fonda. Cochise is Miguel Inclan, popular villain of Mexican cinema, who delivers all his lines in Spanish. A strong Irish element is present; an Irish tenor appears in the Arizona desert, and the jovial drunken role of Sergeant Mulcahy stereotypically rendered by British-born Victor McLaglen is balanced by humanising depictions of Irish American family life.

Predictably, humanising depictions of Apache family life are utterly absent. As the film progresses the soldiers become doomed by Colonel Thursday's inflexibility and stilted dialogue and meet a Custer-like demise. John Wayne's character tries to keep his word with the Indians and seems sympathetic to their plight. Yet, *Fort Apache* ends with The Duke dutifully plotting another Indian campaign.

While the film attempts to portray Irish American class struggle, the Apache struggle against American colonialism is replaced by the value neutral notion of inevitability; the manifest destiny of westward expansion. Assemble the troops; westward expansion is inevitable. The same recurring theme, Indians as obstacles to civilisation, also plays out in what has been called the greatest western ever made, *The Searchers*.

John Ford's *The Searchers* is considered by many to be his most influential and perhaps most admired film. So why would we Indians laugh at it? The plot is loosely based on the real life story of Cynthia Ann Parker, captured by Comanches in Texas. However, much of the film is shot hundreds of miles away from Texas in Monument Valley, Ford's favourite western film locale. That's like shooting *The Quiet Man* in the Swiss Alps purely for scenic effect. Irish people would notice something like that, wouldn't they?

The Searchers opens with an idyllic American family falling prey to bloodthirsty Indians. Only a little girl is spared, taken as a captive. Duke Wayne and his accomplice spend the rest of the movie trying to track her down. I'll explain why my relatives and I laughed at the Indian villain, Scar, played by German-born actor Heinrich von Kleinbach. Let's say an Indian was playing the role of a German while dressed as a teutonic stereotype. Don't you think most Europeans would notice?

There were other moments; Scar uttering a string of allegedly Comanche sentences including a butchered version of 'bellagonna', Navajo for white man. It's like someone trying to stumble through Portuguese while calling it Comanche. The Indian costumes are an unholy mix of contemporary Navajo and generic Plains Indian period clothing. Alleged tribal traditions become a minefield of distortion and fantasy. We noticed all that, too.

In one scene, rescued white female captives babble mindlessly, victims of Comanche savagery. The real Cynthia Parker was so well treated that after being 'rescued' she tried to escape back to her Comanche family but died in white captivity, reportedly from a broken heart, something the film script neglects to mention. At the film's end a racist, Indian-hating Duke Wayne finds dramatic redemption. Not so for his white-hating counterpart, Chief Scar, who is potted at the first handy opportunity.

With *Cheyenne Autumn* John Ford became more reflective: 'I had wanted to make it for a long time. I've killed more Indians than Custer, Beecher and Chivington put together, and people in Europe always want to know about the Indians. There are two sides to every story, but I wanted to show their point of view for a change. Let's face it, we've treated them very badly – it's a blot on our shield; we've cheated and robbed, killed, murdered, massacred and everything else, but they kill one white man and, God, out come the troops.'

By 1964, when *Cheyenne Autumn* was released, popular trends had shifted. America passed the 1964 Civil Rights Act and a counter-culture based on anti-establishment politics was gathering steam. In 1964, Beatlemania swept across America. Music and art, including film, were being transformed. America's dual Indian icon obligingly alternated from drunken murdering savage to noble spiritual savage. Ford's attempt to apologise on film to Indian Country was very well timed.

It was a mixed apology. Once more a Hollywood western invoked one of the designated handful of magic tribal names, but to tell a darker and truer story of epic flight and persecution. Again the lead Indian roles were occupied by others; Ricardo Montalban, Sal Mineo, Carmen D'Antonio, Victor Jory, Gilbert Roland. And although the film purported to show an Indian point of view, no Indians were used as key consultants.

Nevertheless, *Cheyenne Autumn* was an omen for its time, a weathervane in a shifting social wind. The film's portrayal of Indians as victims seemed to perk up some of my cousins, who, although not 19th century Cheyennes, began seeing themselves as rare, fascinating creatures anyway. In reality, John Ford never killed a single Indian. Again constrained by a 19th century storyline, Ford only succeeded in making amends to all the fantasy Indians who dove off horses for him while pretending they'd been shot.

During the year *Cheyenne Autumn* was released, Indian infant mortality was three times the American national average and poverty rates for Indians were among the very highest. Mississippi Choctaws couldn't enter stores or restaurants. Life expectancy for Indian males was forty-five years. The American government was trying to terminate tribal sovereignty and their Indian relocation programme was emptying reservations, consigning families to inner city slums. But there was a resurgence of tribal tradition starting as well.

Those would have been Indian points of view worth exploring on film. Better than almost anyone, John Ford understood the global Indian fetish. The world likes their Indians well feathered and at least a hundred years old. Introducing existing Indian points of view to moviegoers would have been like introducing Mickey Mouse fans to an actual rodent; the illusion is far more desirable. As both apology and breakthrough filmmaking *Cheyenne Autumn* is limited by genre, and by an all too familiar palette.

My favourite John Ford western, but only because I don't like any of the others, is *The Man Who Shot Liberty Valance* which as I recall doesn't have any Indians in it at all. The film does have Woody Strode, who plays John Wayne's black manservant, Pompey. It was nice that Ford cast a black actor in a black role. Apparently playing a black man was too much of an artistic stretch for von Kleinbach or even Sal Mineo. Strode's character, although a subservient one, conveys dignity and power of presence.

Mexican characters in John Ford movies don't fare as well; for the most part they are either comically subservient or preoccupied as dancers and guitar strummers. Colonialist cinema changes the narrative, disseminating, through an immensely powerful medium, lies and distortions about national motives, agendas, and the nature of people. And with every new screening old prejudices are perpetuated. Osama Bin Laden had a military code name; to the US Navy Seals who killed him he was known as 'Geronimo'.

Audiences who have had their central nervous systems hot-wired with surround sound and cutting edge cinematography become easily transported into storyline, their faces reflecting the glow of the screen like torchlight from a Nuremberg rally. When you own the myth you can do anything you want with it; poetic licence becomes reality. Millions have walked away from John Ford's visual myths about the American West imbued with a dire certainty that they know what an Indian is.

Also with dire certainty, many Indian children learn what Indians are expected to be like from watching Hollywood westerns. At intertribal social dances called 'powwows' grease paint and feathers have reached a crescendo, the line between myth and tradition becoming more blurred. It's the most insidious form of colonialism; altering self-perception. We laughed at westerns but we still can't escape their effects.

Similar perhaps is the stage Irish used by Maureen O'Hara in John Ford's *The Thin Grey Line*. O'Hara has a native Dublin accent but adopted a 'begorrah' type affectation for Ford that was akin in intent to the pidgin English spoken by Hollywood's fantasy Indians. Despite his Irish heritage, John Ford was a Yank with fairly mainstream sensibilities. He understood the misperceptions of American audiences because he shared them. And because he shared such biases, Ford was able to reaffirm them.

Bias and misperception should never be reaffirmed. As Ireland embraces *The Informer*, *The Grapes of Wrath*, *How Green Was My Valley*, and *The Quiet Man*, it must also more carefully examine films like *Stagecoach*, *Fort Apache*, *The Searchers* and *Cheyenne Autumn*. The ongoing challenge for Indians is to not be perceived as extras from a John Ford movie. Perhaps in Ireland, a country that has also suffered brutal and protracted colonisation, that challenge can be more deeply felt and understood.

Sometimes on hot, sticky summer nights I caught fireflies with my cousins as the adults visited on front porches in town. Mostly they talked about family matters, though at times their conversations turned to fears of witchcraft. And there were dinners of tanchi la bona, pork with hominy corn, and banaha, cornmeal shuck bread, only now the corn came from stores. Then we would drive up to Tulsa, where we lived near my grandparents.

Hayree say he goin' in da ah-mee in Nofimbo anokfillit ha.

My Aunt Lizzie

There were times my folks would go to Indian doctors, medicine people and I would wait in the car with my mother and brother while my father would enter a doorway at night, old houses in the country and we would sit on the front seat under a blanket and sometimes we would fall asleep or I would get bored and sing. I remember my mother saying once on the way home that she didn't think there were any good doctors left.

My father wanted to send me to Catholic school, but my mother objected. She'd been busy exploring Protestant churches; Baptist, Pentecostal, Disciples of Christ, Presbyterian, Methodist, Lutheran, and was dragging my little brother and I along. No faith seemed to please her. After lingering on through drudging sermons and youth classes involving strangers and Bible verses she would soon grow restless, criticise the minister, and then we'd go off to another congregation somewhere to sit among a different set of pews.

Fah-rends-zuh! Ah sed-duh … fah-rends-zuh! Ah hev good-duh newsza for you tuh-day-yuh! Glow-rah! For ah hev cum unto you yea, verily with thee word-ah uva thee living gyod-duh haw lay loo yah! And so fah-rends-zah … ah say unto you fah-rends-zah … let-tuh thee peepul-la … yea ah sed-duh … let-tuh thee peepul-la … uva thee wun and-duh only … living gyod-duh … rejoice … sah! Glow-rah … glow-rah …

Sermon fragment remembered from childhood

She had her many good moments, but coloured by an ongoing anger that wasn't always obvious. Her instincts were strong, and when I wanted to know the future I would ask her questions while she was distracted with housework. Her off-hand replies would come true. She said that spirits sometimes came around, but these were mostly family ghosts whom she already knew. Although my mother sometimes had ghosts for company, she and my father seemed to have few living friends. I can't recall a single family dinner with guests present.

There's a spirit in this house. But it's a good spirit.

My mother

Sometimes when my mother and brother were away together and my father had enough alcohol in him to feel mellow he would talk about his life, or he told me stories. Then he spoke of High Hill and the people who had lived and died there during his childhood. At times his memories would quicken as if they were being filled by unseen relatives. Maybe these were some of the spirits my mother felt. But if my father was part of the remains of a genuine tribal community, my mother's tribal bloodline ties were much fainter.

Once I think my father saw and felt clearly before sight became clouded by feeling. He'd been forced to learn English and of many things never used in his all-Choctaw community; clocks, bank accounts, books, American flags. His vision was still good concerning family, spirituality, and possessions; he was generous with what he had. But within him culture shame rolled as dark clouds before the sun, and in his eyes an inner anger sometimes flashed like sudden lightning bursts over lifeways once beautiful, but which had been destroyed.

Did you ever think of the white man as a destroyer? That's all he is, a destroyer. Everywhere he goes there's trouble.

My father

Another world waited outside our door. My best friend Tony sent away for a formula made from household ingredients. When the mixture dried it caused a harmless explosion on contact. We smeared it on toilet seats, door knobs, inside shoes. I know what we did was awful, but back then we thought it was brilliant. We found a dumpster that attracted *Playboy* magazines, and we'd sit inside to explore the mysteries of the female form.

In winter we built snow forts and sailed down icy hills on sheets of cardboard. Our gang played marbles and had bicycle races, sometimes crashing in a pile at the bottom of a steep hill when one or two of us failed to make the turn. At Tony's house we'd stay up late to watch scary movies. We played pick-up games of baseball in the street or in fields. It was a working class neighbourhood of small, neat houses that hasn't changed much.

In the early 1960s powwows were starting to appear in cities, and I would go to a local armoury with friends to watch circles of feathers, buckskin and beadwork turning around a centre drum of singers, songs echoing from the

walls. In summer nearby Mohawk Park had powwows, and my parents would visit people they knew among a sprawling camp of canvas tents, cook fires, lawn chairs, cars going and coming, feather bustles hanging, children playing and running. Choctaws called the powwow people *okloshi nukshopa*; wild tribes.

We got a car blocking the road … 1952 Chevy, black with a coat hanger radio antenna. No licence plate but somebody said they seen it driving around White Eagle or maybe Calumet …

Powwow announcement; Mohawk Park

And my grandmother loved me. Small and slender with lank black hair, she always thought the best of me, and made me something to eat whenever I came by. My grandparents kept a small house in the pine hills. Sometimes we went there and I would stay in the woods all day. As far as my grandmother was concerned I was perfect and she was happy when we were together. She liked to work the earth, and her yard had many flowers.

Everything will turn out right. Let worry roll off you like water off a duck's back.

My grandmother

White kids sometimes called me 'Injun Joe', 'dirty Injun' or made whooping sounds as they patted their hands over their mouths. Driving past certain neighbourhoods I remember my parents saying we could never move to those places because the people there didn't rent to Indian families. All the restaurants had signs that read 'We Reserve the Right to Refuse Service to Anyone' and there were times when we walked out of cafes after being deliberately ignored. Indians lived scattered throughout Tulsa, but in small, non-threatening numbers.

Oklahoma was home, and there was recurring stability in knowing and being known. Then in 1963 my parents moved to California again. I didn't want to go, but my grandmother said I had to. My new school was segregated into whites and Mexicans, and once more I didn't fit in. When the school counsellor asked what nationality I was, I replied, 'Choctaw'. She frowned. 'From Oklahoma,' I added. She stared, puzzled. 'I'm Indian,' I volunteered. 'Oh are your parents from India?' she asked, brightening.

Most of the white kids were into surfing. They bleached their hair blonde and wore Saint Christopher medals and iron crosses and spoke of Gordon and Hansen surf boards, shooting the pier, hanging ten, the Banzai Pipeline. Meanwhile my father was getting drunk more often, becoming more violent. I had to be careful around him because he hit me. One night he came home and put his fist through a window again. Then he made me gamble for my paper route monies, blood from his cuts splattering the cards. Police began showing up at our door.

> You learn about life by the accidents you have, over and over again, and your father is always in your head when that stuff happens. Writing, most of the time, for most people, is an accident and your father is there for that, too. You know, I taught writing for a while and whenever somebody would tell me they were going to write about their dad, I would tell them they might as well go write about killing puppies because neither story was going to work. It just doesn't work. Your father won't let it happen.
>
> *Kurt Vonnegut*

School wasn't going well. The white kids thought I was Asian. They called me Charley Jap and Wong Fing, slanting their eyes with their fingers and purring 'Ah sooo' when I passed by. 'Banzai!' they would also yell. Sometimes there were fights after school and they would shout 'Watch out for his karate kicks!' to my opponents. Besides being seen as a young defender of oriental manhood, I found school boring. I wanted to go back to Oklahoma and be with my friends and my grandmother. I got the chance when I turned fourteen.

My mother had been making extra money, so my parents decided to send me to military school. I'd seen war movies which portrayed soldiers as being glorious and brave. I was going to learn how to be a soldier and it would be cool, I thought. But Oklahoma Military Academy was in many ways bizarre, although so highly rated that after graduation and army boot camp you were awarded a real officer's commission. The school also had real army instructors, and for teenage types in 1965, OMA was a seriously gung-ho place.

We learned how to march and drill, and how to take apart, clean, and fire our M-1 carbines. We were up by six each morning and double-timed when we weren't in formation. Any mistake required twenty or thirty push-ups; 'One sir, two sir, three sir ...' In the chow hall we squared our food, picking up a fork or glass in deliberate, slow motion angular movements, taking a quick sip or mouthful. Our bed blankets had to be tucked so tight that you could bounce a coin off them. And we went on bivouac, living in two-man tents to play war games.

Out in the field we were taught how to map coordinates and how to identify night landmarks, taught elementary camouflage and the element of surprise. In our military science classes we were shown how to stop a sucking chest wound, the walls festooned with posters of prisoners bravely resisting torture. We had constant inspections, and I learned how to spit-shine my combat boots until they gleamed like mirrors and polish my brass epaulettes and belt buckle into an acceptable radiance. I couldn't say school was boring anymore.

71

Sound off
One two!
Once more
Three four!
Bust your nuts
One two three four one two ... three four!
Marching cadence from Oklahoma Military Academy

Some cadets found bizarre ways to avoid being picked on. One of them was overweight, uncoordinated Vincent who would voluntarily stick his head down a toilet and pull the handle, always good for laughs. No one needed to humiliate Vincent; he'd do it for you. He convinced bullies that other dimensions rolled by at night and if you only ran fast enough it was possible to catch up with one and enter it. On some nights half of our barracks would be outside chasing other dimensions, led by Vincent. I figured it was his little private joke.

After all we aren't savages really ...
William Golding, Lord of the Flies

Our company barracks were run by older cadets, with no adult supervision. There was a secret clique called the 'Silent Seven' that wore pillow cases with eye slits and who carried entrenching tools. They'd visit you at night if you made mistakes during drill. I was visited while I slept. It was a rude awakening. Suddenly a blanket would be thrown over my head, and I would be hit with small, flat shovels. The visits didn't improve my performance.

I regularly made mistakes during drill practice, but it wasn't because I didn't try. I had a slight foot deformity and curvature of the spine, which meant that I couldn't square my shoulders exactly straight or march in an exact straight line. At fourteen I was small and skinny and my rifle had a difficult breech to open. Sometimes on the drill field during the order 'inspection arms' I'd struggle with my M-1. None of this pleased my drill sergeant.

What the fuck is your problem Injun? Are you some kind of a red retard?
My drill sergeant

Maybe it was all designed to separate men from boys, or turn boys into men, or it was a rite of passage, or tough love, or some crabwise defence of the American Way. I didn't care. I hated the place. When we were finally allowed weekend passes I caught a bus to Tulsa. A lady across from me noticed my military visor cap, navy blue coat, insignia, brass buttons and fourragere and asked if I was in the Chinese army. 'Ah sooo.' I purred. She nodded wisely. But I got to see my friends and I visited my grandmother, who said I looked great in my uniform.

It was 1966. I wanted to quit military school and live in Tulsa, but my grandfather said I couldn't stay at his house. I asked my parents if I could come home. They were reluctant, figuring the discipline was doing me good. Finally they gave in and I caught the bus back. By then they had moved to another small town in California. My new school had the familiar Mexican and white separation but also had black and Asian students.

Ours was an Indian version of *The Grapes of Wrath*. Arriving in from Oklahoma thirty years after the big dust bowl exodus but still looking for the Big Rock Candy Mountain, my folks were being swept along by the odd restlessness they had picked up during the Second World War. Our identities were quickly submerged beneath teeming millions all looking to burrow their way inside the American Dream. Over time my parents would manage to slap together enough loose pieces of that dream to enjoy a middle-class lifestyle for maybe a year or so.

Great sandy flatlands encircled the town, an arid domain of tumbleweeds, lizards, cactuses, sagebrush and rattlesnakes. The sprawling isolation of small town living was made bearable by air conditioning. No one seemed to know the more ancient history of the place we inhabited. There were no area creation stories that the locals knew of, nor did they seem to know how to touch the land except through scenic hikes, or by riding dune buggies and motorbikes out into the desert to leave long scars across the dry, brown face of the earth.

When we're in nature we can quickly sense the spirit of the land is familiar. We may not know where we are, but we feel a maternal tie to the earth if we want to. In towns, the longing for where we've been before must translate into a new sense of place. People do that for us. It's the human touch that slowly pulls us into a community and makes it familiar. Slowly I made new friends but, like myself, none of them fit easily into any racial or social order.

Mario was a Japanese–Italian kid raised in Rome. Paulie was the son of a wealthy Mexican landowner. He and his mother had fled Mexico under mysterious circumstances. Andy was an overweight white kid rejected by his peer group. Juan was black and Mexican with straight hair. Alonzo was Mexican, adopted by a white couple and unable to relate to his people. Dominic was culturally Mexican but didn't care to relate to his people.

Dominic, Juan, and Mario were good looking guys, but for looks, style, and ability to pick up girls, Paulie was the star of our group. Paulie was a bit short but he had a weightlifter's arms and shoulders, and he was a good boxer. Although he lived in a run-down house, Paulie had been raised giving orders to poor Mexicans who had worked on his father's large estates. So he avoided fellow Mexicans, clinging to a vanished sense of status.

This Car Doesn't Run On Friendship

Sign posted on the dashboard of my friend Paulie's car

Juan's Mexican mother spoke Spanish to him which he didn't understand, and he responded with his standard, 'Si, mama.' Juan's black father had a good job, but felt his white co-workers disrespected him. I was the only one who spent time at Juan's house with his black friends. Dominic was from Mexico, and I had a crush on his sister, Consuela. One day Dominic quit school, found a job and went to work. After that his smiles were tired and sleepy.

Dominic liked to try and bleach his hair blonde like a surfer, but it was too dark and always turned red. Andy was friendly and talkative, his folks were white middle class. Besides being overweight and immature there wasn't much wrong with Andy. Alonzo was Andy's friend. His adoptive white parents were also middle class. He was short and dark, didn't want to speak Spanish, and was only allowed to see us at Andy's house.

My best friend was Mario. He had black, wavy hair and was tall and muscular, olive coloured with broad cheekbones and slanted eyes. Mario's paternal relatives had been civilian prisoners in California's Japanese intern-ment camps, and his father had served in the Japanese–American battalion during the Second World War. Mario's parents met in Rome during the war; his mother had been one of Benito Mussolini's secretaries. Theirs was the only house I've been in where bowls of rice were served with Italian wine. And Mario's mother was nice.

You a good a boy, eh? You like a to draw.

My friend Mario's mother

To please her I painted a Fascist axe and bundle, which she proudly dis-played on her refrigerator, my only attempt at fascist art. Mario spoke English with an Italian accent, and was somewhat of an intellectual, influenced by Rome's politics. Eventually Mario would teach me to think critically, and to speak up, on long evening walks around town when the air was cooler. We would have plenty of time for walking. After Paulie started getting even more popular with the ladies our group wasn't able to pile into his junky old car and go cruising as much.

Maybe you know how that is, none of the rest of your friends have cars so you're reduced to walking and hanging out. So we took over Andy's garage, which had a record player and a pool table. We shot pool and listened to vinyl records but didn't talk much about school because none of us liked it. All of us felt an unspoken alienation towards school. Except for Andy, it was hard for us to be enthused about the place. Not only were all of the teachers white, so was the curriculum.

The school elite were well-off white kids who drove better cars than our teachers, their new rides gleaming imperiously with reflected neon as they slow-cruised down Main Street. During pep rallies I sat with the Mexican kids in the top bleacher rows. Our section didn't stand to cheer, even when the mascot performed or the all-white cheerleaders did flips or shouted at us through bullhorns. Our apathy always annoyed the cheerleaders.

What's wrong with you kids? Don't you have any school spirit?

A cheerleader at Pecan Valley High School

The rest of us talked about girls, but only Dominic and Paulie had girl-friends. To me, relationships were as mysterious as love songs on the radio. When Paulie bragged that he could take Dominic's girlfriend away with a single phone call I dared him to try, betting him five dollars that he couldn't. I felt it was a safe bet because Dominic's girlfriend had vowed that she would always be true. I explained all this to Paulie, who nodded as he dialled the number. I listened in on the conversation. Three minutes later I'd lost five dollars I didn't have.

Pay me the money or no more ridings in my car.

My friend, Paulie

Consuela, Dominic's sister, was slim and pretty and we saw each other a while before she went back to Mexico. Once we sat close together at the ball field and talked about the future. After my shyness left I told her that one day I would be an Indian artist like my father. She nodded but I could tell she didn't understand, and maybe I didn't either. Consuela and I went to Mass together, and on the church steps she casually reached up and straightened my tie, which felt wonderful. But I was too shy to ask Consuela for a real date.

My first kiss happened in 1967 with Winnie May, a black girl. I'd been going to band practice near Juan's house and was thought of as a band member, which was odd since I didn't play an instrument. Sometimes I would try and sing. The band was learning the Motown hits we were hearing on the radio. The kiss came after band practice behind someone's house. Winnie May was grinding her hips into some of the guys while holding them in a standing embrace. She came up and ground on me for a while, and then she kissed me.

75

Our little town was in the Imperial Valley where summer temperatures soared to 115 degrees. In the evenings Mario and I would go walking through the whiff of feed lots and he would expound on other mysteries that surrounded us. Through Mario I found my voice for debate; he would raise issues which we'd discuss. 'What is truth?' was a constant theme. He also railed against socialism, and we debated Free Will, most probably to annoyingly adolescent conclusions. Then I'd walk back home to the Mexican side of town.

What is truth? Is it something we can see? Show me truth.

My friend Mario

Those walk-and-talk discussions introduced me to the idea that there is wisdom in the ordinary, and that life is worth thinking about. Mario was like a smart big brother. Later he would finish a doctorate and teach philosophy. In time, my parents moved to a more prosperous neighbourhood, as close as they ever got to the great American middle class. With nicer surroundings came older conflicts. But I wouldn't be staying much longer.

Mario invited me to a political discussion held in the home of a Mormon family. On the coffee table was a book called *He Walked the Americas* about a white-bearded prophet that once came among various Indian tribes. Written by a non-Mormon, the book's cover illustration was in the traditional style of Indian art my father had painted in. The book intrigued me, and I became friends with the family. Soon they asked me to move in with them. My mother seemed relieved. So it was that I was introduced to the Mormon faith.

The Book of Mormon is a true record of God's dealings with the ancient peoples of the Americas.

Elder Hull, missionary, Church of Jesus Christ of Latter Day Saints

After a while my mother became worried about me falling into the clutches of what she called an un-godly religion. I also think that in a small town it didn't reflect well on her to have one of her sons living with strangers. My father's only concern was that the other family were nahullo, white people. They decided to send me to boarding school again, but this time to an experimental Bureau of Indian Affairs school in Santa Fe, New Mexico.

They figured an art school would suit me since I liked to draw. Entry into the Institute of American Indian Arts required sketches of a shoe and a bicycle but I submitted an Apache fire dancer painted in the older genre I'd seen my father use. The school accepted me anyway. I was leaving behind more family drama. My little brother would start to rebel, and, unknown to my father, my

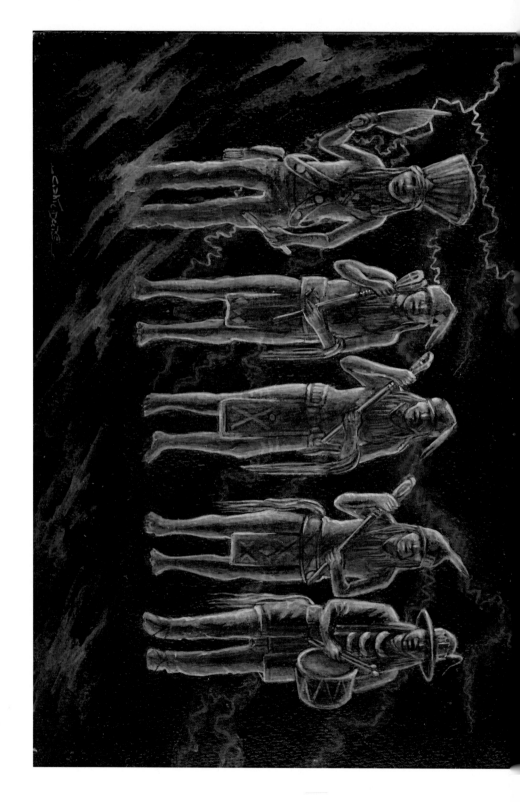

mother was plotting divorce. But something else was waiting down the highway and in 1968 I was being sent off to find whatever that was.

> Again, you can't connect the dots looking forward; you can only connect them looking backwards. So you have to trust that the dots will somehow connect in your future. You have to trust in something – your gut, destiny, life, karma, whatever. This approach has never let me down, and it has made all the difference in my life.
>
> *Steve Jobs*

We don't always remember the day that came to take us from the last places we were when we were seen as children, when we awoke to a morning somewhere beyond our parents. I remember that morning. I was on a bus to Santa Fe. Sometimes I still feel traces from a night I wouldn't come back from, looking out of a bus window into neon and darkness, moving away from faces of days I once knew so clearly but, like everyone else, couldn't stay in anymore.

Santa Fe's adobes shone yellow ocher and earth pink in the late summer sun as the bus pulled into the station. At the Institute there were Indian kids from all over America. Unlike my last boarding school, the place had an amazing amount of freedom. This would have been alright if I would have handled my goings and comings more maturely. I didn't. Most of the students were from remote reservation areas, and with easy access to alcohol many of them began to drink like fishes. My new friends and I were different; we drank like winos.

It didn't take long to make new friends. There was Dan, a Crow from Montana and my room-mate Rob who was a Yakima from Washington State and Richie, a Ute from Idaho, and Melvin, a Lakota from South Dakota. There were the two Lujan sisters from Taos, and others who floated in and out of our little circle. Richie, Dan, Melvin and I were on very limited budgets so we became connoisseurs of cheap wines like Twister, Orange Rock, Tokay, Mission White Port, and Thunderbird; a wine that has 17.5% alcohol by volume.

> What's the word? Thunderbird.
> How's it sold? Good and cold.
> What's the Jive? Bird's alive.
> What's the price? Thirty twice.
>
> *Radio jingle from the 1960s*

My shyness left me when I drank. I felt alright Jack, and the world became a wonderful place filled with excitement and adventure. We were all underage so we always had to get a runner, someone over eighteen to buy our wine. We'd take up a collection, pay the runner extra and send them off to the Garden Spot, a liquor store close to the school. Runners were important, for within the wine shadows girls appeared.

Probably because of all those sixties love songs I was hearing on the radio I still had romantic ideas of what being with girls would be like, but I found that talking to them under the stars in a nearby city park was pretty basic. After a few swigs, or more, girls sometimes wanted to kiss, and sometimes they wanted sex. But my second sexual encounter didn't happen while drinking. It occurred after school in an almost empty classroom.

A female classmate, Zena, approached one of my friends and I, and suddenly began to fondle us. She had a crazed look, it was a bizarre incident, and I had the feeling that more than sex may have been involved since she didn't want to do anything else but grab at us. Otherwise she was like Winnie May on steroids. Later on, somehow, Zena became my first official girlfriend. By then she had quit surprising guys and had become shy, but she did offer to do my laundry.

Zena's ex-boyfriend wanted her back and he had a gang. And the gang started following us. They all dressed like cowboys and walked sort of bowlegged which made the gang very easy to spot, although they attempted to operate like spies on a mission. Two of them acted as scouts, signalling two others whenever we approached. Then the four of them would tail us at a distance, shifting from side to side, ducking behind trees when we'd turn around. They were kind of creepy, and it was hard for Zena and I to be alone together.

Finally the ex-boyfriend sent in an apprentice medicine man, a fellow student who wore sunglasses, even at night. And one night I left a basketball game for my dorm room to get a half-pint of Bacardi; by then my friends and I had graduated from wine to rum. From the hall I noticed that my door was ajar and the light was on. As I crept up to the doorway I heard soft chants. I burst through the door and surprised the guy with the sunglasses.

He was holding what looked like a gourd. Instinctively I grabbed him by his arm and slung him towards the door. He slid across the polished wood floor, hit a wall, adjusted his sunglasses and ran off. The guy was sick for several days. Maybe his little ceremony did affect Zena and me, because shortly afterwards I broke up with her. I liked Zena, she was smart and pretty and had a great shape but our relationship had gotten very weird. And while love songs on the radio included break-ups they didn't have much to say about witchcraft.

In 1969 I was transferred to Carter Seminary, another boarding school in Oklahoma. The following year I met my future wife in Kansas at Haskell Indian Junior College. Lori was quiet and pretty, dark with long black hair. We became close, walking around campus with arms locked, going to town together and talking of marriage and the future. We hadn't met each other's relatives yet but we had religious experiences in common; she had briefly been on the Mormon Church's Placement Programme, living with a church family in Colorado.

When Haskell's school year ended we caught the bus to Yuma, Arizona, where my mother and brother had moved after my mother had divorced my father. Lori and I married in 1971 on the Quechan Indian Reservation in the Church's meeting house there. Following the wedding ceremony several older Quechan ladies presented us with a hand-sewn quilt. Later we were told that the cloth for the quilt had come from a bordello. We stayed with my mother that summer and worked briefly in the surrounding fields, paid to pick grapefruit.

Choctaws aren't a Plains tribe, which made me seem suspect to my new in-laws, all of them Kiowas, Comanches, and Apaches. My sisters-in-law knew the outdated custom of the eldest sister's husband and his claim on younger sisters as wives. They seldom came near me, just to be sure. The family practiced mother-in-law avoidance, which was actually alright. My brothers-in-laws didn't have much to say, either. In many Indian families son-in-laws are kept outside family circles, seen as part-time handymen and occasional financial contributors.

One should never know too precisely whom one has married.

Friedrich Nietzsche

But my father-in-law loved to joke and talk, and sometimes he repeated old stories that his grandfather told. Tall and quiet with white hair, his grandfather was also living in the house and was a respected Indian doctor who used yellowhammer feathers to locate ailments in people, moving the feathers over the bodies of his patients as a woodpecker looks for grubs hiding inside a tree, or as a douser looks for water. After he located a malady he'd make a light scratch, place his mouth over it and by applying suction, remove the ailment.

He didn't wear beadwork or feathers. But that bent old man in the bent straw hat and old maroon shirt, that man in the khaki pants and the bull hide shoes, that old Indian man who the farmers wouldn't give rides to when they saw him walking to town; that man was born in a tipi, and he could make you whole again. There had been sick babies brought to him in winter from cold, drafty houses, little Indian babies whom the white doctors had given up on.

And he had taken pneumonia out of their lungs, saving many lives. Then one day a white man from Texas came to visit my in-laws. He'd once worked at a frontier theme park firing off a cannon. The cannon backfired, shooting black powder into his hand. Dermatologists removed most of the residue but had left black powder granules they couldn't get to embedded between his fingers, which caused him constant pain.

The old man had sucked the rest of the powder out except for a few specks, which the visitor showed me. He said he hadn't been in pain since. My father-in-law kept a buffalo medicine bundle which was renewed each year. His large extended family would camp on the premises and put up a tipi where the male members would gather to renew the bundle. There would be outdoor cook fires and visiting among the camps. After the bundle renewal ceremony everyone would bless themselves with cedar smoke and go home.

> A long time ago there was an encampment of people who were starving. One morning a little boy awoke in his tipi and said, 'Get up mother, I smell buffalo.' The people were desperate so they followed the boy, and he led them to a buffalo herd. The men were getting ready to attack the herd, but the little boy made them wait. He drew a circle in the ground around the herd.
>
> The hunters found that the circle had created an invisible pen. The boy told the men to only kill as many buffalo as they needed, which they did. Then the boy rubbed out part of the circle and the rest of the herd escaped through it. Those little boy's words to his mother are the words we use in our bundle song. That buffalo medicine bundle is for food, clothing and shelter blessings for our family, those things which the buffalo provide.
>
> *My former father-in-law*

Back in 1973 Lori's area was made up of poor Indian families and better off white neighbours with little socialising between the two groups. Down a dirt road, past barbed wire fences and washed out gullies and pastures was the small town of Carnegie and its worn bricked main street, pot holed roads, slow moving farmers, all white police force and its all white city council. Indian children routinely dropped out of Carnegie's schools and there was a fierce sense in the Indian community of having been cheated, of always being on the outside.

Many Indian community members attended peyote meetings, sweat lodges, or missionary churches, spiritual observances involving prayer and sacrifice. For many as well, marriage was only temporary and infidelities were eagerly anticipated. There was heavy drinking in the community and children were often born out of wedlock. Mixed in with ceremonies, prayers, and healings were brittle marriages and shifting sexual liaisons. In my wife's family these two seeming opposites coexisted without a sense of guilt or contradiction.

> I don't care if you're married
> Sixteen times
> I still love you
> I'll get you yet ...
>
> *49 song from Oklahoma*

I'd been working at Indian City USA near Anadarko, Oklahoma, as an artist-in-residence. We moved to Anadarko briefly, and then we moved again to Tulsa. We got an apartment near my grandparents and I continued to sell paintings. Lori went into labour one night and despite our headlights going off and on we made the 40 mile drive to Claremore Indian Hospital in time for our first child to be born. It was 1974 and we just had a baby boy. But he might have been our last. The chances had been good that Lori could have been sterilised.

> One of the people who initiated the government investigation into IHS sterilisa-
> tion policy was Dr Connie Uri, a Choctaw Indian physician working at the
> Claremore, Oklahoma IHS facilities. Dr Uri had noticed in the hospital records
> that a large amount of sterilisation surgeries had been performed. She then
> conducted her own interviews with the women involved and found that many
> had received the operation a day or two after childbirth. In the month of July
> 1974 alone there were forty-eight sterilisations performed and several hundred
> had already been conducted in the last two years.
>
> *Akwesasne Notes, 1974:22*

It was an American government policy designed to decrease the Indian population through sterilisation of Indian women at Indian Health Service (IHS) facilities. Lori had been asked while she was groggy with pain pills and lying in a hospital bed to agree to sterilisation but she refused. During that time there were many other female patients at Claremore Indian Hospital who were sterilised, many without their knowledge or consent.

Our first child was wondrous, and we would push him around the neighbourhood in his stroller. He went with us everywhere, and we bought him a red baby Pendleton blanket. We took him to powwows and laid his Pendleton down by our chairs so he could roll around and play. When he was a newborn he went with us to the Choctaw Fair in Mississippi, and I carried him to the top of Nanih Waiya, the ancient Choctaw mound.

Once his mother brought him into a peyote meeting. It was morning time, and I was holding him on my lap. Sunlight shone through the tipi and the fire was turning to ash. The traditional breakfast was going around, and everyone in the circle was taking bites of the corn, meat, and fruit and sipping the water. I had been up all night in the ceremony and thought how wonderful it was that I had my little son with me at such a special time.

> This day has never been seen. This day has never been told. Yesterday is no more. Tomorrow has not been promised us.
>
> *Frankie Roubideaux, Iowa elder; Speaking in a peyote meeting*

Then I felt a wetness on my knee. I asked if my son and I could be excused and Frankie Roubideaux, the old man running the meeting stared sternly for several long moments before he gave us permission to leave the tipi. I'd been all dressed up in a white shirt, silver scarf slide, new boots and a Chief Joseph Pendleton blanket. Babies I learned, don't care if you're trying to look cool. But it was great to be near my grandmother, and she loved Lori. My grandma called our firstborn baby her 'chief' and she spoiled him more than she ever had me.

Children and marriage can make you fat somehow, and I began gaining weight. It seemed that pressure to produce paintings caused me undue stress. I seldom drank and never around my family, but I started to put off painting, our only source of income. There was something else, an unresolved anger that I'd carried from my growing up years that I didn't know how to talk about. Like my parents I began staring into space, becoming either sullen or at times overreacting.

> As poignantly seen in figure 3 (a) the dourly afflicted countenance of the classic morose male demeanour is ideally characterised by a strong protrusion of the lower lip so as to produce a subtle spasmodic but nevertheless woefully apparent quivering episode glumly accentuated by a fully perturbed knitting of the eyebrows held firmly in a strained 'V' or distressed 'dying seagull' shaped pattern.
>
> The North American Encyclopedia of Classical Frowning, *p. 82*

In the 1980s we had another boy and girl, both different, and both of them beautiful. We'd been blessed with healthy, intelligent, good looking kids. Our next little girl came to us in a special way. One of Lori's sisters had been abandoning her baby daughter. I'd seen the baby and was concerned. When the mother went drinking she left the baby alone in a playpen surrounded by cats. I sent word that if the mother didn't want her baby then we would take care of her. A week or so later the mother came down to visit us.

She asked if we could watch her baby while she looked for work. Seventeen years went by without a card, visit or phone call. The first few days our new little daughter made soft mewing sounds that she had learned from the cats. She just fitted into the stair-step pattern of the rest of our children, and she grew up to be sweet and caring, intelligent and very pretty. Later she had her own baby, born with a skin allergy. The doctors asked her to find out the baby's family medical history. So my daughter called her birth father. I wondered if they would bond.

That would be alright, I thought. In tribal societies children often have more than one set of related parents for it ensures that there won't be any orphans. During their phone conversation my daughter's birth father said he was sorry he hadn't been there for her while she was growing up because she'd never had the chance to be a daddy's girl. My daughter told him that she'd always been a daddy's girl. That she always had me.

> Hopefully we were all daddy's little girl. He was and hopefully still is wrapped around our little finger. Not to take advantage of, more just for the comfort of knowing he is there.
>
> *Violette DeSantis*

We were blessed with two more healthy, beautiful sons. My painting career had high points and also years when I struggled. My wife wanted to stay in the home, and I sometimes put my brushes aside for other jobs. In 1982 we settled outside Ada, a small town where my mother and grandmother had begun to share a house after my grandfather died. Now our children were like seven stair steps without much separation in age.

Where we once lived there is a slow paced mix of the American South and the Cowboy West, ranches, pick-up trucks. It's the last place where there is an abundance of green grass and fat shade trees, a bit further west and the land changes to rolling plains and afterwards its mostly different kinds of desert and mountains and skinny trees clear to the Pacific. There are Chickasaws and Seminoles and Choctaws, hidden dance grounds and Indian churches and throughout the sunny months, the obsession of Indian fast pitch softball.

North of where we lived dancers move around ceremonial fires on summer nights. Without knowing you might miss them unless you're out driving a dark dirt road and through an open window you hear singing. Beyond the wild plums of mid-spring and the cornfields of summer, on past the possum grapes of fall there is a long winter hush, then everyone it seems is waiting to pick wild onions and feel the early spring again.

Our home was on the bend of a curving gravel road at the edge of a small woods. We were in a rural tribal housing area among thirteen other homes that locals called the 'Indian Circle'. In winter we were sometimes snowed in, unable to drive to the highway. Summers were drenched in Oklahoma wet heat, but in their turn our seven children roamed the circle and laughed and played through it all. It was our place of refuge.

Baby nosi, cho-cho in tamaha ki'liya.

> 'Baby sleep and we'll go to pig town'
> Choctaw lullaby

Their mother and I told them stories we'd heard growing up, and sometimes I sang them old songs; sunrise walk dance, raccoon dance, stealing partners, and other times my four sons and I practiced with our ball sticks. Sometimes we went to ceremonies at Kellyville or Gar Creek or New Tulsa, and it was very good to see our children shining in those tribal circles. Otherwise, there were odd pictures in my head of an ideal family that didn't fit who we were.

Those pictures I think were loosely based on *Leave it to Beaver* reruns. The show was about the Cleavers; a wholesome, white, middle-class American family. Ward Cleaver invariably sported a tie and June, the mother, always wore pearl necklaces and had perfectly coiffed hair. There was oldest son Wally, steady and reliable, and then young Theodore, widely known as The Beaver. The scariest thing that ever happened to that family was having socially challenged Eddie Haskell over for dinner.

We were never the Cleavers. We often struggled as I painted for a living, though there were interludes when it felt like we were on a financial cruise ship of sorts. My idea was to keep everyone safe like Mr Cleaver did, although how the guy made money was a global mystery. For I was usually behind in paying bills, and always chasing Christmas. And one late December a couple of major bills I'd been postponing until after the holidays caught up with me.

Because I hadn't done any Christmas shopping yet I was able to pay the bills right away, but with money meant for presents. The Oklahoma galleries had quit buying artwork the week before, so I decided to knock out a quick stack of paintings, chance selling them in New Mexico, and then buy Christmas. Three days later my friend Sammy Billy and I took off in his truck for Albuquerque, making the run in ten hours. But the Indian art galleries in Albuquerque had closed for the holidays as well, except for one.

The owner was willing to trade but didn't want to spend any money, and he was about to shut down, too. I picked out turquoise and silver jewellery, a Taos drum, chile ristras, bags of roasted pinon nuts, an adobe oven incense burner, and a Navajo rug. Sammy wanted to visit relatives afterwards so we spent the night with them in town, and then there were deer and buffalo dances before daylight on Christmas morning in the church at Zia Pueblo and not a priest in sight. As we sped back to Oklahoma I wondered; was Christmas really necessary?

It seemed like a lot of trouble. I'd heard how some Mississippi Choctaw families weren't sure what Christmas was, and didn't ever have presents. I arrived home late Christmas afternoon, and my seven children were waiting. 'Merry Christmas!' I said, handing out the unwrapped gifts. There was a long and fairly awkward silence. My kids had been expecting the toys they'd been seeing on television; toys covered in papers and bows and placed under a decorated tree, and to be opened on Christmas morning, not late in the afternoon.

In those years my wife and I would wait up Christmas Eve until our children slept, uncover hidden dolls and plastic gizmos and quietly with the door well shut wrap them in bright boxes. Somewhere between sunrise and breakfast we'd watch the children turn the floor into a primal flaying ground of scattered wrappings and torn cardboard. But they were our times. And I see how they went too fast.

Fast like scattered papers and bows or a quick stack of paintings or a truck speeding in from Albuquerque. People say you can't buy Christmas, it's about baby Jesus or chestnuts roasting on an open fire. I still don't know if Christmas is necessary, but I know you can buy it. So if you have children who expect toys for Christmas and you don't buy those toys and wrap them in a timely fashion then you'll need a good explanation, like maybe Santa is in rehab or something. But I know now those bright boxes also held memories. And that's what we can't buy.

> Shi boy, my family were well off. We had a warm hogan, lots of sheep and crops, and when we needed money we made silver and turquoise jewellery, or we wove rugs to take to the trading post. We had everything. Then a social worker came and told us that because our hogan had a dirt floor and didn't use electricity or running water we were poor. We had everything until that woman told us we were poor.
>
> *My friend Sammy Billy, Navajo*

While working at home I learned how to tune out the noise of my children so well that I can paint through anything except maybe spontaneous combustion. And I can't sense or listen to my adult children the way I do other people. Within each of them are small childhood faces I still see playing, crying, laughing. I hear their voices from moments when we were close and living as a family, when there was constancy of presence and sound, trips into town and family meals. I still feel echoes of who I and my children once were.

My eldest daughter would give me one of my worst scares. She attended a mostly white rural high school and started hanging around a big farm girl who had become her protector. The two became close friends, and one day they decided to run away together. There were no traces of them found anywhere, and the big farm girl's family hadn't a clue as to where they might have run off to. I blanketed the area with fliers and made trips to all the area police stations and county sheriffs offices. I talked to all of both girls' friends.

Then I did it over again. And again. At night I couldn't sleep. Making matters worse was my friend, a former policeman, who kept dreaming up dire scenarios, including the idea that the girls had been sold into prostitution. Finally someone suggested I contact the farm girl's former employer, a fast food chain. Their computer records showed that the farm girl had applied for work with them in eastern Colorado. She had given an address.

Grabbing his service revolver, my friend sprang into action, taking me on a dawn raid into Colorado. What dark dangers would we have to rescue them from, he speculated. We found the girls and they were alright, living quietly in a trailer park. They had just started jobs. My daughter got in the truck, and we went home. That was years ago, and I'd like to think she now realises how the experience affected me. But I doubt it.

> Any astronomer can predict with absolute accuracy just where every star in the universe will be at 11.30 tonight. He can make no such prediction about his teenage daughter.
>
> *James T. Adams*

My parents were the last of their immediate family lines. Our numbers had slimmed, and we were quietly fading. Of two children, only I married. Now those lines will continue. There is a blossoming again, my seven shining children have given me grandchildren. It's true, grandchildren are special. My second oldest daughter has a little four-year-old girl who treats me like a big doll. She combs my hair or tries to, and brings me unopened cans of food on paper plates.

Once as I held a baby granddaughter I noticed her steady gaze, as if she were about to speak. A very intelligent look, I thought. Smart girl, and probably gets that from me, I figured. 'What is it baby?' I asked. 'What is it you're trying to say?' She continued to stare, her little eyebrows knitting in concentration. If only she could talk, I thought. This little girl has a wisdom beyond her years. Then I discovered she'd been concentrating on filling her diaper.

Good friends are relatives you weren't given through your parents but you needed them anyway. I miss good friends I've left. I can't remember saying goodbye to anyone and maybe it's because I thought I'd return from other places. All of my friends root me to shared places where they and I are known like hills or trees or memories can be known, and from where unfamiliar winds can't blow us too far away.

> Grandson, it's better to make friends than to make brothers because a brother can treat you any way they want and you're still brothers. But to keep a friend you got to treat them good.
>
> *Bill Panther*

In 1995 my grandmother died. She was a kind and loving light who taught me to care for others, an accomplished example of generosity and the importance of family and friends. I wondered why her love of company hadn't at least affected my mother, for after she and my father divorced they both turned into recluses. When I'd visit them in their homes they'd smile and I could see a flickering of affection. Then their eyes would cloud over.

In 2003 I left my wife. She and I got along most of the time as friends and we could always talk, but our bond as husband and wife had slipped away many years before. I had stayed for our children and the idea that if all of us held hands and kept walking together, one day the fog would lift and there we'd be in sunshine, holding hands. It wasn't a plan, it was a metaphor.

> Trying to forget someone you love is like trying to remember someone you never knew.
>
> *Anonymous*

In 2004 I married again. My new wife, Maxine, was Jicarilla Apache and Oklahoma Choctaw, a descendant of the Apache chief, Velarde. Raised in Oklahoma, she had spent most of her childhood summers on the Jicarilla reservation in New Mexico. We had met in a group discussion for a Choctaw education project. Maxine has a doctorate in philosophy, and is a highly paid consultant for tribes and American government agencies. She was on planes a lot flying to and from reviews, consultancies, and meetings all over America.

Dulce, New Mexico was the second all-Indian town I'd seen and the effect is always memorable. The Jicarilla Apache make up almost all the town's residents and all of the city council. The schools are all-Indian, the stores are run by Indians and the police force is tribal. Dulce has issues like funding, street repairs and so forth which are common to other small towns. It's the American model realised on a tribal community level.

Maxine and I had gotten off to a rough start. One of my relatives was facing serious legal charges and Maxine offered to take me to a Navajo medicine man on their behalf. We drove to New Mexico and met with the man in a hogan, a Navajo house made of timbers with an earth floor. The medicine man looked into the coals of a fire and prescribed a ceremony. I was given several things to stay away from, including blood and arguing.

Driving back, Maxine and I argued as we passed a roadside accident. Later that day we had an accident of our own, hitting a pick-up truck broadside. Besides body trauma, Maxine suffered foot injuries. My face was smashed against the windshield, the end of my nose almost cut off. My right arm was broken in half, and I watched it rotate in the wind waiting for an ambulance. With my share of the insurance monies I hired a lawyer for my relative. A lie detector test cleared them of prior knowledge and wrong intent, resulting in a light sentence.

Later I tried showing my scars to some of my Choctaw friends, thinking they'd be impressed. They eagerly started pulling up their shirts and pants legs to display much bigger scars than mine while talking about all the car accidents they had barely survived. One of my friends announced that he had been left braindead for two hours. Another had sailed over a cliff. Another friend said that he had been in ten car wrecks including a fiery crash. After that I changed the subject and didn't mention my little accident again.

Maxine wanted a traditional Choctaw wedding. I asked a friend, an older man who was a chanter, to conduct the services at Maxine's family church in Oklahoma, a small Indian church out in the country. A wedding pole had been put up, decorated with ribbons and after a quick head start I had to chase Maxine. If she had reached the pole before I caught her the wedding would have been off. My male relatives and I had to come in from the woods, whooping, to the wedding. There were certain things both families had to do.

> We used to have another part of our wedding ceremony where the bride would pretend to hide, and her new in-laws would go find her. Then the groom would pretend to hide, and his new in-laws would go find him. One time this guy took off in a car and it took his future in-laws three days to run him down.
>
> *Harry James, Choctaw elder*

My friend gave a wedding talk in Choctaw describing the marital obliga-
tions of Maxine and I. Later it was pointed out that he hadn't mentioned anything about me working hard. Before traditional Choctaw weddings the bride's
family inspects the future groom's hands to see whether or not they're cal-
loused, the sign of a good provider. A red blanket was held above us, and our
relatives threw money on it as wedding gifts. Everyone joined in the Choctaw
wedding dance, and then went to the church's fellowship hall to eat.

We had combined a Christian service with Indian traditions, which was rare.
Afterwards Maxine and I moved to Mississippi, where she began working for
the Choctaw tribal government. The Mississippi Choctaw are very old-school;
most of their children speak Choctaw. I'd been in Mississippi a few times before
and had boarding school friends in many of the seven reservation communities.
Living there, I was drafted into a traditional medicine circle. The members were
Choctaw doctors and they asked me to join them.

While we were in Mississippi, Maxine saw on the Internet that my former
mother-in-law, her daughter and one of her granddaughters had drowned,
swept off a bridge by floodwaters as they were coming home from a powwow.
Maxine drove me to Nanih Waiya mound to pray for the family. As I stood on
the mound the cries of many owls swirled around me three times, slow and
deliberate. In tribal cultures owls announce death.

The sounds were high pitched and loud. The first two swirls lasted about
half a minute each, the third was shorter. I knew the longer swirls were for the
two adults drowned, the last for the granddaughter. Later, I asked Maxine if
she had heard anything; She hadn't. The sounds were for me alone, and then I
discovered something. I learned that blood ties endure beyond divorce or
dying. Children are a spirit bond, a certainty.

I had gone back to painting but in 2006 with Maxine's encouragement I
finished my art degree. But Maxine and I were arguing. She was displeased
much of the time, and I never seemed to be what she had in mind. We separated
in 2008 and would divorce two years later. We were together seven years,
more or less, before our relationship fell apart. Then in 2009 Bacone College in
Oklahoma hired me to teach Choctaw studies.

Through their later years my parents spoke wistfully of my brother, who
never visited though our father always kept a bedroom ready for him at his
house. Finally Josh wrote to them, and we learned of drugs, of his years hiding
in subways of faraway cities and his recovery. By then our little childhood
family was scattered. After their divorce my parents never saw or talked to
each other again. Of the two, my mother passed away first.

She lapsed into a coma and for a while she was kept alive by machines. At the funeral home I spent time with her body alone, and I cried by her coffin until I felt her spirit enter the room. I sensed what she wanted me to know; she was alright and I would be, too. Four years later my father became ill. On a spring day I drove him to High Hill for the last time. We parked and ate fried chicken in front of the small white church. He had travelled the world, lived in many places. On that day he looked around, smiled and said, 'I finally made it home.'

> When a Choctaw dies their spirit goes to the west and then travels along the Milky Way. A portal opens and the spirit enters it. When you look up into the Milky Way and see a star that glimmers a little brighter than the others, they say it's a Choctaw going home.
>
> *Ken York, Choctaw elder*

After my father died I dreamed of The Beautiful Dance. I was at the back of a crowd and it was sunset. Everyone seemed to be waiting. I was standing next to a cousin who as a teenager had gone to sleep drunk on the train tracks near town. That was how he had died. I saw living people I knew, and I thought that we all must be having the same dream. My cousin was young and he was smiling and it was nice to be visiting with him I thought.

'We should see the camps,' he said, so we left. We came to a big tent like army surplus stores used to sell. There was an old woman with her hair worn up, in the way older Choctaw ladies used to fix their hair. She asked if we wanted to eat. Food was laid out on a makeshift table. Then I remembered what my father said and it was too late; I'd gone away with a cousin who was dead. I know now that one day I'll be over at that place again when The Beautiful Dance will be for me. It will be sunset then and all my relatives will be there in the crowd, waiting.

CHAPTER 3
Paintings

EIGHT GRAND, SWISS

'Bobby, you are thinking so much. For you only the best tattoo maestro in Zurich. I have to show you how. It is so simple to try. Believe me.'

'Let me think about that some more, Giovanni,' Bobby offered. He had sold his soul many times in the art business, but he had never completely sold out before. It was where the Henshaws wanted the tattoo; that was the problem.

'No more thinking, my friend. The Mr and Mrs Henshaws are at the hotel two days, nothing more. Then they go to Belgium. You must begin right away. I have lost money with your experiments. Now there is no more time for what you want. The Henshaws have lotta money. They are wanted to pay eight thousand Swiss francs for you. One day of art, nothing more. Eight grand, they have agreed. You must do it. We need money, my friend, OK?'

Bobby stared at a spot somewhere above Giovanni's head and tried to look inspired. 'How about doing a hotel show? We still have eighteen big originals left. We could get some television coverage, newspaper stories; free publicity. I bet the venue would be free. They might even give me a free hotel room. What about that?'

'Forget about this Bobby. Nobody in Zurich understands what you paint now. Your business-suit Indians, your beaded syringes. Who wants to buy them? Only two they sell. Nothing more. Where are your buffalo hunts, warriors and the feathers? You are depressing people my friend. Believe me. Also you have told me this hotel idea of yours before. Do you remember?'

'Why can't it be another kind of tattoo, like maybe flowers or butterflies or something? That would be a lot more suitable if you think about it.'

'I say to you Bobby no more thinking, OK? The Henshaws have art from you already they love so much. They want a tattoo and give you money. What is the problem? You think too much, my friend. Art is art, my friend. Money is money, OK? Do your art and get the money. It is so simple. You need money, OK? I need money, OK? I have lost money on you this time, OK? We need money, my friend. Money. Eight grand, Swiss.'

'Yeah Giovanni you keep saying all that, but why can't they pick another body part? Maybe her shoulder or ankle or arm, or even her forehead.'

Dr Giovanni frowned. 'In Zurich there is nothing for you. If you don't do this, ask your Inca friends will they let you play with them.' Giovanni stared Bobby down, making him fidget. 'Can you play the guitar, my friend? How well can you play? To be the Indian bum playing for loose change? You will lose all your big belly, my friend. Because I have no more money for you, OK? No more money for you. Believe me. No more money. You must make this tattoo. Eight thousand Swiss francs only for one day, Bobby. Fantastic. You must do this, OK? Eight grand, Swiss. Fantastic.'

Spirits In The Rain, Waylon Gary White Deer

PAINTINGS: 1953 –

'Cause if you want to make a living you got to put on a good show.
(Johnny Lee)

My first memories of painting are from the time when my parents were working at Intermountain Indian School in Utah. It must have been 1953 or 1954. Intermountain was an all Navajo school, and the students there created traditional Yei paintings, Navajo gods, on white painted wood backgrounds using black ink. The starkness of that black-and-white imagery left an early visual imprint, and sometimes I see the faces of those Yei even now.

We moved into a duplex on campus and next door to Allan Houser, a Chiricahua Apache artist who'd almost been born a prisoner of war. Allan Houser's parents had belonged to Geronimo's band, imprisoned at Fort Sill, Oklahoma. Allan would become a famous artist. In those days he and my father were friends and painted together. Allan Houser had once been a student at the old Dorothy Dunn Studio in Santa Fe.

Dorothy Dunn had promoted a two-dimensional painting style very similar to what was evolving in Oklahoma, and also somewhat similar to traditional Yei pictorials. My father, too, painted old-school Indian art, influenced by our next door neighbour at Intermountain. I remember my father working late at night at our kitchen table finishing images of horses and riders, deer, and stickball players. Through his paintings you could feel the tribal circle glow.

He also painted Apache fire dancers, again influenced by Houser. My father said that the little people helped him mix his colours late at night, when the house was quiet. From an early age I knew that I wanted to paint like him. Much later I would be sent to the same Indian boarding school campus that Allan Houser had attended. By then the Dorothy Dunn Studio had been re-placed by IAIA, the Institute of American Indian Arts, but located on the same campus.

It was in 1968 that I first thought seriously about painting for a living, walking to my dormitory during a Christmas snowstorm. I'd stayed through the holidays, and the deserted IAIA campus was covered in white, like a blank canvas waiting for answers. Was my ambition really to paint like my father? If so, then why weren't there classes at the Institute for traditional Indian painting? Allan Houser taught at the school, and there was theatre, jewellery making, sculpture, modern dance, music, graphics, writing, and abstract expressionist painting.

Unfortunately, I hadn't made a good impression on my father's old friend. I'd shown up drunk for the first day of his sculpture class, and Mr Houser had gently escorted me to my dorm room. I'd taken sculpture only because traditional painting wasn't offered at the Institute. There were older campus murals of a thunderbird, women pounding corn, and a buffalo hunt, but the school had branded the flat, pictorial imagery as 'Bambi' art. The murals were largely ignored, left over from the campus' Dorothy Dunn Studio era.

Indians for too long have painted themselves in the white man's frame of reference. It's what I call the 'Bambi' school of art, a childlike, over-romantic view of Indians.

Fritz Scholder, German, French, English and Luiseno.
Painting Instructor, Institute of American Indian Arts

At the time I didn't understand Humanism, the philosophical underpinning of European and American art which glorifies individualism. Humanism emphasises 'me', while tribal communalism emphasises 'we'. The tribal circle is 'we' adaptive, but if changes in its aesthetics are forced or if they're reinvented then tribal concepts can become distorted. Such distortions are like the seeming clarity of an amusement park mirror. The Institute was a 'me' humanist mirror that bent tribal imagery, and we were expected to find ourselves in its eclectic reflections.

Although he didn't identify as an Indian there was no raging debate among Indian artists over Fritz Scholder's term 'Bambi' art. Then as now, white art critics and money were the defining voices of the Indian art world, with most of the money and critics solidly on the side of what was trendy. Fast becoming trendy then was 'Pop Indian' abstract expressionism. This rapidly emerging fusion of abstract expressionist painting and tribal imagery was being led by Fritz Scholder in Santa Fe and at the Institute, the school I was attending.

Indian visual artists are often treated as mute. Although their creations are partially regarded as self evident, their artistic intent is most usually explained for them by others. The artist used red. Are they angry? Let's answer that. On the same school campus and in two different eras the Indian boarding school system went far beyond interpreting artistic intent. In two different eras the Bureau of Indian Affairs created and promoted two major Indian art movements.

In 1962 when the Dorothy Dunn Studio was reborn as the Institute of American Indian Arts, painting styles shifted from 'Bambi' to 'Pop Indian'. Yet the same Indian boarding school policies used to mainstream tribal youth remained quietly intact. Reinventing tribal art forms was taught by the Institute as a 'me' vehicle of assimilation, taking students from what was perceived as the old 'we' tribal past into what was promoted as a more relevant and individualistic future. Such an agenda coloured not only painting but all the arts taught at IAIA.

Classic Indian jewellery making was discouraged, reinvented eclectic forms that suggested tribal imagery were offered instead. Dance was theatrically mainstream, although based on Indian themes. Tribal music was denatured by choral arrangements and other western constructs. Plays, essays, and poetry were produced by casting tribal storylines into more commonly accepted literary forms. Although there were no Indian audiences or collectors for such offerings, a large mainstream American market was eager for them.

Dictating tribal art movements had a history. During the earlier Santa Fe Indian School 'Bambi' era of the 1930s, Dorothy Dunn, a white art instructor, had promoted a pictorial style of Pueblo art in which several noted Southwest Indian painters were already working. Dunn assumed that all Indians were natural artists, and believed traditional Indian art was the best painting style for her students to learn. The notion that all Indians are gifted artists is plainly racist, and restricting creative expression is just plain wrong.

> She [Dorothy Dunn] trained us all the same way. Her style lacked originality and creativity.
>
> *Allan Houser*

Allan Houser attended Dorothy Dunn's Studio School and found it restrictive. Some critics further claim that Dunn taught a false style, a childlike and romanticised idealisation of Indian realities; 'Bambi' art. However, a decade earlier six young Kiowa painters had enrolled in a special programme at the University of Oklahoma. Most of them had already received basic art lessons from a Choctaw nun at Saint Patrick's Mission School. Known as the Kiowa Six, they were allowed to explore painting as a tribal group without instruction or interference.

Independently, the Kiowa Six developed a painting style almost identical to the style later taught at the Dorothy Dunn Studio. Their combined portfolio served as a template for Oklahoma traditional Indian painting, a genre which continues intertribally. Racism and creative restrictions aside, if Dorothy Dunn was teaching her students 'Bambi' art then why did two unrelated groups of Indian painters evolve into the same general painting idiom?

Because Dorothy Dunn's studio style was valid. Only her exclusion of other painting genres was wrong. The Kiowa artists were cultural heirs to the two-dimensional imagery depicted on tipis, hide paintings and in Plains ledger drawings. Stylistically similar, two-dimensional Southwest kiva paintings, pottery motifs and sand paintings influenced Dunn's southwestern students. Such parallel traditions were the origins of a confluent painting style.

> During this period these six artists developed what is commonly referred to as the Kiowa style. Like traditional Kiowa painting, the figures in these paintings were drawn on a plain background. Within the lines colour was used as a flat filler. This opaque paint was more solid than traditional vegetable dyes or pencil and ink. Partly because of this technique, Kiowa-style paintings, commonly of individual dancers or ceremonies, emphasise design.
>
> Visions and Voices: Native American Painting
> *Lydia L. Wyckoff, University of New Mexico Press 1996*

Dunn's studio approach may have produced more rigidity than originality, but it is condescending to say that her students or the Kiowa Six couldn't tell the difference between tribal expression and childlike romanticism. Most likely the mainstream public had romantic ideas about Indians that may have to an extent influenced the works of both groups. If true, then the same market forces must have also overtaken the later IAIA painters, as many of their works had enough feathered imagery to outfit the aviaries of several large zoos.

In its formative years traditional Indian painting was an expression of cultural nationalism. The Studio artists and the Kiowa Six painted tribal ceremonies when spiritual freedoms were being suppressed, tribal solidarity when tribal lines of authority were attacked, tribal dress when American clothing was promoted as civilised. And they celebrated the tribal circle when Indian schoolchildren were being taught culture shame.

> [Dorothy Dunn] did a lot for us. She made us realise how important our Indian ways were because we had been made to feel ashamed of them. She gave us something we could be proud of.
>
> *Geronima Cruz Montoya, Ohkay Owingeh,*
> *Student, The Studio School, Santa Fe Indian School*

With less good intent, IAIA taught art with a humanist agenda using reinvented tribal imagery while excluding traditional tribal genres. I remember the stunned look on a student's face after he had tried to submit a painting of a beautifully flowing turquoise horse for an art assignment. He'd just come from painting class and was holding the piece by the dormitory stairs uncertainly, wondering whether or not to throw it away.

The style was classic traditional Indian art, but it had been dismissed as cliché, as 'Bambi' art. I'd grown up with that painting style. Yet the same cultural rhythms which traditional artists drew from also influenced students at the Institute. The most prolific of the IAIA painters were those who were able to dip their brushes into collective realities and express the timeless communal tribal voice through changing idioms.

> I felt it to be a compliment when I was told that I had destroyed the traditional
> style of Indian art for I was doing what I thought had to be done.
>> *Fritz Scholder, Painting Instructor, Institute of American Indian Arts*

Like elsewhere, at the Institute the communal voice was sometimes expressed by group silence, a familiar solidarity which was easily shattered. Once our English class was visited by a trio in coats and ties who were recruiting students with initiative for a tribal youth leadership programme. The man doing most of the talking tossed a pen and writing pad on the floor, and said he wanted someone to take notes. That's how they'd find out who the go-getter among us was. The trio smiled expectantly as we sat silent and motionless.

When I was growing up Indians usually tried to sit at the back of the class, many dropped out of school, and questions from white authority figures were routinely answered with 'I don't know'. Years later my friend Alan would say that First Nations peoples were probably much more assertive before we were colonised, that being shy in public is a recent thing, and wasn't always normative. That makes a certain kind of sense; colonisation undoubtedly altered behaviour.

> Teacher to Indian student: Are you ignorant or just apathetic?
> Indian student: I don't know and I don't care.
>> *Joke told in Oklahoma*

Then again, although the Institute's students were from different tribal backgrounds, a 'we' set of social nuances was widely shared. It was considered rude and nervy to put yourself forward, polite and well mannered to consider the group. We had our own leaders anyway, and anyone with an urge to be too 'me' assertive without their group's approval would have been teased and then ignored. So we all sat quiet as the trio in suits scanned the room while waiting for a go-getter to appear.

Suddenly someone broke ranks, lay down on the floor, grabbed the pen and writing pad, looked up at the man and asked, 'Could you repeat that, sir?' It was Darren. He was from a big city, and his trendy social circle reminded me of the mainstream school elites I'd noticed in other places. Looking down at Darren it occurred to me that his solitary act was a transition into the new, modern 'me' world, an assertive place where the Institute wanted the rest of us to go. Or maybe Darren had been there all along.

In 1969 I left the Institute and was enrolled at Carter Seminary, an Oklahoma Indian boarding school. There was a dulling confinement at Carter. I quit school and went to live with my grandmother. I worked in a cafe and was promoted from washing dishes to frying hamburgers. It was wonderful to be with my grandmother again, but our reunion wouldn't last long. I didn't drink around my grandparents, but my grandfather didn't want me at his house.

Dick West, a renowned Cheyenne artist, was teaching art at Haskell Indian Junior College up in Kansas. Dr West painted Oklahoma traditional style. I didn't seem to have any other places to go to and I didn't want to fry burgers for a living. I passed a high school equivalency exam and applied to Haskell. In late summer of 1970 I checked into a dormitory at Haskell wondering what sort of room-mates I'd been assigned. One of them was Phil. A Delaware from Oklahoma, he'd informally studied traditional painting with Osage artist Loren Pahsetopah.

Phil's painting techniques were advanced, and he soon got us access to the art room in the evenings where we painted and talked Indian art. It seemed then that I had arrived at a place where I was supposed to be. Dick West let us pursue whatever painting styles we wanted, and besides correcting our drawings he left us to develop on our own. I liked his approach, even when he made gruff, teasing comments about our sketches while calling us 'buck' or 'buck-o' And it was fun to paint with Phil, to learn from observing his high skill level.

> Your Indian has a bread head buck-o ... his skull is abnormally long. See? Got that, buck? Bread head. Is he a contortionist too? Because his arms are backwards. Look how they bend. Or is that a woman? He's got a big hefty chest on him for a man. Yeah, looks like he might take a size 40 D cup. And is that supposed to be a Choctaw? Then why is he wearing hard-sole moccasins? Southeastern Indians wore one-piece moccasins. Got that, buck-o? One-piece moccasins. Move your elbow and let me straighten out your Indian for you, buck ...
>
> Dr W. Richard West, Southern Cheyenne,
> Painting Instructor, Haskell Indian Junior College

Besides traditional Indian painting, Dick West created in other styles including abstract symbolism. His centrepiece Christianity series was naturalistic, employing familiar mainstream three-dimensionality. His religious paintings questioned the routine depiction of Jesus Christ as a white European. Dick West painted Jesus as a Cheyenne, for its time a heretical notion in Bible Belt Oklahoma. His Cheyenne Jesus hung on a cross flanked by two Pawnees acting as Roman centurions. The Pawnee had been arch enemies of the Cheyenne.

Phil and I were from Oklahoma where a strong traditional Indian painting style was evolving. We developed in the flat 'we' style without thinking much about it, the traditional idiom was what we loved working in and had been exposed to, I through my father's paintings and his early friendship with Allan Houser. Unlike at the Institute, outside influences were encouraged at Haskell but weren't used to replace or reinvent traditional art forms. Dr West knew the ongoing legacy of Indian art, and the differences between adaptation and reinvention.

> The Indian artist must be allowed freedoms to absorb influences outside of his own art forms and see the promise of a new lane of expression that should keep the Indian's art the art form termed 'Native American painting' and I give my student every opportunity to execute it … I have always felt that the term abstraction has been a part of the Indian's thinking longer than most European contemporary influences and perhaps in a (truer) form.
>
> Dr W. Richard West, Southern Cheyenne,
> Painting Instructor, Haskell Indian Junior College

Dr West seemed sort of old, but still physically powerful. He was big and had the presence of a retired athlete, his voice deep and sonorous. On cold winter mornings when I'd be walking towards campus from a distant married student housing complex, Dr West would sometimes come barreling by in his braids and army surplus jeep with its 'Custer Had It Coming' sticker. He'd stop suddenly and intone, 'Get in, buck,' and we'd roar off towards the school. Sometimes he'd dryly ask, 'How come you Indians like to walk so much?'

Once he told about the time when a teacher had beaten him at Concho Indian School. Afterwards he visited his grandmother, camped in a tipi near the school. When she saw the bruises on him she and several old Cheyenne ladies angrily descended on the school, butchering knives drawn, looking for the offending teacher. The man fled his classroom, and the students climbed to the tops of the buildings to report down to the old women below in Cheyenne which way the man was running. The teacher escaped, but barely.

We had to submit three paintings each semester with very little actual instruction, but I tried to improve my sketches so I wouldn't have to hear any bread head or size 40 D cup comments. Finally I did a small painting that Dr

West seemed to like because he intoned, 'Give me this calibre in oil,' as he walked by. The painting went missing and I asked Dr West if he'd seen it. 'Gave it away,' was all he said. Later I found out that he'd chosen the painting as a gift for a visiting dignitary, the best compliment, although unexplained, he ever gave me.

> The sun arced bright beyond the window as his hand dipped again and again into the water glass, the mix looking like milk and tea, the colours drying dull, layering the palette in swathes. He mixed an apple green and then a vermillion, filling in more buffalo outlines, rounding white and wild each wide, rolling eye. At times he would stretch and yawn before dipping the brush again. Outside the traffic peaked and lulled as the water glass muddied, the sun moving through the long afternoon until the small room turned as grey as his paint water. Bobby switched on a lamp, and all the colours glowed back again strong and alive.
>
> Spirits In The Rain, *Waylon Gary White Deer*

Not long after I married and graduated from Haskell I began to paint for a living. It was 1973 and we had moved to Southwestern Oklahoma so Lori could be with her family a while. The area has a legacy of traditional Indian painters like the Kiowa Six, Blackbear Bosin, Rance Hood, Archie Blackowl, and Robert Redbird. There were Indian shops in Anadarko I sold to. I'd paint in the evenings on the dining table until morning, when my mother-in-law would start breakfast. She'd place a cup of coffee on the table, a cue to put away my brushes.

I'd wash my face, pick up my stack of paintings, head out the door, walk down the dirt road towards the highway, hitch a ride twenty-seven miles into town and try to sell art. Usually the shops paid me half cash, half trade. I'd return with silverwork, beadwork, or sometimes feather fans, all of which I spread out over the kitchen table. My sisters-in-law would grab the trade stuff and I would give my in-laws most of the cash to buy groceries with. I'd sleep till supper and then start over. My in-laws were mildly impressed, and began offering me rides.

> Now chief I just can't go twenty dollars apiece for them paintings. My wife's been in the hospital and it's too damn hot for any good sales. I got a lot of high dollar inventory on my hands and I think there's still a couple of your paintings left over from the last time you was in here. Well you can try the museum if you want. Yep. They might buy from you. Hold on a minute. Would you take half in trade?
>
> *Art buyer at the old McKee's Indian Store, Anadarko, Oklahoma*

My regular rounds were the Southern Plains Museum, Indian City USA, Roberts Indian Store, McKee's Indian Store, and the home of a wholesale art buyer. After I sold all my quick little paintings I'd give my in-laws grocery and fuel money and climb into the back of their pick-up truck for the ride home. I didn't drink around my in-laws and except for painting I kept a low profile. Then Indian City asked me to be their resident artist. Lori was pregnant with our first child and had morning sickness. Her parent's house was hot and crowded.

We moved into a cheap motel room in Anadarko where we had air conditioning, colour television and maid service, and we began eating in restaurants. To maintain our pleasant but fragile lifestyle I still painted all night, then put on a required ribbon shirt and hitch-hiked to the scenic bluffs of Indian City, USA, built overlooking the site of the Tonkawa Massacre, which occurred when several tribes combined forces to attack a single remaining Tonkawa encampment. Apparently the tribes had become fed up with the Tonkawa's ritual cannibalism.

> You are about to turn back the pages of history ... These are the Tonkawa Hills ... Named for the Tonkawa Indian Massacre on October 24, 1864 ...
>
> *Road signage on the way up to Indian City, USA*

Indian City featured a large gift shop and conducted tours of their recreated Indian village. They sat me under a willow arbour at the village entrance. Guides in tribal regalia would escort groups of tourists by, and after their tours were over the groups would stroll past me again. My father-in-law also worked at Indian City and sang for a troupe of war dancers that performed next to my arbour. Sometimes the tourists would get distracted by the dancers. For a while I sat unnoticed behind my paintings, thinking that maybe I needed an art agent.

My first art agent of sorts turned out to be a tour guide, an elderly lady who still looked pretty dressed in her tribal clothes, and who was nice to me. But she was bossy to her tour groups. They would leave talkative and meandering, but came back from their excursions walking obediently straight and silent. She would march them over to my paintings and demand that they look at them. Because of her kindnesses I made more sales.

> See that boy's paintings? They're good ones, annit! You want to buy one, don't you!
>
> *Delores Buffalo, Otoe. Tour guide, Indian City USA*

Two Kiowa societies, the Black Leggings and O-Ho-Mah Lodge held their ceremonials below the bluffs at Indian City. Many years later my father-in-law became a tribal chairman and arranged for the purchase of the entire property including the gift shop and village. He became the architect of its revival, building a new road and making repairs. But at the time, like the tour guides and the dancers, we were Indians typecast into a romanticised wonderland that made money for a board of area businessmen who didn't actually like Indians very much.

Soon Lori and I left for Tulsa and moved near my grandparents. The Tulsa Indian art market consisted of a few galleries that I would regularly visit, and I began to pick up commissions. My early paintings were of Choctaw dancers and doctors, stickball paintings, Trail of Tears figures and the powwow scenes popular in traditional painting at that time. My father had remarried a Yuchi and Creek woman, and they invited Lori and I to rent an apartment in the same complex. I set up a painting area in the kitchen where there was good light.

> I have a huge amount of paintings I have to pay taxes on each year. And Christmas sales were way down for some reason. Business hasn't been good so far this year, either. I just don't know why. Hopefully things will improve; we can always hope, can't we? But road construction is diverting traffic away from the gallery again, which never helps of course. And I have several framed pieces I've been holding for people. I wish to God they'd come and pick them all up. Now that would surely help. I'm just not in a position to buy. How much are you asking for this one … really?
>
> *Tulsa gallery owner*

In 1975 my wife and I went to visit her aunt and uncle and everything changed. Robert Redbird was an emerging star in the Indian art world, an heir to the painting traditions of the Kiowa Six. His works were highly charged creations of colour, tradition, and spiritual energy. Supremely confident in his abilities and kind and generous otherwise, he invited me along on his sales tours. He was called 'Stinson' by family members, never Robert, and he had a string of galleries in Arizona and New Mexico that he regularly sold to.

We'd leave Oklahoma by midnight in whatever old car Stinson was driving at the time. Heading across Texas we'd roll into Albuquerque by mid-morning and there we began to make the rounds. He was a lively salesman, talking up his art and exaggerating his success well before gallery owners had a chance to try and intimidate him. He left buyers excitedly convinced and in slight awe of his work. In tribal relationship patterns I was another son-in-law, and he'd proudly introduce me and show off my paintings to help my sales.

> Yeah I just got back from a cultural exchange tour of South America. The state department wants me to travel again but I told them no, I have to make time for my family. This painting? It's called 'Peyote Mystic'. See that bird swirling out of the fire? It's a prayer bird. Yeah. And this one's called 'Sending His Prayers'.

That eagle feather is powerful, and our old folks use them to send their thoughts straight into heaven. It's a strong spiritual piece. And that's cedar smoke. Sometimes when we burn cedar it thunders. That's how we know God hears us. Yeah, thank you. I was inspired by my tribal teachings. Oh hey, meet my son-in-law. He's just getting started, and I want to start him off right. I said, 'Son-in-law, I'm taking you to meet only the good people ...'

Robert Redbird, Kiowa

After we sold our paintings we'd stay overnight and then head out to Phoenix, where there were more shops and galleries. We'd rent motel rooms with adjoining doors so we could paint together. We had breakfast by eight, worked until noon, ate a good lunch, worked till supper, ate again and continued until nine or ten in the evenings. By the end of the week we'd produced another stack of paintings each to sell. After our sales we'd send money home to our families through Western Union telegrams, but kept back monies for expenses.

In Phoenix the nicest of the cheap motels we stayed in were at the far edge of Van Buren Street with its subsequent miles of whores. They'd solicit you in the daytime at traffic lights and in restaurants wearing the same trademark halter tops, shorts, and platform shoes. Dozens of them flocked at street corners and inside stores. It was like driving through an unusual immigrant neighbourhood; Whoreville, maybe. With their friendly aggression, large numbers and obvious economic impact they could have easily become a significant political bloc.

This just in ... following today's surprise announcement that he'd lost the pivotal whore endorsement Senator Prescott's ever-lengthening poll ratings have softened ...

Breaking news from the Prescott campaign

Sometimes we had to take silver and turquoise jewellery in trade, which was our insurance policy of sorts, in case of a bad tour we could pawn the jewellery. When we were selling we wore our trade items; concho belts and concho hat bands, bolo ties, rings, bracelets, watch bands, heshi necklaces, silver collar tabs, silver boot tips and heel guards. Stinson thought the jewellery made us appear successful which it might have, but I didn't like wearing it. I thought we looked like Indian pimps who had crawled out of a jewellery display case.

At his peak, Stinson's large extended family never had to use their kitchen, most of their meals were catered. There were new clothes, cars and vans and nice furnishings, the result of brisk sales and many art awards and honours.

Stinson was happiest when he was painting, his sure brushstrokes rapidly finishing one piece after another for his numerous collectors. From my father-in-law Robert (Stinson) Redbird I picked up a sense of spirituality and dynamic atmosphere as elements in my work, and more confidence marketing my paintings.

> Robert Redbird, native Oklahoman and renowned Kiowa artist, will be honoured on Saturday, June 7, according to a proclamation by Governor Henry. That day has been proclaimed Robert Redbird Day for all the State of Oklahoma … Redbird's art is full of his conviction that Native American culture is a beautiful way of life …
>
> Canku Ota (Many Paths), *31 May 2003, Issue 88*

Although I hadn't much formal painting instruction, I observed and was influenced by three major Indian art movements beginning with the Dorothy Dunn Studio style and my father's works, inspired by his friendship with Allan Houser. At Haskell there had been Dick West, famous within the Oklahoma intertribal style first developed by the Kiowa Six. I'd been exposed to Pop Indian expressionism while at the Institute.

And I'd been mentored by Robert Redbird. Of the three styles, traditional Oklahoma intertribal painting was the one that I developed in. The genre was grassroots and familiar, evolving all around me, and I had also married into it. Gradually I got better, and began to experiment with sweeping compositions and dramatic effects. During those early years I often painted through the night because I couldn't wait to see how my work would turn out.

Now I could paint using a rush of energy from my fingertips down through pencil and brush and constricted in flow only by how well I could draw, how credibly I could wrap drawn outline in colour, how clearly I knew both the seen and told, how skilfully I could mix it all like pigments with the waters of tribal sensibility. In those days I thought of my work as an agreement between my limited voice and those who might somehow be waiting to hear it, a shared coming together somewhere between imagination and expectation.

One late afternoon in 1976 I was walking near the apartment in Tulsa when a long black car pulled up beside me. The window came down and I was asked if I was Gary White Deer. I was wary, suspecting that the driver and his passenger were sent to collect a bill. It turned out they were from Ni-Wo-Di-Hi Galleries in Austin, Texas. They had come up to evaluate my paintings in the Tulsa galleries, they said. The two explained they had been out looking for me. They wanted to sign me to a contract and fly me down to Austin to paint for them.

Down in Austin, Ni-Wo-Di-Hi placed me at a drafting table in front of a large, uncovered picture window. In the Indian art world their gallery was an innovator for its time, publishing limited edition prints. I was told that what was left of their lithographs weren't selling, that they needed a hit. One of the owners drew a sketch of three eagle dancers he wanted painted. My work had to make a good enough litho to pull the gallery out of its lull.

I was twenty five, and under pressure. Every thirty minutes or so one of the gallery owners would pace by the window and look in to see if I was working, which didn't help. I finished the painting and titled it 'Ascending Eagle Prayer', which the gallery renamed 'Search for the Eagles Way'. It became my first print and it was a hit, selling out in less than six months. Ni-Wo-Di-Hi published two more of my images, advertising them in magazines. My reputation as an artist had been secured, and I began receiving more requests for my paintings.

> From a pair of symbolic eagle feathers and a beaded medallion three dancers spiral upward in a quest for the qualities only the eagles possess. Not competing for group honors or individual recognition, each dancer strives to achieve the perfection of life and the purity of spirit seen in the great bird ...
> *'Search for the Eagles Way'*, American Indian Art, Volume 1

I accepted an art residency in Oklahoma, and there were more exhibits and interviews, but if I had arrived in my career I didn't seem to know it. After three years my paints and brushes couldn't sustain the pressure of being good, of daring to be better. I became paralyzed by deadlines, depressed at the idea of producing artwork. With a growing family to support I should have quit painting and done something else for a living, but didn't. I persisted as an artist.

So my paintings became quicker overall, many just barely good enough to sell for modest prices. I was back languishing in the Oklahoma art market showing half finished pieces to stony-faced gallery owners for family living expenses. I stayed in that small market until 1989 telling myself that at any moment I would self-inspire and start doing work that would re-establish me as a more respected painter.

In 1990 I turned forty, and emerged from my peculiarity. I was asked to do mural work for a tribal museum on the Tunica-Biloxi Reservation in Louisiana, and we all moved there for five months. It was a small tribal nation, and I became a person of interest for their two rival tribal political factions who had their only two tribal policemen doubling as opposing community spies. Suddenly I was under surveillance, but reports about what I was up to were mixed.

One sunny afternoon I took a break to lie on the roof of the museum facing skywards with my arms outstretched and my legs dangling over the edge, relaxing and clearing my head of turpentine fumes. One of the tribal cops announced to his group that I was desperately praying to the sun. The other told his political partisans that I had gotten drunk and was passed out on the rooftop. After that I would either get strange smiles or knowing looks, depending.

The creepiest part was painting in the museum at night. Incredibly, the tribe had their own grave goods on display, a collection of dusty pottery, rusty muskets, and a faience plate decorated with the lyrics of a French drinking song. A recording of the lyrics would click on whenever visitors walked by the faience plate, activated by a motion sensor. In late evenings when I was painting alone the recording would sometimes mysteriously play, the sounds echoing eerily like voices of ghosts through the dark empty building.

Verse ami Gregoire
À boire
De ce jus charmant
Je sens que mon âme
S'enflamme
A chaque moment.

> A Gregoire; *the mysterious French drinking song*

In the American South they have stories about crossroads, tales with African origins. A relative once gave me his version of a crossroads story. I always thought of the story as a metaphor for artistic success. Although countless hopefuls have stood at empty southern crossings at midnight with lottery tickets or whatever else pressed between their eager fingers, at my crossroads in life I happened to be holding paintbrushes.

If you want to be a great fiddle player, dress in black and go to a deserted intersection at midnight. Bring your fiddle and a black chicken. Sooner or later a man will come walking by. That man will tune your fiddle and take the chicken in exchange. After your dark encounter you will become a virtuoso.

> *Dan Chisholm, my Shawnee uncle*

And then in 1991 I revisited the Anadarko art scene and met Mr Roscoe, a portly old outlaw millionaire who loved card games, cigars, whiskey, and rich foods. The region is home to a number of well-known Indian painters, silver-smiths, and bead workers. In the middle of all those creative tribal traditions Mr Roscoe had opened up an Indian art gallery. Mr Roscoe spoke with a gruff, smoky twang that made him sound like a hillbilly pirate captain. He wasn't accepting black chickens, but he did have a reputation for making devil's bargains.

Mr Roscoe reveled in wearing cattleman suits, silver bolo ties, and tinted glasses topped off by a J.R. Ewing-style rancher's hat. He dabbled in backroom politics and always had a string of questionable projects going. I knew none of this when he signed me up as the latest in a line of Indian painters he had been promoting. He slapped me on the back and smiled, the cigar clamped between his teeth trailing smoke as we walked to his bank for some money.

The bank had just closed. To my amazement Mr Roscoe began pounding on the door, rattling the glass, shaking his fist and twisting the doorknob, all the while indignantly shouting in his gruff, pirate captain rasp. When the bank manager finally peeked out Mr Roscoe cursed him, loudly insisting that if he had been given his own goddam key, he sure as hell wouldn't have been standing outside the fuckin' door looking like a goddam idiot.

Still agitated, he elbowed his way into the place, waved his cigar around like a smoking revolver, snorted imperiously, and then demanded that the manager hand over a stack of green ex-presidents, pronto. I was wondering whether the old man might have been attempting a bank robbery and was making me his accomplice. But the manager only smiled and coughed nervously, dutifully counting out bills while enduring Mr Roscoe's glowering impatience, obnoxious jokes, thick Corona smoke, and rambling, stream-of-consciousness commentary.

> Wanna know mah secret of success? Yuh pay yoreself first afore yuh pay yore bills. Son, yuh pay yoreself ten per cent of whut yuh take in. Hold to it son, an ah guarantee yew'll always have money.
>
> *Mr Roscoe*

Later I discovered that not only did Mr Roscoe own the bank, but also much of the town he lived in. I was assigned a studio in Mr Roscoe's labyrinth headquarters building, a room that another artist swore was bugged. In the afternoons Mr Roscoe held court, playing poker with his cronies, smoking his big Coronas and swapping tall tales, a bottle of whiskey and a loaded pearl handled six-shooter placed within ready reach in front of him.

It was a lethal mix at best. Employees claimed that he had once shot his own brother in the shoulder for cheating at poker. From his gaming table Mr Roscoe keenly eyeballed gallery customers on a secret television monitor while alternately frowning at his cards. His raucous routine was short-lived. Towards the end of our dealings Mr Roscoe was stricken with cancer, which caused him to turn solemnly to the Bible Belt faith of his childhood.

Other artists reported that a large, open-face King James Bible was prominently displayed on Mr Roscoe's nightstand while he languished in his hospital bed and gazed heavenwards, moaning piously. A number of visitors and nurses were genuinely touched that during his last days Mr Roscoe finally got religious. The ruse seemed to work. Months later he was completely cured and happily pursuing his questionable business deals again.

Many people were wary of him, but I genuinely liked Mr Roscoe. Although never a likely candidate for a sensitivity award and certainly not one to be trifled with he was nevertheless a fine patron of the arts. We did art shows and lithographs together and he advertised me in art magazines. He weaseled out of our contract when he thought he was dying, but that was OK. Mr Roscoe was good to me, and I believe he was good for Indian art as well.

> Giovanni glanced at Bobby and remarked 'With the Incas no playing, OK?'
> Rich Henshaw brightened. 'Is Robert both a painter and a musician?'
> Dr Giovanni stared at Bobby meaningfully. 'The artist should not play the guitar for money. Especially in Zurich.' Everyone laughed.
> 'Back in a second.' Bobby called, leaving the room and walking quickly out the door into the hallway. Slowly the chrome elevator sank towards the lobby, its sheer glass walls flooded by a brilliant sapphire sky. Bobby put his fingers to the moving glass and in precise descent gazed up at all the swift white clouds, billowing plump and supple like great wild herds of fleeing buttocks.
> Spirits In The Rain, *Waylon Gary White Deer*

Shortly after I left Mr Roscoe in 1992 I was asked to do a summer art residency teaching Choctaw kids painting in west Tennessee. Choctaw families had migrated up from Mississippi to Tennessee as sharecroppers in the 1950s, recruited by white landlords during a farmer's strike. Those families formed communities, but had remained somewhat isolated and traditional. During the residency community members asked me to help put together a ceremonial ground. We located some suitably isolated land and we began.

It was very good, that one summer, to see everyone come together on a bluff overlooking verdant bean fields and the broad, winding Mississippi. When we began our dances the lines were full and long. Firelight and moonlight alternately fell and flickered upon the black flat-brimmed hats, beaded mantillas, diamond-patterned shirts, Breton dresses, warrior belts, and flowing ribbons. The thick summer air was full of sound. And my painting students enjoyed the dances much more than they had enjoyed sitting in a classroom with me.

Tali hata pisa chukma.

'Such silver is good to see'
Choctaw Drink Water Dance lyrics;
referring to the crescent moon as a gorget

When my art residency ended I was invited to Zurich to do painting exhibits by a promoter who didn't seem to understand the Swiss painting market. His main interest was in selling Amish quilts which the Swiss hung on their walls as fine art. He was also being paid to show tourists around Switzerland, and I tagged along to see the Alps and Geneva, and Chillon Castle. Our painting venues weren't well advertised and were secondary to his quilt sales. Then I found myself stranded in Zurich for a month while the promoter conducted tours.

I spent a lot of time on the city bus and made a discovery. Although the bus route was circular it was displayed on signs as a straight line with a series of connected dots representing various stops and their schedules. That puzzled me. Since the bus route encircled the city, why were its stops and schedules represented by a line and not a circle? Suddenly it occurred to me. Like all mainstream westerners, the Swiss saw time as infinitely linear. I realised then that I had been raised thinking of time as cyclical, a returning series of circles.

> I only know from my own experience, and I personally feel that there's a cyclical nature to things, so you don't want to start making generalisations about how bad things have become in comparison to the old days.
>
> *Jeffrey Jones*

Switzerland was beautiful, and in 1992 I think I was the most overweight person in the country. Most of the Swiss were reed thin, and after hiking up and down steep streets all week many of them went hiking up and down steeper mountains on weekends. I was surprised to find garage service bays without their almost inevitable oil slicks, tools gleaming and put away. All the farms looked as if armies of gardeners had pruned their way through them. There were flower boxes outside windows, and towns were pristine and picture-perfect.

Only when you left the German-speaking regions and wandered into French Switzerland did sidewalk cracks appear, weeds flourished, and there was vagueness and imprecision. I felt comfortable in those places but I also appreciated the aesthetics of the German Swiss. I'd been brought up thinking that white Americans had the highest standard of living on the planet but it was soon evident that the Swiss drove better cars, had nicer houses, ate better food, wore nicer clothes, made better things, and had a superior quality of life overall.

Not long after that I was approached by an Oklahoma art dealer who became my manager. He began to publish my work as lithographs and featured me in his art calendar. We went travelling America, going to exhibitions and entering art contests, and I began winning awards. Oddly inspired by my Swiss trip, he decided to promote a three-man art show in Germany. I'd been asked by the Chickasaw Nation to build arbours for their national holiday and to organise a dance troupe first. I agreed to zooger their cultural image a bit before I left.

Jimi Hendrix: Hey man why you keep saying I'm dead?

Otto Von Wieghorst: Maybe you chust need a goot zoogering.

Jimi: What's zoogering, Otto?

Otto: Zee art of changing a human profile. It iss what I do.

Jimi: Like, are you experienced?

Otto: Ja, I teach zoogering to zee Associated Press.

Jimi: So I'm still dead but you're alive, right?

Otto: I am a literary character, as you are also at this moment.

Jimi: Hey man you said you teach zoogering to the Associated Press.

Otto: Und zee Associated Press are literary characters also, Ja?

The Chickasaws had lost all of their dances except one; their Gar Fish Dance. Once, the Chickasaws had been British allies and were our enemies. Later, after they signed away their lands they asked the Choctaw for help. We forgave them and allowed them to settle near us. We outnumber their population at about four-to-one, even within some of their own communities. Quite probably, we have always gotten on their nerves.

Just before the Second World War these tribal neighbours had resorted to holding most of their remaining ceremonies hidden deep within a wood, at the bottom of a meteor crater. The real end came, their old folks said, during their last pashofa dance, a four-day healing ritual. The restless spirit of a neglected ceremonial fire possessed the curative fire of the pashofa dance. The people began to sicken within the glow of its corrupted light and so they fled, scattering through the night, abandoning their remaining dances and ceremonies.

I put together a quick dance troupe and tribal dress for the Chickasaws, and then I caught a plane. For the art shows in Stuttgart, Germany, there was myself, an Assiniboine artist and a Pueblo painter. It was a low-budget foray. We set up our artwork in the foyer of a culture hall by the toilets, on the fringe of a German powwow and the sound of drumbeats. Powwows, a form of Plains Indian social dancing, have been spreading like a feathered global conga line.

109

Surprisingly, all of the dancers were German, decked out in period tribal dress.

> If beadwork, horsemanship, teepee building and traditional dancing were Olympic sports, the German team would be medal contenders … a tribe that numbers some 40,000 strong, according to hobbyist organisations.
>
> *James Hagengruber*

We couldn't see the powwow from the foyer, but a steady stream of painted and feathered war dancers and women in buckskin dresses strode past us towards the toilets. Every accessory they wore, from beadwork and silverwork to real eagle feather bustles had been exactingly recreated. Adding to the buzz, *Dances With Wolves* was playing in local movie theaters. My father never quite made it to Germany. He was in Alsace-Lorraine during the Second World War when a German sniper shot him in the neck, which he naturally never forgot.

Pop had reacted to my art trip to Germany as if I were running away to join the Wehrmacht. Worse, terrible acoustics had prompted some of the German powwow dancers to break out in Plains Indian sign language. Unfortunately most of the hand signals I knew weren't Indian and had very rude meanings, but I was tempted to use them anyway. After the powwow we went outside to wait on our ride. Suddenly, photographers came charging across the boulevard.

The German press were eagerly heading in our direction. Now we're getting somewhere, I remember thinking. But we were wearing boots, jeans, and cowboy hats. Although we weren't dressed like movie Indians we weren't expecting to see locals wearing lederhosen, either. However the press scurried past us, swerving instead towards a nearby group of painted and feathered Germans who immediately began preening and granting interviews.

Another non-encounter with the German media occurred at an 'indigenous' press conference we had to attend. We entered the pressroom to find three American Latinos in serapes and berets festooned with feathers and posing as Indians. Reporters and groupies surrounded them. Seated at a table laden with microphones, the trio appeared to be a guerilla junta. It was obvious we'd interrupted some sort of compelling opinion or comment.

The trio hastily hailed us as brothers, but when we asked what tribe they were they evasively mumbled 'indigenous'. After favouring us with strained smiles they wisely stroked their grizzled chins and resumed their movie critique of *Dances With Wolves*, to the fascination of their audience. Despite our boredom they kept eyeing us nervously, as if we might spring to our feet and denounce them as imposters. I whispered to one of the reporters sitting spellbound, asking if she'd heard of the film's sequel, *Dances With Dobermans*. She ignored me.

In the early 1990s there were dozens of little Inca bands scattered throughout Germany, playing for tips in various underground train stations, and tourist spots. I found out that theirs was no random set of concert locations; the bands had German managers who plotted their appearances on computers and rotated the little groups according to strict schedules. Like us, the Incas weren't wearing feathers, accessories that wouldn't have saved any of us from the roving gangs of neo-Nazi skinheads harassing non-whites around the city.

> [Hitler] often praised to his inner circle the efficiency of America's extermination – by starvation and uneven combat – of the red savages who could not be tamed by captivity.
>
> Adolph Hitler, *John Toland, p. 202*

Fortunately, I had been assigned great hosts, a brave couple leading a campaign against the skinheads. More interestingly, the city was in the middle of Oktoberfest. Hans and Uschi explained that there was a hard-fought contest each year between Stuttgart and I think Munich, to see which city could consume the most beer and roasted chickens. I was taken to an amusement park encircled by what looked like enormous circus tents. All of the rides were eerily deserted. As we entered one of the giant pavilions, I found out why.

Drinking styles and their theme music varies with cultures. Oklahoma cowboy types like to do their drinking in honkytonks, where dusty standards like Okie from Muscogee and Red Necks, White Socks, and Blue Ribbon Beer blare from jukeboxes. Affronts, real or imagined, can quickly shatter the beery tedium, and then folks will start kicking, punching, swearing, biting, and swinging billiard sticks before you can swallow your tobacco.

Honkytonks and hard-core Indian bars have this much in common; they both make you feel like telling the folks inside to quit being annoying, and no, they do not have permission to pass out, pinch asses, vomit, break windows, hit children, sob uncontrollably, lose jobs, punch noses, wreck pick-up trucks, or hug fire hydrants while screeching like howler monkeys. The pubs in Catholic Ireland on the other hand are famous for the craic.

The craic is a lively creature found lurking in pubs with dark wood furnishings and attracted to traditional music sessions or the occasional party piece. The craic often makes the rounds with its loquacious associate, the chat, a compulsive conversationalist and expert shape thrower. Yet there are those nights after last orders in Dublin city centre when the chat has gone quiet and the craic has caught a ride, leaving everyone else to stiffly converge on the taxi ranks like well-behaved zombies to go home and act crazy in private.

But I digress. It was during Oktoberfest in Stuttgart that I witnessed drinking choreography. Inside each giant pavilion were scores of long wooden tables and benches, holding about one thousand stein-waving drinkers. The great tents were clammy from body heat. Raised bleachers featured shrill brass bands that cranked out popular show tunes. Huge heraldry banners hung from lofty ceilings, and chicken rotisseries solidly ringed the canvas walls.

Throngs at the tables swung their beer steins in unison while they swayed in perfect cadence, crooning lustily along with their very loud bands. The concert was punctuated with breaks so that beer maids could fetch the multitudes fresh draughts of lager, photographers could solicit souvenir snapshots, and more roast chickens could be consumed. Like clockwork, the brass bands would crank up again, and once more the sea of tables would begin to sway and croon. There were at least six such giant tents for a total of around 6,000 imbibers.

It was their crack beer-and-chicken team on their way to breaking the Stuttgart–Munich record. It was also the largest, most efficient, best disciplined, and most impressively organised group of drunks that I have ever seen. Shortly after that I said goodbye to Germany and caught a flight to Oklahoma. Back home again, the Chickasaw Administration were anxious to keep their dance troupe going, and offered me a full-time position. I quickly moved up the food chain to become director of cultural resources and morphed into an office Indian.

I put my paints and brushes aside for three years, from 1992 to 1995 until after developing a tribal dance troupe, entering into regular negotiations with American agencies, supervising two museums, making two trips to Ireland to help with humanitarian projects, and after getting caught by tribal politics, I was asked to resign. Less than a week later Don Mullan rang again. Could I come to New York, and then to Ireland? There was an art project I could do that might be interesting, he said. And that's how I got back into painting.

If I'm going to Hell, I'm going there playing the piano.

Jerry Lee Lewis

Suddenly Don and I were piling into taxis together in New York. There was a definite buzz on the streets of The Big Apple and at all hours, like a current running through the city. The feeling strongly reminded me of another place. From time to time friends and others have told me that at certain spots the

earth's energy lines cross. That was the explanation they gave me the time I stayed in northern New Mexico to paint at the mouth of the long stretch of canyon that climbs from Velarde all the way to Taos. It's a narrow, winding route.

> Nimrod needed the great clear sky, the endless sensation of flight. As they drove on the last embers of sun vanished from the tops of everything, twilight coming fast. They entered the canyon at Velarde. The river was always rocky and narrow there, tumbling swiftly down from the snow mountains. Quickly they were washed in deep canyon shadow ...
>
> Spirits In The Rain, *Waylon Gary White Deer*

Indian friends in the area also said they were under constant attack by wolf people who would come in at night using secret canyon trails to commit acts of sorcery. There was an influence running through the area that attracted the unusual and spiritual; a crossroads. I began to notice a similar odd tug on the streets of Manhattan, and I wondered what kinds of shadows a landscape with so many late night crossroads might draw.

Don and I stayed in New York at Iona College with the Christian Brothers. We were a train ride away from Manhattan, but New Rochelle was still very congested. A friend who had played host to a van full of Swiss tourists once told me that he had watched them taking photos of deserted Oklahoma crossroads. In Switzerland, like Manhattan, you almost never see an intersection devoid of vehicles, and his Swiss visitors were impressed.

I never told Don my Uncle Dan's crossroads story, but while we were in New York I did buy Don a chicken sandwich just to complete the metaphor. So if you find yourself waiting at one of life's deserted intersections one dark night and Don happens to stroll by, offer him a chicken, or at least a chicken sandwich. You won't have to give up your soul, but surrender any doubts because if Don believes in you they won't be needed. But there's always a chance that a van full of Swiss tourists will show up with cameras and ruin everything.

The Christian Brothers lived in a large manor-style house and served as college faculty. Beyond the comfort of their tiny rooms their amenities seemed to be food, booze, and television. In the afternoons a fully stocked liquor cart awaited them. Then their chef would trot out an array of exotic snacks. Evenings meals were semi-formal affairs, great food that was only a run-up to the highlight of their day – watching television game shows.

Don't tell me what you believe in. I'll observe how you behave and I will make my own determination.

> *Alex Trebek, host of the hit television game show* Jeopardy!

Each of the Brothers had their own beat-up recliner ranged in a semi-circle. After dinner they would ease into the worn loungers and shout and laugh at the TV like schoolboys. These particular Christian Brothers seemed to be a happy group. One of them taught me a painting technique involving sheets of wrinkled plastic and German inks that I couldn't wait to try. Soon there was a plane to catch and then I was buying art supplies in Dublin on O'Connell Street.

> On Raglan Road on an autumn day I saw her first and knew
> That her dark hair would weave a snare that I might one day rue;
> I saw the danger, yet I walked along the enchanted way ...
>
> Raglan Road, *Patrick Kavanagh*

Don had organised an art residency in Clare, outside of Carrigaholt. One of Don's old school friends had been persuaded to sponsor the residency, and it was his family's empty summer house that I would be using. From the front windows you could watch ships glide soundlessly past you on their way to Kerry. I was left on my own to produce enough paintings for some credible art shows. For exercise I took daily walks along the beach into town.

I learned to keep an ear out for the sea so that I could hurry back to the house on the cliff before the great grey waves of late afternoon came pounding over my rocky little shortcut. It was a time of twin-track, decommissioning and the divorce referendum, and I had a one month deadline to produce twenty paintings. I rose early and worked late. I hitch-hiked into Kilkee for art supplies, and had good luck getting rides from Travellers. It was a solitary and sometimes lonely routine.

One morning, someone I'd once casually spoken to rang. Declan had been raised in a poor section of Dublin but fled to the west of Ireland where he married a local girl, learned Irish, and then proceeded to wade up to his goatee in local folklore. He lived in a *gaeltacht*, an all-Irish-speaking region. Declan was so insistent I come visit him that I decided to put aside my brushes for a bit and hop on the bus. Besides, I had never been to Connemara.

> It is better to travel well than to arrive.
>
> *Buddha*

En route I had to change buses in Ennis. With the bus door left tantalisingly open, the driver slowly checked his paperwork, thoughtfully chewed his breakfast, re-checked his paperwork, and then helped his single remaining passenger off the bus, an enormous old lady who was probably his mother, all of which seemed to take forever as his passengers stood outside waiting in the rain, shivering. These white folks ain't acting like white folks I observed with amazement.

In America, white folks left standing in cold rain beside a dry, warm, almost empty bus would have started rioting in mere seconds. Or a special someone would have coolly strode to the fore, and with the menacing civility of a British line officer, sorted things out. Having enough right white stuff is the internal equivalent of crackling phosphorescent hair and skin so radiantly lucent that if such a blinding glow were externalised as great shooting rays, then all the world's creatures great and small would have to wear safety goggles.

I shall have a word with your superior. Immejutly.
The Royal Adventures of Sir Percival 'Vinnie the Rat' Pimpington,
Londinium Press

It was my first noticing, I believe, of the after effects of colonialism in Ireland. But Declan was Mr Energy Pill of 1996, and he had a proposal. As we bumped and skidded recklessly in his car along the Connemara coastline he explained his plan. He and I would cut turf, load it into a currach and sail to the Aran Islands. We would become prosperous turf merchants, braving the deadly tides in true Irish fashion without the benefit of life preservers. If we did happen to drown, then the locals would compose sean-nós songs in our honour.

Wisely I returned to Carrigaholt and started on the last of twenty paintings. Don and the sponsor would be coming soon, and I had to have my show ready. I had worked within four or five different styles, and the subjects ranged from the Choctaw Trail of Tears, to the crinkly plastic wrap and ink technique I'd just learned at Iona College. Then the Miami police called. Would I bring a dance troupe to Florida? I organised a new troupe by telephone from Clare, one free of tribal politics.

They were all friends and family and I named us the Southeastern Intertribal Dancers. The new troupe were flown into Miami from Oklahoma, and I was brought in from Shannon Airport. In contrast to the rocky chill of Carrigaholt, the beaches of South Florida were balmy with warm, sparkling sand. It was good to see my friends and relatives dressed up and ready to dance, and we had a great time visiting and looking around.

It is not every day that we are needed. But at this place, at this moment of time, all mankind is us, whether we like it or not. Let us make the most of it, before it is too late!
Waiting for Godot, *Samuel Beckett*

115

Local police were promoting the festival, and from the way they were throwing cash around I began to suspect that confiscated crime monies were involved. We danced in a city park. Four days later I was back in County Clare. Though I worked late and rose early the days passed too quickly. I'll always be grateful to the house's owner for sponsoring my painting residency. It was a crucial time for my family and I, and his sponsorship was a great kindness. All too soon Don arrived with the sponsor. Finally, it was show-and-tell time. Unfortunately, the paintings were met with a less enthusiastic reception than I had hoped. Don and I left Clare for Dublin that day.

A day or two later Don and I parked in front of the American embassy. He stared out the window and sighed. So this is how it ends, I mused. I'm being deported.

> A guilty conscience needs to confess. A work of art is a confession.
>
> *Albert Camus*

It turned out Don only wanted to pay Jean Kennedy-Smith a social call. While we were waiting in the embassy foyer I checked out the paintings that they had hanging from their ceilings, an American exhibition that featured images of enormous severed red hands and giant flying eyeballs.

I nudged Don and remarked that my work was a little 'lighter' than what was on display, and that the ambassador might give me an exhibit. Don was doubtful, but asked me to bring up my portfolio. Fortunately, the ambassador loved the Clare images. She agreed to give us a solo exhibit and volunteered to open it for us. It was great news.

> In very general terms, Gary White Deer is a modernist artist, but he does not embrace just one sort of modernist approach; his work can range from neo-realism and something close to abstraction and then to the Mexican/Southwest style … Diversity and variety are the hallmarks of his work.
>
> *Internet excerpt*

The embassy exhibit was well attended. I thought it would be our final venue, but Don had other plans. The paintings would travel to Derry in the north of Ireland. Derry's Nationalist community solidly supported the show, a measure of the respect they had for Don. Our theme was to show the Famine link and solidarity, and Don persuaded John Hume to open the exhibition at the Calgach Centre.

Next the show was back in Dublin at the Bank of Ireland's Culture Centre. We had just finished up a successful exhibit in Derry, and another Dublin show would be the last venue. Sitting around in Don's parlour one afternoon,

I noticed a television programme about buffaloes in Ireland. The owner of Perry's Crisps had imported a small herd. I idly called Don to the screen, and while the buffaloes stared blankly into the parlour he had another inspiration.

> An idea that is not dangerous is unworthy of being called an idea at all.
>
> *Oscar Wilde*

Within an hour we were up in Meath, not far from Tara, looking at the herd. Ray, the owner of the buffaloes, was friendly and accommodating. We were allowed to stand inside the fence a few feet away from a couple of the larger bulls. Don's sudden idea was to have a buffalo at the exhibit opening. We needed a strong personality to top the American ambassador and John Hume, who'd opened our previous shows.

Ray told Don it wouldn't be like bringing a good-natured cow to a social event. Buffaloes would always be wild, Ray explained, even ones born in captivity. It was why they were behind an electric fence. Ray had plans for their tempestuous natures. He wanted to market buffalo steaks, and sell buffalo flavoured crisps. The herd and I both knew the limits of fences and the feeling of waiting inside them as time slowly runs out.

We left the buffaloes standing dark against the vivid green of an Irish pasture. There was a dullness to the herd, as if they could feel their spirits slowly being planned and managed away. I sympathised with those buffalo in Meath. Maybe you know that feeling, too. Then, swiftly, the day of the show arrived and there we were again. We opened without a buffalo but to a good crowd. After our final 1996 exhibit no more paintings remained.

> Whatever you do, or dream you can, begin it. Boldness has genius and power and magic in it.
>
> *Johann Wolfgang von Goethe*

Don and I would travel together a while longer, fundraising for humanitarian organisations. Then he would write *Eyewitness Bloody Sunday*, which launched a major investigation by the British government into the 1972 murders of fourteen unarmed Catholics by British paratroopers. I remember sharing a room at Iona College with Don the night it occurred to him that army snipers might have been positioned on the Derry Walls. The next morning he was on a boat to Staten Island to consult with an American ballistics expert.

In 2002, and with a lot of help from my friend Kitt, Don put together a final exhibition for me in New York, at the Irish Cultural Centre. Around this same time I was also invited to do a painting workshop on the Garvaghy Road, in

Portadown, Ulster. It was an invitation through strange circumstances. I'd received a call from a Dublin woman who was visiting the Lakota. She claimed she'd seen me in a vision being anointed by angels and that I was to help her accomplish great things for the youth of the world. Would I come to Ireland and help her, she asked.

She booked flights to Ireland for me and a small group of dancers and we toured Dublin, Donabate, Balbriggan and West Belfast. Her second project involved an art residency in Portadown, Co. Armagh, Northern Ireland. In Portadown, Orange Order marches pass through Catholic neighbourhoods on their way to the epicentre of their origins, Drumcree Church. Celebrating continuing British and Protestant rule in the Irish north, the marches down Garvaghy Road had ignited sectarian violence and civil unrest for over one hundred years.

> Man tells his aspiration in his God; but in his demon he shows his depth of experience.
>
> *Margaret Fuller*

My art residency was based in the last Protestant house on Garvaghy Road. The owner was in hospital, and very kindly donated space for an art workshop with local Catholic young people. It was a tense time. I was staying with a man whose wife, a civil rights lawyer, had been murdered by Protestant paramilitaries. He seemed lost and dazed, his small children were missing their mother, and a numbing sadness enveloped their home. The kids I tutored had to leave the town's businesses by sunset each day or risk death or injury.

In spite of the constant strain of being under siege, the art workshop was a success, and after it was over I took the train back to Dublin. While I had been away an odd thing happened. The woman who said she'd had a vision about me reported that after her brother had seen me off to catch the train up to Portadown he had begun drinking heavily. While talking to him she said that something unseen ripped through his shirt, leaving burning scratches. Suddenly he began speaking in another voice, saying, 'I will destroy your Indian.'

Then he howled as bite marks appeared on his side. After her brother calmed down the woman sent for a priest, who couldn't explain the marks and scratches. I talked with her brother, and he showed me long scratches and what looked to be bite marks. He said his memory of that evening was clear except for the unseen attack and of speaking in another voice. Whatever happened to him remains a mystery.

At one point, she looked at me and saw a demon, a totally demonic figure. For whatever reason, either because it's true about me or because of her own grasping at something, it was pretty bad.

Jack Nicholson

My next residency was a youth art project in West Belfast, another Catholic enclave in the middle of a large, hostile Protestant area. I was working out of a neighbourhood community centre, and Gerry, the centre's director invited me to his home to give me a very pointed tour. His doors, he said, were really metal covered with wood panelling. Turning on his television he clicked to eight different views of the outside of his house.

Eight surveillance cameras surrounded the property, video sentinels positioned to catch approaching Loyalist death squads. Gerry recounted how one of his teenage daughters had recently fled a dance when she realised that paramilitaries had spotted her and were 'baying for her blood'. Getting into his car, Gerry informed me that after the door opened should we hear a sound like a small bird chirping we would have ten seconds to get away before the car exploded. I began accepting rides from Gerry with more attentive interest.

I had my students paint on large panels, and I asked them to compose a quote that expressed how they felt about the time and place they were in. There was mural art all around them, nationalist images of Bobby Sands, who was one of the hunger strikers, Loyalist murals of King Billy and paintings of masked men with automatic weapons in neighbourhoods the children couldn't enter. But they could enter a place that their paints and brushes created, a place they could know as their own.

I'd like to think I gave those kids an encouraging experience. If they had been Protestants it wouldn't have made any difference; all children deserve hope, safety, and happiness. Soon enough my residency ended and I left West Belfast and flew home. Other exhibits, residencies, and travels would follow. But my paintings never shone better for me than when laid against blind darkness, when there would be a sudden sense that an act of creation is light.

Surely all art is the result of one's having been in danger, of having gone through an experience all the way to the end, where no one can go any further.

Rainer Maria Rilke

There were those many times when I painted for a utility bill or to feed everyone. Often my hand would blur too quickly while I worked the imagery, and the instrument I was using became dulled and tired and blunted and I didn't always do my best work, then. I've learned not to use my paints and brushes just to make a living, that there are useful things I may say or do for people with them. And I can see and sense all that now.

So I sharpen the instrument and try to be of service. My painting styles sometimes change but the work I'm most proud of are the images that have what I saw in my father's paintings, a thing that makes the tribal circle glow. And then I see the faces of those Yei again and the rhythms of my father's horses and riders and stickball players become creation songs, and it's true what he once said that sometimes late at night I'm prompted to mix certain colours.

In later years I showed my father a portrait I'd finished of a woman lost in reflection. He'd never had much to say about my paintings. That morning he stood before the canvas portrait motionless, squinting and frowning, peering into the woman's features. Then he smiled, raised his hands and moved them through the air like a symphony conductor; slowly, fluidly, serenely, gracefully, as if hearing an exquisite music. It's been my nicest moment in art.

CHAPTER 4
Politics and Performances

THE PRETTY-COLOURED WAGON

A man went out early one morning to pray. As he turned towards the east he saw a shadow pass before the face of the sun. The man looked closely and saw that the shadow was a wagon of the prettiest shades and colours, and with wheels that shone. Looking closer, the man could see a crowd of Indians walking behind, every one of them wanting to ride in the pretty-coloured wagon.

As the shining wheels turned faster, the crowd began to chase after the wagon, every one still wanting to ride. The man watched as mothers threw their babies away to catch up with the pretty-coloured wagon. Then he knew that he had seen the future.

Later, after the man told the people what he had seen, he held up a piece of paper money. 'This was the colour of the wagon,' he said to them. Then he held up a coin saying, 'And these were its wheels.'

Family story

POLITICS AND PERFORMANCES: 1992 –

I am not a demon. I am a lizard, a shark, a heat-seeking panther. I want to be Bob Dylan on acid playing the accordion.
(Nicolas Cage)

Indians in business suits always seem interesting, as do Indians in beadwork and feathers and at one time during a varied career I regularly wore both, though not at the same time. On most days I should have also been wearing shark repellent. Initially I was asked by a tribal regime to recreate a dance culture for them that had faded away. But beneath the blush and sparkle of beads and feathers the waters of tribal governments often run murky.

> Such a system produces, with dire predictability, a people lacking in self confidence and easily bullied by outsiders. Doctors, dentists, lawyers, engineers and architects are produced in over-abundance, to meet the career aspirations of the new elite, but most are then exported as free, instant experts to the First World: and so it is with most native critics. The more gifted amongst them are often simply internalisers of the imperial mode.
>
> *Declan Kiberd*

My first exposure to tribal politics was in 1977. I attended a campaign rally for David Gardner, who was running for Choctaw Principal Chief. The American government was allowing the first free Choctaw elections since before Oklahoma Statehood in the early 1900s. Gardener's rally was packed into a high school gymnasium and, curiously, the enthused crowd looked to be all white. One of Gardner's campaign promises had been to lower the minimum blood quantum for tribal membership from one-quarter to any amount, no matter how small.

I stood and proposed a petition to keep the minimum blood quantum for tribal membership at one-quarter Choctaw. For the first time in my life I was booed by a crowd. Old white ladies were shouting at me and shaking their fists. The gym was filled with political supporters who were all much less Choctaw than the minimum, and who were seeking not only full tribal membership but full tribal benefits. Gardner won the election and soon afterwards Oklahoma Choctaw membership rolls were swamped with thousands of new applicants.

> Politics, n. Poly 'many' + Tics 'blood-sucking parasites'
>
> *Larry Hardiman*

121

In the early 1980s my former father-in-law was elected Kiowa tribal chairman. I observed from the sidelines as tribal politics grew more rowdy and contentious. His political opponents would bring large guitar amplifiers to tribal meetings, plug them in, and shout back at him from the audience through microphones. But he took the idea of true tribal sovereignty seriously enough to alarm American officials with his projects.

His intertribal horse racing track would have competed with powerful national business interests that were building their own racetrack in Oklahoma. The project drew massive political pressure and was shut down. He also proposed charging water usage fees for Lawton, a good sized city and home to a US army base. He'd realised that a small creek on Indian land fed the town's large water reservoir. The city council panicked.

Another time, I went with him to inspect a petroleum refinery that was for sale. He wanted to buy the refinery, convert oil pumped on tribal lands into gasoline, build a string of tribal filling stations and sell fuel at much lower prices than any competitor could. Suddenly his home was raided by Federal Agents looking for illegal feathers, and there were investigations of alleged tax violations. Both events were clear enough messages.

Ada, Oklahoma, the small rural town I live in is Chickasaw tribal headquarters. When I returned from Germany in 1992 I was offered a position with the Chickasaw Nation. I was wary about working for any tribal government. Tribal politics seemed too contentious, tribal governments too controlled. I remembered the weird surveillance I had been under by tribal police on the Tunica–Biloxi Reservation. But in the end I decided to again put my painting career on hold, for with a guaranteed pay cheque I could provide more security for my family.

'What is a Chickasaw?'

Dallas Morning News, *7 March 2011*

With the Chickasaws' success in business has come dramatic growth in tribal population. Since 2001, the Chickasaws, who have 48,000 members, have added 10,000 adults to their rolls. In 2009 alone, 3,400 people received new Chickasaw citizenship cards.

What is driving this growth? The answer lies in the tribe's rules for membership. The Chickasaws require prospective members to prove only that one of their ancestors was among those on the so-called Dawes Rolls around the turn of the century – a sort of federal inventory of who did and did not have Indian blood.

Under those rules, it is possible to have very little Indian blood and be considered a Chickasaw, which means that Chickasaws incorporate a wide range of physical types. Today, they tend to look like a cross-section of America, and include everything from blond or red-headed Caucasians to African-Americans, Hispanics and, of course, American Indians.

Today, there are only an estimated 500 full-blood Chickasaws left. The new members are simply people who can prove lineage to the Dawes Rolls. In hard economic times, things like free health care, college scholarships and the raft of human services available begin to look better and better.

'It shows you how much times have changed,' says a former tribal official who asked not to be identified. 'When I was growing up in the Chickasaw Nation in Oklahoma, nobody wanted to be an Indian. There were a lot of people who were, like, 'Oh, those damn Indians, always with their hands out.' But then we started making money and these same people went up to their attics, dug through their family Bibles and proved their descent from a Chickasaw citizen.'

All of which begs the question: Should a tribe that does not look like Native Americans, does not speak a native language, has no special tribal religion (most Chickasaws are Christians) and makes hundreds of millions of dollars still be treated as a tribe and given federal money?

Most Indians bristle at the question. 'I'll tell you what,' says US Rep. Tom Cole, R-Okla., a Chickasaw. 'You can have the money back if we get our land back. You have to recognise the federal obligation, the trust obligation to the tribe. Basically all treaties, most of which have been violated, are exchanges of either sovereignty or land for some level of support quite often in perpetuity.'

As for tribal identity, Chickasaw Gov. Bill Anoatubby puts it this way: 'Being a Chickasaw is who you are, in your heart. I know that I feel at home. There is a yearning inside that gets filled. It is part of you. It makes you whole.'

S.C. Gwynne and Gary Jacobson

The Chickasaw administration began claiming the dances and regalia I put together for them as their very own primordial traditions, unaltered since before Columbus took that big wrong turn. We achieved a repertoire of a half-dozen very simple dances, and our troupe swelled to over two-dozen members, all Chickasaw tribal employees. Schools and festivals were booking us for performances, and we were regularly travelling out-of-state.

Sure we were sanitised, pre-packaged and a bit ironic, kind of like the ground-up commodity buffalo meat the US government now distributes to Indian families, but our gigs met the quick and slender purposes of a requested cultural makeover. The tribal regime was very pleased with it all. After a small interval I was offered the position of historic preservation officer, and shortly after that I was promoted to department director and assigned a staff of eight. As required, I began wearing a coat and tie, and had a secretary and a speakerphone.

In those days the Oklahoma Choctaw political administration was attempting a cultural revival as well, but their notions of Choctaw identity were puzzling. Hallways at tribal headquarters were festooned with old Indian mannikins about three feet high; after turning a corner visitors would encounter a wide-eyed gang of little dummies staring at them, and not office dummies, either. The centrepiece of the long-running display was a fake headdress that hung from the doorknob of a vacant office.

Perhaps inadvertently, pottery from the graves of other tribes would later appear on shelves. Then the administration began to sponsor wholesale cultural borrowings from other tribes. New but negligible tribal membership criteria and a corresponding hunger for cultural identity had given the office regime a mandate. Although the Six-Town revival and other grassroots lifeways had helped to ensure the continuation of tribal community ethos, the administration seemingly couldn't tell imbedded tribal realities from mainstream American perceptions.

Eventually the office regime would resort to promoting a handy tribal fair version of Mississippi Choctaw culture for public consumption. A political quest for Oklahoma Choctaw identity would finally be resolved through cultural importation rather than revitalisation, and in the end not many Oklahoma Choctaws seemed to notice. But there were similar importations in the cultural initiatives I was asked to put together for the Chickasaws.

It's the thing itself that's essential.

Alan Cook, Muscogee Creek

My friend Alan used to talk about 'the thing itself', that is, the essential nature of a tribal understanding, and not the cultural expression that dresses it up. Such understandings are carried forward by a group as continuity; ethos. Cultural expressions can change a bit, but 'the thing itself' marks who you are through lifeways rather than identity activities only. And when continuity is broken it can't be recovered by importation, reinvention, or even by reenacting the appearance it once wore.

So I think we are the people for our times, and essential understandings as our group carried them forward are more vulnerable now. Of all the 'isms' we know, it's consumerism that seems to be the most transcendent. People everywhere want to smile into cell phones and wear London Olympics t-shirts. And more often now we build cargo cults out of cultural expressions hoping to catch time spirits. But as tribal spirit moving through time, 'the thing itself' really lingers within tribal lifeways; the daily act of living and seeing communally.

> Back when I was a boy I hitched a ride on a train to Atoka to watch the Choctaws play stickball against the Chickasaws. Each morning the Choctaw players walked to the field in a long line with their medicine man in front of them. He was small, almost a midget and he wore a big black hat and cowboy boots. An owl would fly in front of the Choctaw line, diving and swooping.
>
> The Choctaws were mad and wouldn't give up because the Chickasaws were using black players, instead of an all Chickasaw team. That game went on for two weeks until finally the county sheriff came out and broke it up because too many men were getting hurt.
>
> *Armon Holden, my Chickasaw uncle*

Much of my time with the Chickasaws was spent consulting with federal and state agencies about protecting tribal burials and traditional cultural properties. The Americans have historic preservation laws that apply to tribes, and the consultations were supposed to be government-to-government. But the rules we played by had been set by the Americans. Departments of transportation, Army bases, highway construction programmes and pothunters were all involved in digging up the ground and unearthing tribal burials. It was my job to protect those sites.

> The past is not dead, it is not even past.
>
> *William Faulkner*

Beneath the lands they call America are millions of Indian graves, and many other places are ancient sacred sites. Routinely, Americans have been looting, building on top of, or paving over such places. American law allows tribes to negotiate for preservation if there is a federal tie involving land, permits, or monies but desecrations on private lands have no remedies other than what state governments allow, minimal protection at best.

When it was a new discipline, archaeology was given a lucrative mandate to collect skulls from people of colour from around the world. The scientific community wanted to measure the size of the brain cavities to prove they were smaller overall than those of white folks. There may also be something primal about digging an Indian grave in the name of science. A human war trophy is a version of an ultimate defeat, a way of humiliating your enemy.

Many tribal burials and sacred sites are now hundreds of miles from where tribal nations have been removed to. I spent a lot of time on planes travelling to Alabama, Northern Mississippi and Tennessee, all part of the ancient

Chickasaw homeland before the removals. I, and representatives from other tribes would face off against archaeologists and American government officials at conference tables in the American South, negotiating memorandums of agreement to protect tribal burials and sacred places.

Our side usually shared a tribal conversation feature consisting of a brief silent pause. The silent pause means that what you just said is respected enough not to be blurted over with a quick response. American officials sometimes mistook the pause for agreement or even fascination and would drone on like they were speeding through a red light. One archaeologist misread the silent pause so completely that he came to believe he was on a roll, telling jokes and stories blissfully uninterrupted as if he were working a lounge in Vegas.

Indian grave looting in the American South is a major growth industry, with burial pots and other funerary objects often going for several thousand dollars on the international black market. Pothunters frequently sell drugs besides robbing Indian graves, and they like to carry guns. Because of my official tribal involvement, I began receiving death threats from pothunters who vowed that I would never leave their woods alive.

I've had death threats, if you can imagine.

Pat Boone

When the office phone rang with news of a burial washout on an island in the middle of Lake Texoma I straightened my tie, rang the tribal motor pool, and sauntered out the door, on my way to my first on-site consultation. I arrived late and missed my boat, but fast-talked my way aboard a small, motorised sailboat with a limited two-person wheel deck. The husband-and-wife crew had me stand at the edge of the bow, holding to a mast cable with one hand, my briefcase in the other. The morning sun shimmered across calm, brilliant waters.

I stared out at the glinting expanse of placid lake in my new suit feeling like James Bond as we motored away from the dock and headed for Treasure Island, the actual name of my destination. But almost as soon as we cast off and began to move, a strange wind flapped my tie, and then thunder rumbled across the length of darkening skyline. Soon lightning began to flash while great black mists swirled in. With the thunder, sudden sheets of dense, slanted rain lashed down, stinging my face and hands, but my hosts plowed doggedly ahead.

Only my firm grip on the cable wire kept me on board as the boat banked into a wide, sliding arc. As Treasure Island bobbed into view my hosts shouted,

'See if you can make it nowww …' I'd no choice but to jump overboard. In seconds their little boat disappeared into the storm. Waves lapped at my chest but I kept my feet and struggled ashore, briefcase in hand. Figures in pith helmets huddled beneath a canopy some distance away. They were the archaeologists from Texas I was to consult with, and as I slogged closer they began to take notice.

With no explanatory boat in sight they stared as if I were a drowning victim who hadn't realised his fate. While lurching along, oozing water, it occurred to me that like clerical collars or glow-in-the-dark suspenders, suits are best left to those who can wear them convincingly. Eventually the day returned to warm and sunny calm, and I began to dry out. With the archaeologists and my discount clothing both shrinking from me I inspected the burial, a mass grave old enough to be ancestral Wichita and dating from the 1500s.

All the remains had been exposed with only the streaks of the red ochre they had been buried with to shield them from the wind and rain. Besides suspecting me of being a haint, the Texans seemed to have had a more profound ignorance. Treasure Island had once been a mountaintop. Those that had once buried their dead so close to the heavens never thought that one day a strange people would flood the valley and desecrate the grave. I told the bone jockeys I would follow up on security, and then I caught a skiff to shore.

Whatever comes out of the ground should be put back into the ground.
Wilson T., Choctaw doctor or medicine man

There were only ripples as the skiff skimmed across tranquil waters. I had been baptised into my new vocation. It had been a curious service, attended by both the quick and the dead. Back at the office I settled into a routine of phone calls, meetings, and paperwork. Several weeks went by before concerned citizens in Huntsville, Alabama called the office to report that bulldozers were taking down an ancient burial mound in part of the old Chickasaw homeland, a mound that ran for almost a mile along the Tennessee River.

In America, private property rights are sacred. Because the mound was on private property, American federal laws couldn't stop the desecration. While the State of Alabama had jurisdiction over the protection of its burials, Indian grave disturbances were a misdemeanour punishable by a fifty dollar fine; far less than a mere slap on the wrist to a large commercial operation. The concerned citizens, all of them white, had asked for help from tribal government as a last resort. The degree of violation and destruction was amazing.

I'll show you where your grandparents are. You have aunts and uncles buried there, too. It's the same hill where your grandparents used to have their double cabin. No one goes there anymore, and there aren't any names on the headstones. They're just rocks that the family made square. I think I can remember who is buried where, according to the rocks. But we'll have to be careful because a white man owns the land, now. He runs cattle on it.

My Uncle John

Trucks carrying burial earth mixed with chipped slivers of human remains were continually leaving the mound to have their loads divided into sacks and sold as topsoil. Flowerbeds and vegetable gardens in the region were speckled with fragments of human bones. I scheduled an on-site meeting with a concerned citizen's group and a few archaeologists, and then booked a plane to Huntsville. We met on a spring morning amid the roar of bulldozers.

There were choking clouds of red dust and giant yellow earthmovers. Soil would be torn away by the dozer blades, until another long row of graves appeared, the top of each burial covered with white shell. Earthmovers would charge up the side of the great mound and scrape down another layer of earth, tearing open more graves, scattering their shell coverings and gouging out the skeletons. Larger remains were thrown upon a growing pile of jumbled human bones, and once more the dump trucks would be loaded with earth.

At night, pothunters gathered to burrow through the piles of bones and open graves for ancient pots, effigy pipes, spear points, incised shell gorgets, copper inlaid maces and other grave goods that brought premium prices from a global collectors market. Turning to the archaeologists, I asked them to identify an intact human remain among all the white fragments that littered the plowed red clay. They all bent down and examined the ground while taking careful, evenly spaced paces, conducting what bone jockeys call a walkover survey.

It went against my instincts to search out and take from the dead, but I felt that I needed a verifiable human remain as evidence in case the destruction of tribal graves was ever denied or contested in court. Soon I was watching the crowd suspiciously bunch together, increasing their strides, none of them looking up but all of them suddenly turning like a school of fish, casually pacing further and further away from me.

Something was very wrong. I glanced around in time to see a huge bulldozer with its blade tilted forward, lumbering swiftly in my direction like a yellow dinosaur. Despite my stomach going queasy I decided to stand my ground. Besides, it would have looked bad to have appeared taken by surprise.

I crossed my arms and stared silently, just like an old-time movie Indian. But I flinched before the giant machine lurched to a stop, six feet away.

> A white man came to my grandfather and tried to run him off his land. The man had legal papers and a gun. My grandfather was wearing a long blanket. As the man reached for his weapon my grandfather parted his blanket. He had been holding a 30.30 rifle underneath. So my grandfather raised his rifle and shot the man.
>
> *Chebon White Cloud, Otoe-Creek*

Thinking fast, I did what old-time movie Indians are never supposed to do; I lied through my teeth. I told the driver, an angry man with red hair, that we were exploring old Chickasaw village sites. Amazingly he nodded and roared back towards the mound. The crowd returned, sauntering towards me as if they had been away picking daisies. I shot them all mean looks for not warning me about the dozer. Then an intact human bone was found.

My sense was that it belonged to a little girl. I placed the little remain in my briefcase, along with a signed statement from an archaeologist attesting that the femur was human and from the site. Right away I rang the Army Corps of Engineers, a federal agency with limited shoreline authority along major waterways. That weekend a Corps representative and I met at the mound. Despite the signed statement and the scatterings of human bones, she was only interested in a dirt pile that covered part of a nearby marsh.

It was in fact pay dirt; soil that constituted an illegal wetland fill of an endangered waterfowl habitat, a violation of the Clean Water Act. Under American federal law it's a grave federal offence to disturb endangered waterfowl. We had found a federal law which could bypass state law and private property rights. That weekend I caught a flight home, and on Monday morning the citizen's group rang me at the tribal office in Ada.

They were waiting for the arrival of a Corps of Engineers official, and then they gave me a play-by-play report. The workday had begun, and the bulldozer operators were firing up their engines. Since our visit, the topsoil operation had brought in attack dogs. The little group reported that a long black car had driven up to the mound and parked. Dogs were leaping wildly, restrained by their handlers. I listened at the other end of the phone.

A man was getting out of the car holding papers; the bulldozer drivers were shouting and waving their arms; then they shut down their awful machines, leaving only the sound of baying dogs. The little group was celebrating. The Army Corps of Engineers had slapped an injunction on the topsoil operation for the Clean Water Act violation. And there was a fine; fifty thousand dollars for each day they remained in business.

As befits the classically disturbed mien gazing evermore into the hinterlands of despair, the corners of the mouth shall be drawn and puckered, eyeballs kept dull and free of gleam, the closed sobriety of the lips naught disturbed save for the sudden sneer or rueful laugh.

The North American Encyclopedia of Classical Frowning, *p. 37*

Months later the dance troupe I had organised for the Chickasaws performed at the Burritt Museum in Huntsville, Alabama. I had brought along the remains of the little girl, and on a cool, grey morning I took the dancers to the great mound. We were standing beneath clouds fat with impending rain, dressed in ribbon shirts and long dresses, black hats circled by beadwork, the hair of the women caught by silver combs. A vast plowed field stretched before us and we began to walk somewhere towards the middle of it. We were there to rebury.

Then two archaeologists came driving up unannounced, carrying a cardboard box filled with bone fragments. They wanted to return the violated shards they had collected back to final earth. The sense to do that had never occurred to them before, somehow. They alerted us that others had also arrived. Up a dirt road and hidden behind a tree line were five cars. Shielded by the trees, pothunters were waiting for us to leave so they could dig up the bones once again to see whether any new artefacts had been placed in the grave.

I walked up the road to the cars, their windows rolled down, about three persons in each vehicle, men and women, staring silently. I felt prompted to tell them that they would never find the grave, but I didn't know why I said that. None of the pothunters said anything, and I walked back to the group. We dug a circular hole as a whirlwind spun across the plowed field, picking up grit. My sense was that the whirlwind was a spirit.

For the past few nights ghosts have knocked on our door. I get up to open the door, but of course I can't see anyone. They came to warn me that someone had left the door unlocked again. Was that you?

My mother

As the little whirlwind reached us it thumped against the cardboard box and blew bone dust up my nose, which startled me. An elder began singing Choctaw Hymn 112, *Lament unto Death*. Just as we quickly finished the reburial and were leaving the field, the clouds finally burst open and a straight and heavy rain fell, soaking everything. The dry, red earth became smoothed and evened and glossed with rainwater and soon all traces of our footprints and the little round grave we had just dug were completely washed away.

Nitak kanima fehna ho
Si ai illi hokma
Anki aba binili mut
Is sa halanlashke

'Some day when I die, Father who sits on high, take my hand'
Choctaw Hymn 112

One result of my efforts was friendly contact with the towns and cities within ancestral tribal homeland areas. Residents of Memphis, Tennessee wanted to host a Chickasaw homecoming. There was a positive response from the tribal regime, so I worked with the residents to put together an official tribal return. The dance troupe was to play a major role in the event, which involved a Trail of Tears in reverse. We would cross the Mississippi River from its western bank on a massive Corps of Engineers barge, over to Memphis.

Downtown Memphis seemed filled with expectation. A crowd had gathered to welcome us. The dance troupe joined in with the Tennessee Choctaw, who had come out in force to support the homecoming. Both groups merged and spiralled in soft flashes of beadwork and graceful twists of ribbons as old songs echoed off the buildings and down the alleyways. Days before the barge trip and the homecoming I had driven north out of Memphis to see Ittibachafa. The dance arbours had fallen in, and the ball pole was beginning to lean.

It was at Memphis in 1830 that American soldiers had first ordered Choctaw warriors, exhausted mothers and their hungry babies, tired and sick children and frail grandparents onto cholera-infected boats and barges in the dead of winter, barefoot and without blankets, exiling them to faraway western lands that would later be called Oklahoma. In 1994 my little staff and I had managed to organise a triumphant intertribal return.

> In the whole scene there was an air of ruin and destruction, something which betrayed a final and irrevocable adieu; one couldn't watch without feeling one's heart wrung. The Indians were tranquil, but sombre and taciturn. There was one who could speak English and of whom I asked why the Choctaws were leaving their country. 'To be free,' he answered, could never get any other reason out of him. We ... watch the expulsion ... of one of the most celebrated and ancient American peoples.
>
> *Alexis de Tocqueville;*
> *witnessing the forced removal of Choctaws from Memphis, 1831*

After the activities were over my assistant, who happened to be named Elvis, jumped into the car and we cruised past Graceland towards the Mississippi River. Watching city lights shimmer down upon the cold, fast waters, the ghosts of the Choctaw removals, Ittibachafa, and Graceland too, all seemed close. It had been an odd homecoming. Then later that summer a small-town festival in northern Mississippi booked the dance troupe.

Northern Mississippi was an ancient Chickasaw homeland area that I'd been to often, negotiating to protect old village sites and burials. A few whites there claimed Chickasaw ancestry, but Kyle Cunningham was the most insistent. A silver-haired, white southerner with a big moustache, Kyle was the self-proclaimed 'chief' of the Mississippi Chickasaw, although the tribe had all been removed to Oklahoma by the 1850s.

Kyle had once presented the tribal legislature a clump of dried mud, claiming it was a chink from the last Chickasaw council house built before the American removals. Pushing his luck, he had me examine what he insisted was a carved likeness of the Spanish conquistador Hernando Desoto, supposedly crafted by an Indian during the 1540s. He solemnly paraded the little nugget out under glass, like Larry London serving up the earth's very last alleged *Varanus Komodoensis* at Carmine (aka Jimmy the Toucan) Sabatini's fabulous Gourmet Club.

The 'carving' turned out to be a small, ordinary piece of sandstone daubed with oil to suggest a facial outline. A statement of authenticity that Kyle himself had worked up accompanied the beleaguered lithic. I guess I didn't take the presentation seriously enough. When the dance troupe came to town Kyle rang the mayor's office to threaten that if I didn't leave by sundown I would be shot, the same sort of decree that the Klan once gave to blacks in segregated southern towns. For some reason no one had thought to arrest Kyle.

Not one of the troupe members had yet thought to learn how to sing for a single dance, so instead of laying low I had to go sing for them, flanked by a wary police escort who sullenly eyed the crowd as they mumbled into their radios. I began to enjoy veering off in another direction just to see if my escort could keep up. The dancers kept a prudent distance and probably took bets as to where the first bullet would strike.

On my return, tribal headquarters seemed embarrassed that I'd received a threat on my life. All the death and shame in the air was odd because I hadn't tried to provoke or mortify. Elvis, a former military policeman, insisted on checking my car for bombs each time I left the office. If I hadn't exactly knocked on death's door I'd managed to ring his doorbell once or twice before running off. Death is embarrassed when you do that.

Then Don Mullan called again. The Chieftains were performing at Southern Methodist University in Dallas, and the semi-elected Oklahoma Choctaw chief wanted to make the Chieftain's leader, Paddy Moloney, an honorary Choctaw chief. 'Honorary Choctaw Chief' was a title that Don had already received and he wanted me there for the ceremony. Why wouldn't a Chieftain already be a chief, I wondered. It seemed confusing.

Let the music speak for itself.

Paddy Moloney

Handing out Hollywood western style feathered bonnets is a flashy way of giving someone the key to your city; nice enough as long as your honouree doesn't show up trying to unlock doors or lead war parties. The war bonnet routine got worse whenever the chief startled honourees by presenting them with jars of moonshine labelled 'Panther Piss'. Don turned down the chief's offer of war bonnets for all the Chieftains, even with a few jars thrown in. Maybe a band of feathered-up honorary chiefs crazed on moonshine was too scary an idea.

You can tell it's good if you light it and a blue flame comes up; that means it's good moonshine and it won't make you go blind.

Johnny Knoxville

After a statewide search, a lone war bonnet was finally cornered in the window of a trading post in Pawnee, and the tribal jet was sent to fetch it. During the first moments of the concert I knew that whether I had heard of the Chieftains or not, the rest of the world certainly had. Then at intermission Choctaw officials crowned Paddy Moloney. We joined the Chieftains backstage, and they were very gracious to us.

While we were backstage Paddy Moloney poured me my very first Guinness, from a can and into a plastic cup. Matt Molloy offered me a proper pint should I ever find my way to his pub in County Mayo. Then Paddy offered me poteen if I would come to visit him. 'Potcheen?' I echoed. 'Say, is that anything like panther piss?' It was March of 1995. I would soon be leaving for my first visit to Ireland, though I didn't know it yet.

Meanwhile, Don Mullan called again. He was a director at Concern Worldwide. Don's latest plan was, as always, inspired. Two peoples bonded by famine and removals were now in a position to help feed the world's hungry. Don wanted to come to Oklahoma again to appeal to the Choctaw Council for a charitable donation. He was optimistic, for he had cultivated a good working relationship with the quasi-elected Choctaw chief, Hollis Roberts.

Hollis Roberts' term as Chief ran from 1978 to 1997, when he was convicted of one count of Aggravated Sexual Abuse and two counts of Abusive Sexual Contact.

Choctaw Nation of Oklahoma

Don had put together a history scrapbook from Famine times, placed within a photo album. I read of Skibbereen, as the haunting faces of Bridget McDonald and her small children stared back at me. I read passages from *Mo Scéal Féin*, telling the story of Cait Buckley and her family who died at Macroom, Co. Cork. I learned of mass graves, of 'taking the soup', of absentee landlords and Famine roads. I read of coffin ships and Penal Laws.

And I read of the plantation system, of those who died at Doolough, and of so many more who died with the hungry grass in their mouths. I read of Trevalyn and the potato blight, workhouses, and how through the years of the Famine, food was leaving Irish ports bound for England as over a million Irish men, women, and children perished. The solidarity of our two peoples was the basis of Don's appeal to the Choctaw Council.

There had always been rumours about the chief, alleging bribery and sexploitation, but Hollis Roberts had survived his accusers and without any term limits was headed for two straight decades of executive office. I didn't want to offend my Chickasaw employers by appearing at a Choctaw Council meeting. Despite this sage realisation, I soon found myself at Choctaw tribal headquarters anyway, having agreed to stand with Don before the Council.

> After the reading of a letter from the Irish Relief Committee of Memphis ... the chairman spoke of 'Old Erin' as men of Irish feeling and Irish blood alone can speak; he said, 'It is not words she wanted, but substantial food.' A subscription list was then opened, and in a short time $170 were subscribed and paid ... you will perceive the names of many full-blooded Choctaw Indians, who knew nothing more, cared for nothing more, than the fact that across the Big Water, there were thousands of human beings starving to death ...
>
> *Eyewitness account of Col. G.W. Clarke,*
> *Published in the* Arkansas Intelligencer, *March 1847*

Don and I made a strong appeal, but the Council's hearts were not moved; the Somali Famine victims were denied assistance. We had merely been two people asking for money on a busy morning. It was a dismissive result far different than the 1847 Choctaw donation to Ireland. In a general way I understood what might have gone wrong. In 1847 ordinary, non-tribal government Choctaw people were appealed to. In 1995 we had appealed to tribal politicians.

It's an unfortunate neocolonial system. Oklahoma Choctaw chief executives have been able to create self-perpetuating regimes that are sanctioned, enforced, and significantly funded by the American government's Bureau of Indian Affairs. An amazing three-quarters of tribal voters live outside the Choctaw Nation. The only effective way to solicit the critical absentee votes of the Choctaw diaspora is through the voter registration list, names and addresses the regime keeps secret.

Besides denying access to the voter list and a subsequent monopoly on postal electioneering, political censorship by the tribal newspaper, use of the tribal jet, expected employee support, no term limits, and with all campaign costs paid for by tribal monies, the incumbent chief executive has one final advantage; their hand-picked employees count all the ballots. The system is so overwhelmingly one-sided that beginning in the 2003 election no one attempted to run against the incumbent chief.

> I'm not a dictator. It's just that I have a grumpy face.
>
> *Augusto Pinochet*

In April of 1995 I received permission from my Chickasaw employers to help Don Mullan with humanitarian projects in Ireland. I was an Afri Famine commemoration walk leader in Co. Mayo, and there followed a whirlwind schedule of appearances, interviews, and lectures. At the end of our tour I exhibited my artwork in London. More interviews and lectures followed, all part of Don's initiative linking the Great Famine to modern world hunger issues.

Responses to the eleven day tour were enthusiastic. It had been an amazing first trip to Ireland. Less than a month later, Don called again. He wanted us to attend President Robinson's visit to Oklahoma Choctaw tribal headquarters. Once more I quietly took time away from my employers. Her Excellency was made an honorary Choctaw chief, although I'm not sure about the complimentary jar of moonshine. We'd been kept away from greeting the President.

> Earlier in the month I met one of the members of the tribe, the artist Gary White Deer, who brought me a beautiful painting. He explained to me that taking part in that (Afri) walk and remembering the past between the Choctaw Nation and the Irish people and re-linking our peoples is completing the circle. I have used that expression recently at a major conference on world hunger in New York. I spoke of the generosity of the Choctaw people and this idea of completing the circle.
>
> *President Mary Robinson,*
> *Choctaw Nation of Oklahoma tribal headquarters, 1995*

'Completing the Circle' was Don's phrase. He found it suspicious that although it was through his projects that the President of Ireland ultimately visited tribal headquarters, their officials prevented us from speaking to her. Don still claims that I was seen as a threat by the tribal regime and after his association with me, a known apathetic, they began ignoring him. How big a threat could I have been? Contact explosives on the regime's toilet seats? Refilling moonshine jars with Oolong tea?

> Contact explosives are rarely encountered in the classroom, owing to their unstable nature and the associated danger of detonation. However, using the following method, a small quantity of dry ... crystals can be used to produce an impressive 'crack' and a beautiful cloud of purple ... vapour ...
>
> Demonstrations to Capture the Student's Imagination,
> *Adrian Guy of Blundell's School, Royal Society of Chemistry*

My Chickasaw dance troupe was now appearing at venues like the Gallup Inter-Tribal Ceremonials. That annual event featured fourteen tribal groups, including Apache fire dancers, Navajo butterfly dancers, Taos buffalo dancers, Zuni olla maidens, and the finale of each evening's show, Los Voladores, aerial flyers from Mexico who whirled down from a giant wooden pole attached to woven cords. At Gallup we passed in review before grandstands that had witnessed flying hoofs and airborne Indian cowboys only hours before.

When the floodlights shut off a speck of hush fell, the cue for all the troupes to take their seats around the freshly raked dirt and manure of the arena. Then shafts of luminous round light struck the arena floor and quivered while overhead, loudspeakers boomed loud enough to set your teeth on edge. It seemed for many of the dance troupes that performing within those golden circles of light was like being touched by the incandescent fingers of an entertainment god.

Highlighting each evening's performance was the show-stopping Mexican Indian flyers finale, which required elaborate preparation. First, the great eighty foot high column of wood was splashed with tequila to appease it, or at least try to get it in a good mood. Next, the plucky flyers shinnied up thick, dangling ropes to teeter near the top of the great pole. They braced on something like a big pinwheel and got busy coiling ropes around their waists. Their flight was an ancient ritual meant to symbolise eagles soaring before the sun.

As Los Voladores prepared for flight, their leader danced, beat a drum, and played a flute on a tiny wooden platform atop the pole without any life-saving restraints. Then the flyers started unwinding from their waist ropes, whirling their way downward. And then they revolved towards the ground in ever-widening spirals until with rope ends secured around their ankles, the flyers unfurled Mexican flags, shouting jubilantly.

You have become the Tree of Life …
In your boughs our home shall be
We will be your flowers.

Los Voladores, Song of the Flyers

Indian dance troupes were nothing new. In 1540 Choctaw women as a distractive strategy performed several polite social dances for the Spanish adventurer and sociopath Hernando Desoto, whose men, being European soldiers, were looking for women and gold. Dance performances went well until one of the Spanish expedition's caballeros wantonly stabbed an Indian bystander. The finale was a spectacular shower of arrows.

There's no business like show business.

Irving Berlin

The audiences that peered down from the dusky height of the Gallup grandstands at us had different motives, some genuine, others dire fantasies. But all the dance troupes seemed delighted to hustle towards the spotlight, a mesmerising glow that showcased their slightest movements, graced them with bedazzling sparkle, and flung their magnified silhouettes against dramatic red rock mesas that for an eternal instant rang with waves of validating applause.

If there were one magnified silhouette that did not like me at Chickasaw headquarters, it was their lieutenant governor, my supervisor. Number Two resented that I was an outsider leading what appeared to be a tribal cultural renaissance while representing his tribe in sensitive negotiations. He also had a reputation for firing people. Attracted by the travel and perceived glamour, a tribal legislator was after my job. My assistant had the same ambitions. He came to staff meetings with a hidden recorder hoping I'd say something incriminating.

Enforcement is the long overdue step to protect our Nation from external threats in a time of war. And then once we do that, we can effectively discuss a guest worker programme.

J.D. Hayworth

Fired office workers are usually never seen again, mostly because their ex-fellow workers tend to ignore them as if they were dead. This, despite all of the office parties, birthday and sympathy card signings, Christmas present exchanges, chummy conversations, weddings, funerals, baby showers, confidential meetings, department picnics, beneficial alliances, personal favours, cheerful memos, charity donations, spontaneously pleasant remarks, calculated compliments, voluntary overtime, or cosy lunches they may have been party to.

Being fired is like a shark attack; one chomp and you go under, leaving behind faint ripples. It's often a ruthless and sneaky process out of the 'Reprimands and Revenge' section of the American Dream manual. Long-term tribal employees never made waves and curried favour, wise behaviour for survival in the American model which tribes copy. I was loyal and worked hard, but I was neither a political partisan nor a Chickasaw. I wondered how long I could exist in such a universe.

Jimi Hendrix: Hey man, if we're literary characters, do we exist?

Otto Von Wieghorst: Ja, somewhere between imagination und expectation.

Jimi: Will I live tomorrow?

Otto: Vell, I chust can't say ...

Jimi: Say what?

Otto: If I am correct, our god iss a writer with a deadline.

Jimi: Sounds like a pissed off god, man.

Otto: Und you would prefer a vengeful deity?

Jimi: Same difference, Otto.

Otto: You see Chimmie, we are being written into zee past. For us, und maybe for everyone, time flows backwards. Or maybe it iss the voice uff time returning und returning.

Jimi: You're freakin' me out, man.

Otto: Ja, heaven iss the pages uff a book waiting to be turned. Over und over.

Jimi: But I'm still dead, right, man?

Otto: We haff been zoogered into existence by zee Great Writer in zee Sky. Time, und all uff creation iss a mysterious deadline.

Jimi: 'Scuse me man while I kiss the sky.

During this period I served on the board of a national Indian organisation that had numerous ongoing feuds and high levels of political intrigue, most of it not at all subtle. Indian board members liked to engage in office warfare more than their white counterparts it seemed, similar behaviour to what I was witnessing in tribal government. Where were our old communal values, I wondered. Where were our old traditions of coming together?

Once, while we were on a board retreat, a white facilitator asked us all to hold hands and, without saying anything, move as a group to the other side of the room. One of our members casually pointed with their lips and away we all went. The facilitator was amazed, and said that other groups found such an exercise designed to teach cooperation difficult, that there was always a lot of tugging and pulling. I thought, well, we still have our tribal cooperative attitudes, our communal tendencies. They're still in us. What makes us drop them so easily?

> Words have power. Be careful how you use them. They carry the breath and force of life.
>
> *Regina Moore, Pawnee*

Turner Broadcasting was producing a documentary series called *The Native Americans*, and a Cherokee friend asked me to appear in the Southeastern Indians segment. The director seated me next to the now late Wilma Mankiller, a renowned Indian leader and at the time the Cherokee Principal Chief. Feminists have a high regard for the late Chief Mankiller because of her impressive reputation, but also I think because they like her last name, which they tend to equate with something like bold exterminator of male sexist pigs.

I forgot what she said on camera, but Chief Mankiller's remarks to me between takes were fascinating and inspiring. She told me that past leaders had restored tribal governments, her generation had gotten tribal economies going again, but now new leadership was needed to strengthen culture and traditions. One of the quotes that I gave for the Turner programme interview had to do with that same idea, continuity of tradition:

> I think the spirit, is the one thing we have to rely on. It has been handed to us as a live and precious coal. And each generation has to make that decision whether they want to blow on that coal to keep it alive or throw it away … Our language, our histories and culture are like a big ceremonial fire that's been kicked and stomped and scattered … Out in the darkness we can see those coals glowing. But our generation, whether in tribal government or wherever we find ourselves … Choctaw, Cherokee, Chickasaw, Creek, Seminole … are coal gatherers. We bring the coals back, assemble them and breathe on them again, so we can spark a flame around which we might warm ourselves.
>
> The Native Americans, *Waylon Gary White Deer,*
> *Turner Broadcasting 1994*

Then, once again, Don rang. Could I come to Dublin with a special commission? The purchase amount would be 10,000 Irish punt or about 17,000 American dollars. The painting, done on a bodhrán or Irish drum would be bought by the Irish State, the money given to Concern Worldwide to aid famine victims in Somalia. The upcoming trip upset my secretary. She'd heard I would be fired if I went to Dublin again. My Chickasaw employers had no Tribal–Irish Famine connection. Their ancestors had been mercenaries for the British.

It was the second of September 1995. By first light I was in Dublin. After I landed, there followed a handing over of the cheque ceremony between Irish government officials and Concern as the little Irish drum changed hands as well. Don organised another whirlwind tour of lectures and interviews. Too soon I left Ireland, but with the sense that I had made a contribution. But my employers hadn't hired me to go travelling overseas.

They greeted my return from Ireland with stony silence. A chill was in the September air, and as I began returning calls and catching up with paperwork I wondered whether or not my secretary's warning would come true. I felt a brooding tension developing. Then a festival in Louisiana booked the dance troupe, and we boarded the tribal vans to travel to yet another out-of-state gig. Our policy was to travel together in case of van trouble. While I waited on a late arrival the rest of the troupe grew impatient and took off.

> Perhaps there is only one cardinal sin: impatience. Because of impatience we were driven out of Paradise, because of impatience we cannot return.
>
> W.H. Auden

That left an elderly lady, the late arrival, and myself to make the journey on our own. About ten hours into our trip we developed engine trouble. We coasted to a store on the outskirts of a small town, a glowing oasis flanked by shadowy fields. The roadside stop turned out to be a night-time magnet for wine drinkers, frisky women, and anyone else who cared to lurch in from the darkened meadows lured by pulsating neon signage.

I have since concluded that there are times when it may be better to sit in the dark cursing rather than light too bright of a candle. Within minutes drunks swarmed around us, becoming more aggressive as the night wore on, eventually demanding money. Finally one of the festival organisers arrived, just as I was about to bang the main wino over the head with a car tool. The organiser, a no-nonsense white woman, threw herself in front of me and chased all the drunks away, scolding, 'You leave that boy alone!' – So much for macho last stands.

> A good man doesn't just happen. They have to be created by us women. A guy is a lump, like a doughnut. So first you gotta get rid of all the stuff his mom did to him. And then you gotta get rid of all that macho crap they pick up from beer commercials. And then there's my personal favourite ... the male ego.
>
> Rosanne Barr

After allowing us to glimpse her version of enough right white stuff unsheathed against the inebriated like a great flaming sword, the organiser lady whisked us all off to her house, where she fed and bedded us. If we had been overrun by wino hordes, or otherwise hadn't made it, the rest of the troupe would have been stuck, because they still hadn't learned to lead any songs. Later we found them at the festival standing around all dressed up but otherwise immobile. They were waiting on someone to sing for them.

Forgetting that the dancers were also voting members of a political tribal regime, I lined the troupe up beneath the trees and let them have it for abandoning us. They didn't take my point very well. We did the gig and returned home, the dancers dutifully reporting the scolding I'd given them to their tribal politicians. The following week I was summoned to the regime's inner sanctum. Number Two and the personnel director were seated solemnly facing the governor's desk. There was an empty chair between them reserved for me.

All the lights in the room were off except for a small reading lamp. Number Two favoured me with a cold smile, like sunlight on a tombstone. They wanted my resignation. Number Two got angry when I asked for an official reason. Simply put, I was an outsider drawing political heat and my services were no longer required. If they had fired me because of that they would have had to pay me benefits, so they pressured me to quit instead.

It had been a strange time of burials, paperwork, government negotiations, death threats, political intrigue, performance, and trips to Ireland. I'd been asked to create the veneer of a tribal dance culture. And there seemed to have been an odd dysfunction within the tribal office culture I'd inhabited; standard office politics maybe, but with a twist. What had been the dynamic that so often created more envy than efficiency?

> There are three kinds of men. The one that learns by reading. The few who learn by observation. The rest of them have to pee on the electric fence.
>
> *Will Rogers*

After I left tribal government I did art residencies and exhibitions in Ireland. Then I was invited to be an emcee in Centennial Park for the 1996 Summer Olympic Games in Atlanta, and to bring my new dance troupe along. Shortly after we returned to our hotel in Atlanta one evening the largest pipe bomb in US history detonated near where we had danced. The explosion killed two people and injured one hundred and eleven others.

I felt the same strange sensation I'd experienced in Derry when violence seemed close by. There was a body count going on in the America South. The

1995 Oklahoma City bombing that killed 168 people and injured 680 had been in retaliation for Waco, Texas, the 1993 siege where 86 persons were killed. The place they call America was becoming more dangerous. Later, Don and I travelled around Ireland and America fundraising for humanitarian causes until 1998.

In 1999 I was hired as the director for a federal urban Indian programme. My office was in Nashville, but I also supervised two other state offices. I'd no idea why I was hired, except that the Indian board of directors seemed to like me. A week after I started, federal representatives in Washington demanded my resignation. Always suspicious of board hires, the federal representatives said I wasn't qualified. I survived, but the programme's finances were a mess; each past director had used their own accountant.

Our programme mission was to provide job training and assistance to Indians, and we were able to assist many who came to the big city and got stuck. Poor Indian families were relying on an American federal programme for help, and I was being paid to help them. Everyone, including me it seemed, was chasing an American model. From my office I watched an urban Indian diaspora come and go and wondered why we'd stayed dependant on foreign systems for so long.

With such foreign systems come office politics. After I took the job I learned that the board had gone through twelve programme directors in eleven years, and had an extremely toxic relationship with their funder, the US Department of Labor. I also soon found out what had happened to my predecessors. Board members began rummaging through my desk at night, and sat under the time clock in the mornings hoping to catch me running late.

> Destiny is a good thing to accept when it's going your way. When it isn't, don't call it destiny; call it injustice, treachery, or simple bad luck.
>
> *Joseph Heller*

A faction had also been trying for some time to install my secretary as director. In anticipation, she started keeping a daily log on me about alleged policy violations. Most board members worked subordinate day jobs; maybe firing directors was empowering to them. Maybe. I didn't have a clue. I wondered whether the other eleven directors had really been fired or if they'd been executed, their bodies stuffed in empty file cabinets. Quietly, I met with the board attorney. He supported my charge of nepotism; my secretary's sister was a board member.

It was the opening the federal representatives had been waiting for. The board was banned from interfering with my office under penalty of losing the programme. The sister was given a choice; resign from the board or her sibling, my secretary, would have to leave since nepotism violated federal law. It was an obvious decision. The secretary had a family and needed a pay cheque, while all board members served entirely without pay. Surprisingly, the sister chose to stay on the board. So I picked a former programme coordinator as my new secretary.

Following the big board battle I was asked to be in a film, *The Hard Road to Klondike*, and left for a weekend. I needed the break, the board fight had been draining. The film was about the true adventures of an Irishman who struck gold in Alaska and had brushes with Crow Indians along the way. We filmed in Glacier Park and at Crow Agency, Montana. Back in Nashville I grew tired of the constant intrigue and eventually resigned, after first helping to make sure the federal representatives hired my new secretary as my replacement.

Then I resumed painting. In 2002 Don organised a show for me in New York at the Irish Cultural Center. About this time I was asked to bring my dancers to Ireland. A woman had claimed to have seen me in a vision, and wanted me to help her with youth projects. After I returned home an old friend came by to offer me a position as historic preservation officer for the Seminole Nation of Oklahoma, work similar to my Chickasaw experiences. I had a wife and seven children to support, and working for a guaranteed pay cheque again still seemed responsible.

Once more I put down my brushes and entered tribal politics as a member of another tribe. This time I thought I knew what to expect. Council members were unhappy that I wasn't Seminole, which wasn't a surprise. What surprised me was that my friend was afraid of the assistant he'd assigned me. When my alleged assistant wasn't directly refusing work he'd spend quality time at home on full salary. I found out he belonged to a powerful political family; he couldn't be fired, disciplined, made upset, or even looked at cross-eyed.

This town was built on nepotism.

Damon Wayans

More weirdly, my friend and another director both claimed to be my supervisor. Their conflict was part of an ongoing feud I'd walked into, and after a year I was finally let go. The state employment office investigated, ruled unfair dismissal, and the tribe had to pay me unemployment compensation. During that year I'd protected cultural sites and tribal burials, and negotiated agreements with American officials. I was happy with that. But what was the dysfunctional office pattern I'd been noticing – and had even come to expect – lurking in tribal organisations?

It occurred to me that after the conquest 'we' type native institutions were stripped of civil and economic powers and left with cultural nationalism, which alone couldn't feed or protect people. A few short-lived blended systems developed before everyone was redirected towards mainstream 'me' individualism and entrepreneurial capitalism. Yet many tribal people still retain enough 'we' communal spirit to make for a conflicted presence within the American governance models that replaced tribal models, foreign systems now thought of as normal.

For communal peoples, however, those are not normal systems; 'me' dynamics stress competition over cooperation, personal ambition over group welfare. But unlike immigrant groups in America attracted to 'me' systems because their own institutions weren't working properly or were repressive, First Nations societies functioned well overall, and the people they served were content with the traditional 'we' social order before those original government models were taken from them and replaced.

> Out of the Indian approach to life there came a great freedom, an intense and absorbing respect for life, enriching faith in a Supreme Power, and principals of truth, honesty, generosity, equity, and brotherhood as a guide to mundane relations.
>
> *Luther Standing Bear, Oglala Lakota*

Predictably, the competitive systems that replaced cooperative tribal systems work best for those most assimilated as 'me' Americans. Everyone else seems to be caught in versions of a conflicting cultural crossfire that tends to breed envy and resentment over efficiency and 'enterprise'. Limited American style economic development largely defines most modern tribal governments, even as American authorities contemplate their demise, through a process called 'Indian Self-Determination'.

> Indian Self-Determination had two faces: a domestic face which was a social policy which contemplated the eventual assimilation of tribes through economic development, education and the development of Indian management skills; and an international face which was a political policy aimed at deflecting international criticism of the United States in its treatment of Indian tribes.
>
> Neo-Termination and the Reagan Administration:
> US Assimilation Policy with a New Label
> *Rudolph C. Reyser, National Congress of American Indians, 1982*

145

I'm sometimes asked about Leonard Peltier, a Chippewa–Lakota American Indian Movement member. AIM is an intertribal Indian rights group that has described themselves as a warrior society. In 1975 an AIM contingent engaged in a shoot-out with two FBI agents on the Pine Ridge Reservation in which one AIM member and both agents were killed. During this same general period, tribal regime death squads, who were armed at least in part by the Bureau of Indian Affairs, killed over sixty Indian men, women and children at Pine Ridge.

Within this political reign of terror only the tragic killings of the two FBI agents became a paramount focus for American authorities. Following a massive manhunt, Peltier was convicted of the FBI deaths, although the two other AIM members who were charged had already been acquitted for acting in self-defence. Witness intimidation, undue FBI judicial pressure and a misleading ballistics report were key factors in Peltier's conviction. Since his sentencing in 1977, Leonard Peltier has become widely regarded as a political prisoner in America.

> A political prisoner is someone who is out fighting for his or her people's rights and freedoms and is imprisoned for that alone.
>
> *Leonard Peltier*

Peltier has received support from Amnesty International, the Dalai Lama, the European, Italian, and Belgian parliaments, Nelson Mandela, Rigoberta Menchu, Archbishop Desmond Tutu, the United Nations High Commissioner for Human Rights, and the Kennedy Memorial Center for Human Rights. Despite worldwide demands for clemency, Leonard Peltier remains in prison. American authorities have no direct evidence linking him to the killings of their two agents. Does Leonard Peltier's imprisonment serve other purposes?

AIM's short-lived activities had the potential to incite more insurrections against American colonialism. Such social disruptions would have proven problematic for law enforcement but, more tellingly, the legitimacy of America's claim to freedom and democracy would have been directly called into question both at home and abroad. Leonard Peltier serves as a chilling reminder to Indian Country; try to reassert your true tribal sovereignty and you may die in prison, no matter who supports you.

> When we talk of sovereignty, we must be willing to solve our own problems and not go running to the oppressor for relief ... We have been and still are at odds with the most dangerous, well-funded, strongest military and political organisation in the history of the world.
>
> *Leonard Peltier*

You and I know how the world is explained to us. Social and political institutions, technology, and the news media maintain a conventional consciousness, an agreement about how things work. Our job in the world appears to be finding and maintaining our comfort zones; places that through education, hard work, talent, or circumstance make us feel safe and secure. We think most people are good. Everyone is trying, we think. Honest mistakes are made but we also know there's evil in the world, and that bad people sometimes do bad things.

But the world is manageable we tend to believe, because there are explanations. To contemplate the world other than the way it's explained to us intrudes on our comfort zones. It's uncomfortable to think that good people are subverted by bad systems or are unjustly jailed, that wants and needs are often exploited or controlled by powerful hidden agendas. Yet, lying close beneath the reassurance of explanations and the comfort of known convention, the agendas of exploitation and control continue as systems, powerful and often hidden.

Occasionally when our comfort zones are interrupted and explanations don't make sense we begin to suspect the existence of other systems, other agendas. Some of us occupy Wall Street, or wonder at the fluctuating price of fuel. When the world gets comfortable again we tend to doubt the glimpses of the hidden systems we thought we saw. But for others, the world isn't ever that comfortable, safe, or secure so covert systems are more visible, explanations often don't make sense, and exploitation and control are more keenly felt.

Most Indians over time have chosen not to look too closely at hidden systems; the view is too overwhelming. Instead they grudgingly accept a tribal status defined and validated by the Bureau of Indian Affairs, and would find it strange if their tribal nation entered into independent trade agreements with France or China, or declared they weren't bound by American law, or if they began to maintain armed forces like other sovereigns do.

Yet these are all attributes of tribal nationhood, of First Nations as countries which once bore arms, made treaties, and lived by their own systems. True tribal sovereignty should always reserve its fundamental and inherent right to exercise all attributes of nationhood, even if its capacity to do so has been limited, suppressed, or denied. And historically the American government has used all means, including deadly force, to limit tribal sovereignty.

> My people will sleep for one hundred years, but when they awake, it will be the artists who give them their spirit back.
>
> *Louis Riel*

147

There was once a Choctaw nationalist movement that opposed Oklahoma statehood and the loss of tribal lands and sovereignty. By then the western Choctaw had a blended system of government, an official American model whose leaders informally shared 'we' communal values. In time, however, Americanised tribal politicians took control of tribal government and the same conflicting cultural crossfire in tribal politics today played out then, also within the same long shadow of American colonialism.

In 1871 the United States Congress assumed plenary powers over Indian sovereignty, violating the solemn intent of Indian treaties as honoured agreements between nations. American pressure on the Choctaw to accept the allotment of their communally held lands as a prelude to Oklahoma statehood and authority began to mount. Yet the Treaty of Dancing Rabbit Creek, the final Choctaw removal agreement, had guaranteed that:

> No Territory or State shall ever have the right to pass laws for the government of the Choctaw Nation of Red People and their descendants; and that no part of the land granted them shall ever be embraced in any Territory or State …
>
> *1830 Treaty of Dancing Rabbit Creek, Article IV*

After two decades of growing American pressure, Green McCurtain became principal chief. He led the Choctaw pro-American faction, a political party that represented one third of the electorate. Another prominent leader during this period was Jacob B. Jackson. College educated and a full blood Six-Town Choctaw, Jackson had served both in the Choctaw Senate and as National Secretary. Jackson opposed the American government's Dawes Commission and its threatened land allotments intended to dismember the Choctaw State.

The Choctaw people were also overwhelmingly opposed to any change in their national status and the Choctaw National Council appointed a committee to meet with the Dawes Commission to protest 'any dissolution of our present tribal relations or tenure of our lands'. During this time a pan-nationalist movement of grassroots Creek, Seminole, Cherokee, Choctaw and Chickasaw traditionalists began to emerge. Known as the Four Mothers Society, its members opposed land allotments and the dissolution of tribal governments.

The movement eventually grew to 24,000 members. Eufaula Harjo, a Muscogee Creek, and Redbird Smith, Cherokee, were two early leaders but Chitto Harjo, the Muscogee Creek orator was the most influential. His name translated to 'Recklessly Brave Snake Clansman', though white detractors called him 'Crazy Snake'. Because of Chitto Harjo's outspoken leadership, members of the movement were called 'Snakes' by their enemies, a name that the movement also came to use themselves, because, traditionally, animal names were not seen as insults.

The Four Mothers Society sent delegates to Washington, hired a white attorney as a lobbyist and collected membership dues. Closely related, the Creek and Seminole were counted as one by the Society and with the Cherokee, Choctaw, and Chickasaw created the sacred number four. 'Mothers' alluded to matrilineal clan origins. Besides opposition from whites, the Society attracted hostility from Americanised Indians and whites with small amounts of Indian blood. Inevitably, the American government targeted the Four Mothers Society.

> We ask the honourable Dawes Commission to make their report to the Congress of the United States favouring the extension of justice to us and our peaceful homes and ask to be permitted without molestation to possess that which is ours and only ours.
>
> *Choctaw National Council General Resolution, 1896*

But the Nation's sovereignty remained a target of predatory American policies. A flurry of hostile bills were introduced in the American Congress. Oklahoma Territory proposed that tribal nations be forced to accept land allotment with the vast remainder of tribal lands given to white homesteaders. Chief McCurtain hoped to defeat such hostile legislation by convincing the Nation that their only hope was to negotiate the most favourable settlement possible with American authorities.

Then, on 28 June 1898, the American Congress passed the Curtis Act, which demanded the dissolution of tribal governments and the surrender of treaty lands. A pretext for a massive land grab, the Curtis Act carried the implied threat of American military aggression. Faced with forced land allotment and political abdication, tribal nationalists formally organised the Choctaw Snake Band, allied with the Four Mothers Society. Jacob B. Jackson was chosen as band chief.

Starting with a membership of 600, options were meager. The McCurtain government commanded the Choctaw Militia. Armed resistance to the Curtis Act could provoke civil war, giving the Americans an excuse to send troops to aid the McCurtain forces; already there had been sieges, gun battles and assassinations between pro-American tribal partisans and Choctaw nationalists. With armed conflict increasing and the peace and freedom of the Nation in peril, the hopes of the tribal nationalists turned south, beyond the Rio Grande River.

In 1898 Chief Jackson led a Snake Band delegation into Mexico to negotiate Choctaw resettlement. The Snakes proposed to 'sell' their individual land allotments to American authorities before they were assigned, pooling the revenues to buy a sovereign sanctuary. In turn, Mexican officials pledged that a reestablished Choctaw Nation of Mexico could remain free and independent. Chief Jackson only had to convince the Americans to pay the Snakes in cash for the impending theft of the Choctaw estate rather than through small allotted land parcels.

But at home, American style tribal politics were coming to a bitter and divisive end in the looming shadow of dissolution. Disputing an election ballot count, armed partisans began converging on the national capitol at Tuskahoma. Violating Choctaw sovereignty, the US Cavalry entered the Nation on the pretext of helping to settle the dispute. American demands for Chief McCurtain to use more force against the Snake Band rose steadily. McCurtain declined, requesting instead that the Americans themselves take 'prompt action'.

> I have the honour to herewith enclose a resolution adopted by Council, in which I am authorised to respectfully request you to take some action relative to the suppression of the Choctaw Snake Band.
>
> The information I have at hand is such that I believe that unless steps are taken to imprison the leaders of this so-called [sic] Snake Band of Indians that much serious trouble will result from this species of outlawry which they now practice in secret … if prompt steps are taken at once, and a few of their leaders imprisoned, the threatened danger to other fullbloods [sic] who reside in their neighbourhoods may be averted.
>
> I earnestly and respectfully request that you take some action in this matter at your earliest practical moment, in order that the band of fear may be removed from those who desire to select their allotments, but have been restrained from doing so by threats of vengeance from this secret band of Indians who foolishly oppose the present policy of the Government in carrying out the terms of the present Treaties.
>
> *Green McCurtain letter of 22 October 1903 to Indian Agent J. Blain Shoenfelt,*
> *University of Oklahoma Western History Collections: Green McCurtain Collection,*
> *Box 16, Folder 1*

Chitto Harjo was imprisoned at Fort Leavenworth for advocating tribal sovereignty. Later he would be shot down on the porch of his own home, unarmed and without provocation, by newly minted Oklahoma deputies. After he and a companion killed two of the deputies and managed to escape, Chitto Harjo was hidden in the Choctaw pine hills by Daniel Bobb, a Choctaw Snake Band partisan. Never recaptured, Chitto Harjo died of his wounds.

Efforts to preserve the semblance of an Indian state played out against the swift decline of tribal autonomy. The Choctaw education system passed from tribal control in 1901, the tribal courts were dissolved in 1904, and county and district tribal governments were closed out in 1906. Thereafter, the office of principal chief was filled by appointment of the American president and, predictably, Green McCurtain was chosen as the first presidential appointee. Green McCurtain was clearly expected to sign anything the Americans gave him.

> That if the principal chief of the Choctaw, Cherokee, Creek, or Seminole tribe or the governor of the Chickasaw tribe shall refuse or neglect to perform the duties devolving upon him, he may be removed from office by the President of the United States ... If any such executive shall refuse or neglect, for 30 days after notice that any instrument is ready for his signature, to appear at a place to be designated by the Secretary of the Interior and execute the same, such instrument may be approved by the Secretary of the Interior without such execution, and when so approved and recorded shall convey legal title, and such approval shall be conclusive evidence that such executive or Chief refused or neglected after notice to execute such instrument.
>
> *Section 6 of the Disposition Act of 26 April 1906*

After calling allotment opponents an 'ignorant class of fullbloods' Green McCurtain later lamented, 'we are virtually denied any voice in the settlement of our estate. The interior Department has acted with much severity towards the Choctaw people. We can no longer regard the present Secretary of the Interior as a friend ...' (University of Oklahoma Western History Collections: Green McCurtain Collection, Box 16, Folder 1 and Box 22, Folder 22–1) By 1906 the Choctaw Snake Band had 2,000 members, including Chickasaw elements.

> Surely a race of people, desiring to protect the integrity of that race, who love it by reasons of its traditions and their common ancestors and blood, who are proud of the fact that they belong to it may be permitted to protect themselves, if in no other way by emigration. Our educated people inform us that the white man came to this country to avoid conditions which to him were not as bad as the present conditions are to us; that he went across the great ocean and sought new homes in order to avoid things which to him were distasteful and wrong.
>
> All we ask is that we may be permitted to exercise the same privilege. We do not ask any aid from the government of the United States in so doing. We do ask that we may be permitted, in a proper way, by protecting our own, to dispose of that which the government says is ours, and which has been given to us over protest against the distribution, to the end that another home may be furnished, and another nation established.
>
> [W]e ask consideration of this prayer for these reasons: First, it is our desire, and one we make the request with a full knowledge of its importance, both to us and our children. Second, we believe, if it were known, it would be the desire of the white man. He does not want the Indian any more than we want him, and

by carrying out this plan he will get that which he wants – the Indian land. We will leave and trouble him no longer. Third, it is right – it is just. Over our protest a majority, or what is said to be a majority, of voters approved an agreement with the United States changing our social, political, and personal conditions. There is nothing left for us to do but accept conditions as they are. There is no remedy for us except removal.

If the Choctaw and Chickasaw people as a whole were to lose their racial status, to become by a slow process of blood mixture, and through changed conditions, white men in fact ... we do not oppose the carrying out of their desires; but in addition to the reasons given, we believe that the Great Father of all men created the Indian to fill a proper place in the world. That as an Indian he had certain rights, among which is the right to exist as a race, and that in protection of that right, it is our belief that we are fulfilling the purpose of the Divine Creator of mankind.

Choctaw Snake Band Chief Jacob Jackson,
American senatorial committee address, 1906

Ultimately, the American government refused to purchase the Snake Band allotments, and the vision of a Choctaw Nation of Mexico was lost. Reasoned appeals, an adopted American political model and solemn treaty rights were not enough to save the Nation from American invasion. Choctaw lands were again seized and in 1907 Oklahoma Territory became another American state. Immediately, elements of the new state's white citizenry began stealing tribal land allotments through collusion, fraud, bribery, and at times, by murder.

On 4 July 2010 I reorganised the Choctaw Snake Band to re-establish by peaceful means a Choctaw free state. Much broader than 'domestic dependent nation' status, a free state is a form of nationhood from which fully restored tribal sovereignty may be anticipated. In our day and time we are using the concept of resovereignisation to recover our independence. Resovereignisation is the re-empowerment of traditional tribal social, economic and political systems as instruments of full governance from within American style tribal political structures.

Resovereignisation does not mean anti-American. Resovereignisation means respecting the legitimacy of the government of the United States as a separate political entity. Resovereignisation also means respecting others who identify as 'Native American' or 'American Indian'. Resovereignisation affirms our ancient and ongoing rights as members of a nation whose original sovereignty has been repressed, but has never been extinguished.

[T]hose powers which are lawfully vested in an Indian tribe are not in general delegated powers granted by express acts of Congress, but rather limited powers

of an inherent sovereignty which has never been extinguished.
Cohen, Felix S., Federal Indian Law, US Department of the Interior, 1944

Our sovereign rights remain as great as those of other nations, for they were given by the Creator. Our birthrights as independent First Nations are divine, ancient, perpetual, and self-evident. Those rights are expressed through tribal community sovereignty, which means that tribal nationhood resides within bands and communities. Tribal officials and American style governance models only represent our sovereignty, representations which have largely been compromised.

If a band or community having a continuity of tribal language, visual identity, and original custom determines that its American derived governance model consistently opposes sovereign tribal interests, then that band or community may invoke their inherent right to tribal community sovereignty, and govern accordingly. Like coals from a fire being smothered, a band or community may separate from a compromised flame to spark a brighter sovereign blaze around which they may again warm themselves.

Eventual restoration of tribal freedoms will be impossible without sufficient political pressure. That kind of pressure involves moral force, which together with resovereignisation can be used as political leverage to promote, achieve, and sustain decolonisation, for attempts to decolonise without reinstating original tribal institutions almost always recreate and then perpetuate home-grown colonialist models.

Moral force is a powerful tool available to anybody with sufficient courage. It involves saying no to being dehumanised in any way and instead asserting and insisting on our dignity and rights as free human beings ... Moral force is not just a tactical strategy ... Moral force is an affirmation of our common humanity in the midst of our struggles ...

The means we use to achieve our social and political objectives tell us about the goals we have in mind – the type of world we want to bring about. Moral force requires moral courage because at the time it is employed its position on the side of justice is not necessarily recognised or accepted. Indeed, it is inevitably contested. Moral courage is standing up and taking your position in the always ambiguous uncertain ground of the present. History will determine who was right but history belongs to the future.

Mark Garavan, Afri

I propose a blended political system. Features of government such as a commerce department, a department of education, a justice department or a department of foreign affairs would report to governance authorities which may include clan mothers, clan and society leaders, a chiefs council and so forth. That's the trick. An external American style political structure designed for contemporary function would be controlled by a traditional tribal system, and not the other way around.

Resovereignisation also means traditional consensus democracy. In decision making involving significant issues, authorities within the traditional model make the wishes of their members known to say, a chiefs council which must then render decisions based on cooperation. Such a process works slower than majority rule contentious democracy but outcomes are almost always respectful of the entire group. Private property rights and individual material accumulation would be secured within longstanding cultural traditions.

The economic model should be a traditional cooperative communal system designed to become self sustaining. If a community or band has declared themselves to be an independent sovereign, then that sovereign needs land to exist on, and enough potential resources, human and otherwise, to develop a semi-closed economy. Initially, members would participate in outside trade markets and conventional employment while evolving increasingly self-sufficient alternatives to dependence upon mainstream economies and energy grids.

> Indian tribes are not now, nor have they ever been a part of the United States or its federal political system.
>
> The desire to achieve Indian self-government, political distinctiveness, and the fulfillment of Indian rights threatens US political stability and its desire to achieve its national, political, economic and social goals.
>
> Treatment of Indian tribes by the United States is a matter of international importance which has long played a part in US foreign relations.
>
> Tribes must exercise political leverage within the United States and within the international community to counter US strategies and policies of dismemberment and assimilation.
>
> Tribal communities must be better informed and work cooperatively toward common goals against the common threat. Communities must be fundamentally reorganised to build semi-closed tribal economies which turn Indian labour and natural resources in direct support of tribal needs rather than the export needs of the US economy. Tribal communities must work toward tribal goals and objectives and not US goals and objectives.
>
> *Rudolph C. Reyser, National Congress of American Indians Analysis Paper, 1982*

It's a process that begins with social, political, cultural, and spiritual re-empowerment. It's why cultural competency; the ongoing articulation of tribal ethos is essential for an independent band or community, for through ceremony and custom, cultural nationalism can be maintained. It is the original tribal word view which makes ceremony and custom work, a communal 'we' ethos instead of mainstream 'me' sensibilities. The cooperative 'we' of traditional tribal culture is then authoratively transposed into political and economic systems.

> [E]verything is still possible and I am as determined as ever. I believe first that the project of a people does not die. It is the project of freedom for a people, it is a project of sovereignty. And since the nation exists, it has the right to its own state. I will work to advance it in that direction.
>
> *Pauline Maoris*

That's what I've learned. The imprint of tribal nationhood survives despite sustained and coercive attempts to transform First Nations into another hyphenated American sub group. That losing our birthrights as free and distinct peoples is unacceptable. That there is moral power in being on the right side of a struggle, of using the peaceful but unwavering force of conviction to pursue and achieve just ends. And that our struggle isn't over.

CHAPTER 5
Ireland

THE AMERICA DEATH

Fred was carefully crossing the wide shoulders of O'Connell Street wearing his Aran jumper and plaid 'Paddy' cap. Though his father had been Czech–Norwegian, Fred was proud to be Irish American. A camera hung from his neck filled with images; his arrival gate at Dublin Airport, ruins at Glendalough, ruins at Slane Hill. There were shots of Tara, and of the Liffey from O'Connell Bridge, and shots of Fred in Galway taken by obliging locals.

For his slide-show presentations back home in Boston Fred wanted to snap a few photos of smiling, red-haired children riding in a cart or doing some other real Irishy thing. He would reward them all with a Euro or two. It was peculiar money and, like the Irish B & Bs, not up to American standards. Why didn't the Irish have motels and accept dollars? Why would an entire country drive on the wrong side of the road?

Fred longed for a familiar sense of direction and an American motel with an ice machine. There were also too many foreigners in Dublin, he observed. Niggers, chinks, and spics, same as in America. His granny had been a Murphy from County Cork. After coming to Boston she had married a Kelly. So he had named his two daughters Kelly and Murphy.

But Kelly had wasted all her golden Irish blood by having kids with a Puerto Rican. For Murphy there was still hope. That was worth thinking about. He'd go there next he decided. He would go to County Cork and ask about the Murphys. That was sure to be ow—

Bystanders were helping Fred to his feet. He had narrowly escaped the American Death; looking and thinking in the wrong direction.

IRELAND: 1992 –

'Blogh na mBlascaoidí'
Mhaireadar in aghaidh na gaoithe:
Ag tógáil clainne
I bhfoscadh na cairreagacha
Cothrom idir spéire agus farraige.

'Blasket Island Fragment'
They lived their lives facing into the wind:
Raised their generations
In the lee of stones
Balanced between sky and sea.

Michael Powell

A final flourish of emerald splendor trailed past us down New York's Fifth Avenue, echoing off the cathedral doors behind us. It was the last of the largest St Patrick's Day parade in the galaxy; a five-hour display of AOH chapters, bagpipe bands, clan societies, dance schools, military units and shouts of *Tíocfaidh ár lá* from NORAID marchers. Cardinal O'Connor had smiled and waved tirelessly through it all, a black-and-scarlet icon braced against the March wind, the wide steps of St Patrick's descending from his feet like a tiered pedestal.

'You want to meet the Cardinal do ya?' Don Mullan ventured matter-of-factly after the parade had ended, motioning me to line up for His Eminence in the church rectory. Like an usher, he walked ahead a few paces, directing me to the back of a long, winding queue that was waiting somberly. Among the sainted naves, I gradually began taking notice of those who were returning from around the corner. There was radiance on their faces and bounce in their steps. Small, remarkable transformations were somehow, somewhere taking place.

I concluded His Eminence had to be in rare form to have that kind of an effect, but I also wondered if there wasn't something else going on. It seemed that maybe a shrouded Celtic mystery was working its ancient magic somewhere down the hushed corridor. So often we grope in blind faith towards the certain dimming of each sunset. For once the universe appeared to have some ready answers, as if it were offering a cup of celestial tea, an extraterrestrial bun, and a quick peek at the religion section of the Cosmic Independent.

It would be a bitter cosmic joke if we destroy ourselves due to atrophy of the imagination.

Martha Gellhorn

Time crawled by tantalisingly slow, like an exotic dancer slithering on her jewelled navel. Those ahead of me disappeared around the corner until my own moment came to encounter the mystery. Then I found that each person was entering what looked like a small white closet door, accompanied by the faint but unmistakable sound of water gurgling. At last I understood their radiant looks. I wasn't waiting to see the Cardinal after all.

Far beyond Irish America, no outside foreign influence has shaped my thoughts about my own Indian people as much as my times in Ireland have. What sheer, well rounded improbabilities had been sorted, neatly racked, and then slammed loose to send me careening like a red billiard ball across the bright and fleeting green of the Irish world? In the summer of 1992 Don Mullan was director of Afri, Action from Ireland. He had received a postcard.

The image was of one of my paintings advertising a Choctaw Walk of the Trail of Tears. Don called from Dublin for permission to use the same image. He wanted the artwork to help raise Somali famine awareness and I said sure, to go ahead. Don was also organising an Afri walk. The walk would retrace the Oklahoma Choctaw removals back to Mississippi. The artwork was soon used on T-shirts promoting both of Don's projects.

1847 was the height of An Gorta Mór, the Great Irish Famine. In April of that year the Choctaw donated $170 to victims of the Great Hunger. At a place called Skullyville, Western Choctaw Nation, ordinary Choctaw tribal members were told by an organisation called the Memphis Committee of people who were suffering as much as they had, and in that same year there were still Choctaws being removed from Mississippi to Oklahoma.

Niles Weekly Register reported that the Choctaw, 'the children of the forest', had donated from 'meager resources' what they could to Famine Ireland. The donation was quickly forgotten and the event remained an obscure historical footnote until Don discerned the divine spark of the story as one poor, dispossessed people reaching out to help another. I was being asked to help Don bring the humanitarian spirit of the little Choctaw donation to the Irish world. To accompany each T-shirt, Don had me write a message:

> When my people were forced from their homelands ... much of the massive loss of Choctaw life was due to hunger ... a few years afterward ... the Irish people were suffering from terrible famine, and ... we sent your people sustenance.

Thus, a bond was made between the Irish and Choctaw nations ... As I mentioned my mother is part Irish. It will be a great and wonderful thing if we reaffirm the bond between our two peoples by feeding the people of Somalia. We will be feeding our own spirits as well.

Waylon Gary White Deer

The Irish–Choctaw Famine link story brimmed with solidarity like an arrow shot through time, waiting to land for almost 150 years. On 7 September 1992 I met Don's Afri walkers. They were over from Ireland, wearing the postcard T-shirts. Ironically, the time arrow seemed to have landed at Arrowhead Lodge, a resort then owned by the Choctaw Nation of Oklahoma, and where I was doing a weekend painting residency. Soon the walkers were filing past the gift shop and out of the hotel lobby to trace the Choctaw removal routes.

During the same week the Afri walkers left for Mississippi I said goodbye to the dance troupe I had just put together for the Chickasaws and flew to Stuttgart to do art exhibitions. But for almost three years ripples set into motion by the small splash of Don's first phone call would rise and swell and nudge and push until one early April morning in 1995 my luggage cart went crashing like a drowsy wave against a wall at Dublin Airport.

Since then I've been back to Ireland for sixteen more trips, invited for a week or, occasionally, for months. My last visit went on for over a year. Many but not all those visits have been my part in projects Don initiated. I've seldom been summoned to spend time in Ireland because of my own perky merits. Directly or in the background there has been the small but lingering Famine link between the Choctaw and the Irish, a bond that has moved forward through time.

My first Irish experiences had begun much earlier, in Oklahoma. Where I live one fairly distinct and persistent ethnic group has historically controlled and exploited what was once called Indian Territory through their overwhelming numbers, control of the economy and the inevitable support of the American military. These same amazingly persistent folks seized Choctaw assets and sovereignty in Mississippi and later in Oklahoma. Exactly who are they?

To horse! Young Jock shall lead the way;
And soud the Warden tak the fray
To mar our riding, I winna say,
But he mote be in jeopardie.

The Feast of Spurs
An old ballad of the Anglo–Scottish Border Marches

Not only for the First Nations communities they negatively affect, but also for this amazing group themselves, questions concerning their origins and identity largely go unspoken. Such questions lead like a dimmed but bloody trail to the Irish North. Why does my hometown telephone directory have more Macs than a golden arches franchise? Because successive waves of Scots and Ulstermen settled in Southern America. Protestant family surnames from the Irish North are rampant throughout the Mid-South and Deep South regions.

There are over 30 million Scots–Irish in the United States. Yet the story of the Ulster Scots in America is one of the least known sagas on the planet. To understand white southern America you must know its Irish origins, and then look beyond Ulster to the once dark and bloody Border Marches region, the 'Debatable Land' that lies between Scotland and England. The original Border Marches folk were English speakers after a fashion, part Scots and part English. They remain a wholly unique but also an ethnically compromised people.

Centuries of warfare instilled in the inhabitants of the perennially contested Anglo–Scottish border land a general social profile that ranged from raw bloodletting to a stubborn determination in daily affairs. A precarious existence made them seek the safety of large family groups. These were not Highland Scots clans, but Lowland gangs united by common surnames and a predatory suspicion of outsiders. Border feuds were fierce; the Johnston-Johnson clan took to decorating their homes with the flayed skins of their bitter rivals, the Maxwells.

> They are a people that will be Scottish when they will and English at their pleasure.
>
> *Border Marches official*

The great riding clans were Reivers, robbers who rustled cattle and marauded with 'lang spear' and 'steill bonnet'. Raiding parties 'rode with the moonlight'. When, in the 1560s, the Scottish Reformation hit the Border Marches as Presbyterianism it was inevitable that the new, post-Catholic version of Lowland Scots Christianity became infused with the same defiant spirit that permeated everyday life. Beginning in the early 1600s the English Crown recruited such families to colonise lands confiscated in Ireland following the Flight of the Earls.

Up for grabs was a territory just a short hop across the Irish Sea, in the province of Ulster, and in 1606 the sea crossing took a mere three hours. No longer living along the Border Marches but not native Irish either, the colonisers settled into a frontier siege mentality and became known as the Ulster Scots or

Scots–Irish. After 400 years their descendants still live in the north of Ireland, a controlling majority with British identity and sympathies.

> They are now dispersed, and when they shall be placed on any land together, the next country will find them ill neighbours, for they are a fractious and naughty people.
>
> *Sir Arthur Chichester, Lord Deputy of Ireland*
> The Ulster Scots, *BBC*

Then a century later the English began imposing religious taxes on them while the Ulster economy soured, kicking off an Ulster Scots exodus to America in the hundreds of thousands, with many of the immigrants eventually settling in the South. Most of the new arrivals who followed the Appalachian Trail down into the southern territories were reborn as frontiersmen, and their sensibilities soon dominated the region. Known in America as the Scots–Irish, they brought with them a frontier siege mentality and a stubborn independence.

Once entrenched in the American South, a milder climate and profound appreciation for leisure permitted the Scots–Irish a slower paced lifestyle than the compulsively industrious Yankees up north pursued. Settlers did covet more Indian lands however. To their great joy, Andrew Jackson, whose parents had been Ulster Scots from Carrickfergus, organised the ethnic cleansing of the southern tribes by the American army through the Indian Removal Act shortly after he became president. The invading colonisers lit bonfires to celebrate.

> Wha daur meddle wi' me?
> Wha daur meddle wi' me?
> My name is Little Jock Elliot
> And wha daur meddle wi' me
>
> *'Little Jock Elliot'*
> *Old ballad of the Scots–English Border Marches*

Some of the interlopers became plantation owners simply by grabbing large chunks of lands made vacant by the Indian removals, just as they had in Ulster. Smaller landowners were often cattle herders, evolving into some of the first American cowboys. Epithets used for white southerners have Ulster origins. Hillbilly or 'hill Billy-boy' referred originally to William of Orange, or 'King Billy' supporters who had settled in Appalachia. 'Cracker' is from the English–Gaelic *craic'er*, originally meaning someone who likes to have a good time.

Clogging, square dancing, moonshine, tall tales, bonfires, quilting, lacework, old fiddle tunes and an appetite for religious and political excitement are all part of the original Ulster legacy in America's southern regions. Cracker sensibilities would spice up American politics and business, influence country and western music, promote southern hill country feuds, and perhaps may have even indirectly contributed to the rise of west coast biker gangs, partial descendants of Depression Era Scots–Irish nomads fleeing Texas, Oklahoma, and Arkansas.

A post civil war exodus from the Deep South had placed multitudes of Scots–Irish once more on the doorstep of Choctaws previously removed to Oklahoma by Andrew Jackson, the president who glares defiantly from the twenty dollar bill. In America there's no higher compliment than being given face time on its currency. Seventeen American presidents have been of Scots–Irish descent, including Bill Clinton and the Bushes.

> To anyone familiar with Border history it was one of those historical coincidences which send a little shudder through the mind: in that moment, thousands of miles and centuries in time away from the 'Debatable Land', the threads came together again … Lyndon Johnson's is a face that everyone in Dumfriesshire knows; the lined, leathery Northern head and rangy, rather loose-jointed frame belong to one of the commonest Border types … Richard Nixon, however, is the perfect example. The blunt, heavy features, the dark complexion, the burly body, and the whole air of dour hardness are as typical of the Anglo–Scottish frontier as the Roman Wall … it is difficult to think of any face that would fit better under a steel bonnet …
>
> *George MacDonald Fraser,* Steel Bonnets

Because of a shortage of Presbyterian ministers, early Scots–Irish churchgoers founded or swelled the ranks of other emerging Protestant sects, creating a southern Bible Beltway of thundering sermons and impassioned altar calls that now overlaps like a giant beer belly across the broad western waistband of an extended Mason–Dixon Line. The Bible Belt includes Tornado Alley, a volatile stretch that ducks for cover each spring while massive, rotating winds snake-tail down from tepid skies to suck hapless souls up into shrouds of reeling black air.

Country and western music carries enduring Ulster roots, and Oklahoma has a tradition of singers like Garth Brooks, Reba McIntyre, Vince Gill, Mel McDaniel, Woody Guthrie, Wanda Jackson, Blake Shelton, and Toby Keith; whose song 'Courtesy of the Red, White and Blue (The Angry American)' was released in response to the World Trade Center attack. Its feisty lyrics are well within the Reiver ballad tradition and the tune is now a battle anthem for the American military.

The town I live in functions as a fairly loose notch on the Bible Belt, although public displays of religion are routine. At times there are less laid-back Scots–Irish manifestations, like when the Ku Klux Klan recruited white school children with dollar bills with a toll-free KKK phone number scrawled on them. Or the day of the World Trade Center attack when locals bought up all the fuel and ammunition and belligerently drove around with full gas tanks and loaded rifles. Then there was the Oklahoma City Bombing, less than two hours up the road.

In the Bible Belt today the Southern Baptist Convention is the majority religion, a denomination having no less than fifty-seven schisms. Perpetual sermonising sustains a religious preoccupation throughout the Deep South and Mid-South regions. Besides the standard call to repentance, the other predominant theme of Bible Belt sermons is the end of the world. Wars, social change, Jews returning to Palestine, the number 666, and most major disasters are all frequently seen as prophetic evidences of an imminent doomsday and subsequent final judgment.

It's called the Bible Belt because the thee-and-thou King James version of the Bible is thumped and quoted as pure gospel, although there are as many interpretations of it as there are denominations. In Bible Belt Oklahoma the real Jesus would be seen as a hippie, a communist, a tree hugger, a weirdo, or even worse, a sissy were he to unwisely wander into a revival tent unannounced. But what if Jesus had been a local? Maybe a hard-drinking, womanising, foreign-hating, gay-bashing, right-wing voting, git-outta-mah-face-by-gawd Okie?

Now it came to pass that Bubba spake unto his disciples saying: 'Git outta mah face by gawd.'

And his disciples answered him thus: 'Nay Master, for the multitude awaits thee. Verily they hunger for thy wisdom and succor. Wilt ye not rise from thy vineyard cup and go amongst them forthwith even as our prophets of old stood upon the mount and beseeched the hosts of Israel?'

And Bubba was wroth for his cup was full, and he went out amongst the multitude saying: 'Mah gawd ah ain't seen so many sissies in all mah life! Don't any of ya'll know whut a John Deere ball cap or a rodeo belt buckle is?'

And the multitude answered him thus: 'Nay Lord, for dwellers are we in divers places and we knoweth not of such things; robes and sandals hath we for rainment.'

And he said unto them: 'Ya'll talk like sissies too. Well that figures. Say, ya'll ain't gay is ya'll?'

Then the centurion Gluteus Maximus spake unto Bubba upon this wise: 'Master behold, we humbly beseech thee thy blessing, for many are they amongst us who are halt and blind, widowed and orphaned. Yea, and verily amongst us also are the poor and downtrodden cast even as chaff before a mighty wind. And lo, the Beluga of Caviara and likewise their bretheren the Gideons, they who leaveth Bibles at our inns, all hath proclaimed glad tidings of thy works and wonders.'

And Bubba said unto the centurion: 'Yore some kinda foreigner. Ain't ya.'

There was a certain woman, a camel whisperer, who arose from the multitude saying: 'Master doth thou not hath remembrance of me? For once didst I lay before thee mine own fruits and of them did ye partake. And woe betides me, for mine house hath been rent asunder and I goeth hither and yon, cursed with a most sore cursing. Behold I am faint with hunger and I thirst. Pity me O Lord in mine afflictions, and I shall kneel anointed before thee all my days in praise and in thanksgiving.'

And thus spake Bubba: 'Baby, you need to pucker up an go snag yorself a man.'

Then one Raoul of Coniferous fell down before Bubba, crying: 'O Lord in whose merciful bosom dwelleth eternal succour, we beg thee to look upon our wretchedness but with favour, for also are we of thy flock, notwithstanding the wickedness of our transgressions. Wilt not thou suffer by thy infinite grace our poor and afflicted that they might enter unto thy most high and holy covenant to be made whole therein?'

And Bubba was wroth and said unto Raoul: 'Ok I get it sissy boy. Ya'll is a tryin to get somethin' fer nothin'. Well it ain't a gonna work! Ya'll need to get off yore lazy butts an get jobs. The Lord helps them what helps themselves. Comprende voo, towel head? Now fill up them goddam offering plates. Mah back hurts. Ah'm a gonna go lie down fer a spell. Say, where's that there camel whisperer?'

The Book of Bubba, *Chapter 3: verses 1–9*

In such a wild, uncharted place the book of God was vital, for it nourished their spirit and laid boundaries for their conduct. Other subjects simply had no relevance.

James Webb, Born Fighting: How the Scots–Irish Shaped America

There is no clearly defined critical mass of pure Scots–Irish. Like most other Americans, Debatable Land descendants are a further ethnic mix. What has survived besides Scots–Irish cultural markers and surnames is ethos; identifiable group sensibilities within a convergent historic profile. Otherwise the Scots–Irish observe a kind of heritage amnesia. Their self-reckoning begins not in the Border Marches or even Ulster but with the American frontier, one reason why any tenuous claims to Indian bloodlines are often important to them.

Because the Oklahoma Choctaw no longer have minimum blood quantum limits for tribal membership, the vast majority of card carrying tribal members have only small traces of Indian ancestry and are visually and in demeanour, Scots–Irish Okies. To the degree that any tribal regime controlled by America's Bureau of Indian Affairs can be truly representative, the Scots–Irish coup d'etat of Oklahoma Choctaw tribal government services amounts to a peculiar kind of wholesale identity theft, a biological form of colonialism which could be called Choctaw Ulsterisation.

Chief Jacob Jackson's prediction about the Oklahoma Choctaw has almost come true; most of the folks now registered as Oklahoma Choctaw are no longer identifiable as Indians. Our immediate colonisers, both internally and externally, are now largely a diaspora extension of Scots lowlanders who once colonised Ulster. Yet, despite a general down-home friendliness, the Scots–Irish are still the people of the long spear and steel bonnet. And they won't go away.

> It is a great comfort to a rambling people to know that somewhere there is a permanent home – perhaps it is the most final of the comforts they ever really know.
> Ben Robertson, Red Hills and Cotton: An Upcountry Memory

This is why my journey into Ireland, or at least to Ulster, really began in Oklahoma. Comparisons between the Border Marches, Ulster, and the Scots–Irish in America, though now convoluted by history and circumstance, are inescapable despite prolonged Scots–Irish heritage amnesia. There is an eerie similarity between Orange Order marches and the stubborn kind of patriotism found in the American South, and other cultural similarities survive as well.

In 1995 I hadn't yet been to Ireland or experienced how its faraway historic events had affected where I lived. There would be a prelude of Don Mullan projects before my first arrival at Dublin Airport. But I was also morphing into a tribal bureaucrat; coming in early, leaving late, working weekends. Because I had to wear a coat and tie I was sometimes mistaken for a salesman or an Indian minister. And my desk was always covered with paperwork.

Maybe you've had a similar job that might have escalated until the world seemed to turn into a pile of paper. Thankfully, Don called again from Dublin. Could I come to Ireland? So I said sure, and after receiving permission to travel from my Chickasaw employers I was on a plane bound for Ireland. I don't remember having any notions about misty glens or harps or castles, but I do recall feeling happy about being out of the office for a while. And I remember Dublin shone with fragile sunlight that first morning when Don drove me from the airport.

Permitted To Land In Ireland
28 April 1995

'Those are real Irish bushes,' I remember thinking as we passed down the airport's long drive towards the roundabout. 'Those are real Irish cars driving on the wrong side of the road,' I also noted. I was less certain, I think, about the giant metal spike sculpture that resembles an upturned tack at the airport's entrance. 'That's a real Irish ... whatever that is,' I duly observed. When we arrived at Don's house his family insisted I have a lie-in.

I would need to be rested because Don had a whirlwind schedule organised. What he had in mind was a Famine awareness tour of Ireland and Britain. It would be eleven non-stop days of lectures, art shows and interviews sponsored by Concern Worldwide. We would be promoting awareness of world hunger by telling the story of the 1847 Choctaw donation. I was also asked to be a leader for the annual Afri Famine Walk in Co. Mayo.

My first reaction to Temple Bar was literal; I see the bar but where's the temple? While I slurped tea someone hung my prints across the walls of a gallery. Soon it was time to go, a road trip was scheduled to Ulster the next morning, my first visit to the Irish North. When we arrived we were warmly received by Derry's mayor, and by some of the Afri walkers who had made the trek from Arrowhead Lodge to Mississippi three years earlier. The next day we drove to Carrickfergus.

Andrew Jackson's parents had been from Carrickfergus. I was to plant a tree of peace at the Andrew Jackson Centre, and do an interview. Carrickfergus was solidly Ulster Scots, and the tree planting one of those little gestures meant to symbolise reconciliation 165 years after Jackson's Indian Removal Act. The small crowd seemed friendly enough until a tall, stout, grey-haired man walked over, glowered down at me and began bellowing. His belligerence was eerily familiar.

> Andrew Jackson was a friend to yer people till ya bit the hand that fed ye, so ye did ... aye, an then he sorted youse out, hae ... aye ... och an yer man shoulda sorted out summa thum wee thran taigs ...
>
> *The old big dude at Carrickfergus*

I could have been in Oklahoma. It was my first inkling of the connection between Oklahoma and Ulster. Later I would research the link but at that moment 300 years of separation seemed to merge. Although Okies and Ulster Scots certainly aren't all tied together by bloodline and history and they certainly don't all think or behave alike, overall you may notice more than a passing family resemblance.

The next day we were in Dublin to film with Gabriel Byrne. I didn't know he was a film star. I don't read fan magazines, don't watch celebrity programmes, and, unless I'm dragged off by someone, I don't go to the movies. Gabriel Byrne was waiting at the entrance to St Stephen's Green, looking sharp in a white shirt and black Armani suit. It was a fashion combo we would see a lot of over the next few days; he'd just returned from the Cannes Film Festival but had forgotten to bring a change of clothes.

Gabriel did some impromptu street interviews. The Irish treat their celebrities with the privacy accorded ordinary people. Celebrities in turn don't fear going out in public. Later I heard that Michael Flatley of *Riverdance* showed up in Ireland flanked by bodyguards. The Irish were quietly amused. I'm glad I had the opportunity to get acquainted with Gabriel Byrne before I knew that he was a big-time movie star.

He turned out to be sort of reserved, but extremely decent and genuine. The next day Don arranged for me to give a reflection at a special Mass of Intercession for the 169 victims of the Oklahoma City Bombing. The Mass was at St Mary's Pro-Cathedral in Dublin. The week before I left for Ireland, Tim McVeigh had detonated a devastating bomb that had rocked Oklahoma City, obliterating the Murrah Federal Building.

> My day's work started a little before five o'clock yesterday, when I began helping
> Ed Sanders mix heating oil with the ammonium nitrate in unit 8's garage …
> The Turner Diaries, *Andrew McDonald aka William Pierce*

The cathedral fell silent as Ambassador Jean Kennedy-Smith gave the first reflection. After church the ambassador asked to be introduced, and she invited Don and I over for tea at her residence. Her personal photographs of John and Robert Kennedy were touching. What to me were familiar images of two assassinated American politicians were to the ambassador treasured memories of her lost brothers Jack and Bobby.

We headed for Mayo the next morning. At Doolough you can feel the spirit of the land strongly.

At Doolough in 1849 the sick and starving walked along that same stretch of waterway to Louisburg to petition the British authorities for food and were turned away. As they made their unsure trek homeward a storm blew hundreds into the sea. The round, barren hills saw it happen. John Pilger spoke and I followed, and then a very long line of Afri walkers set off to give form to memory, tracing the footsteps of the original Doolough Famine walk.

Gabriel Byrne was filming a documentary, *When Ireland Starved*, for National Geographic Explorer in Mayo. It was Don who had suggested the Choctaw Famine donation as the film's subject, and we were to be interviewees. For the first time I saw potato ridges from the 1840s desperately scratched into the cold bare rock of the County Mayo hillsides. Old roads trailed pointlessly across deserted landscapes, remnants of Famine workhouse projects forever leading nowhere.

I can still feel them like a sudden cold hand. While we were filming young girls came bounding across a meadow. Why would schoolgirls appear out of nowhere, I wondered. Their bright forms showed surreal against the grey mists. They were honing in on Gabriel Byrne, waving pens and papers and churning up the turf like land torpedoes. It dawned on me; he really was a movie star. When we returned to Dublin we were received at Áras an Uachtaráin by Mary Robinson. The President of Ireland had a natural welcoming grace, and put us at ease.

The following month President Robinson would visit Choctaw tribal headquarters in Oklahoma to officially thank the tribe for the 1847 donation.

Permitted To Land In Ireland
2 September 1995

Five months after my first visit to Ireland Don again asked me to come back. I knew I was pushing things with my employers, but I was to help fundraise for people in Somalia who were starving, as my people once had. I was almost finished with a bodhrán painting which the Irish State was to buy for 10,000 punt, the money to be given to Concern Worldwide for humanitarian projects.

This time it was raining when I arrived at Dublin Airport. I was spirited away to a B & B where I locked myself in my room to put the finishing touches on the bodhrán painting as Don anxiously pounded on the door and yelled at me about being late. This trip over there wasn't a chance for a lie-in, but I did manage to spread enough paint around by the time we left for the official Tendering of the Cheque ceremony at the Plinth. Everyone gave speeches, but I was too sleepy to pay much attention.

Once more, Don and I left for England where we did lectures, radio and television interviews and press releases, all relating to the Irish–Choctaw Famine link, making comparisons between Famine Ireland and third world peoples of today. Two Irish Concern workers gave me the obligatory walking tour of London. After meandering around looking at public buildings, we found ourselves facing a large stone edifice where a crowd was waiting. One of my guides whispered politely, 'Ammm … can ya ask them what the craic is? We … have Irish accents.'

I still get that. I tell them they are the ones with the accent, not me.

Sean McCurdy

Those two never wanted to ask questions on an English street corner, because back then their Dublin accents could have prompted unreasonable anxiety and anger over the IRA. It turned out we were at Buckingham Palace and the crowd was waiting for the Coldstream Guards. Moving between Irish centres I didn't get much opportunity to chat with the real natives of England, the English. The Irish diaspora always insulated me, a constant bubble that made it seem as if I were still in Ireland. It was like travelling with Choctaws.

A Choctaw car trip to, say, a sports tournament or dance troupe engagement may involve several stops with as many opportunities for outside interaction, but such contacts are minimal. Older passengers speak Choctaw among themselves and some of the younger ones do too. The journey might cover great distances and pass through many towns, but in a larger sense it's as if the group never left home, comfortable and secure in their own company and not quite trusting the world that lies beyond the fleeting shadow of their own group.

The beginning of Canadian cultural nationalism was not 'Am I really that oppressed?' but 'Am I really that boring?'

Margaret Atwood

While I was surprised to find that English locals call the Liverpool Metropolitan Cathedral 'Paddy's Wigwam', Westminster Abbey was a puzzle. Over 3,000 prominent dead people are embedded in its walls and entombed below the paving stones, but for some elusive purpose tourists are encouraged to walk on them. In Indian Country such acts would be considered desecration. I was uncomfortable tromping through an ethereal high rent district for dead British aristocracy and clergy, but as a living being the English treated me relatively well.

The communication of the dead
Is tongued with fire
Beyond the language of the living.

T.S. Eliot

These words grace a tombstone, somewhere near Dylan Thomas's grave, in Westminster Abbey, London. In that grey place, the paving blocks are, quite literally, tombs. Somewhere between when you pay admission and your eyes adjust to that dim light, it occurs to you that you are in the middle of an immense burial ground.

Everywhere there are bodies. Graves line the floor, impossible to avoid, endless chiselled names and descriptions, stepping stones to walk upon. Bodies are buried between the walls. Bodies molder between the relics and altar pieces, and under sculpted mausolea on which Byzantine images of their diminutive occupants stare with fixed expressions past endlessly curious lines of tourists …

Return of the Sacred, Waylon Gary White Deer
Stepping Stones to Common Ground, *Alta Mira Press*

I was staying in more B & Bs. In pre-Celtic Tiger Ireland, bed and breakfasts were frequently a voodoo mix of youth hostel and your granny's spare bedroom. At a B & B you could be assigned your narrow sleeping quarters with the toilet down the hall or up the stairs, and with photos of the owner's deceased pets and family members watching your every move. You were also liable to land up to your eyeballs in lace doilies.

If you really want the old-school B & B experience, move in with relatives for a week and ask them to be unnaturally tidy and civil in exchange for a lucrative commercial fee. Some bed and breakfasts had so many cherished bric-a-brac mementos lying about that one misplaced lurch would have resulted in the permanent enmity of the owners. Others were often little more than cells with miniature televisions mounted like surveillance cameras.

The bath, wherever it happened to be, had a mysterious metal or plastic box with a pull-string and a dial resembling a Geiger counter, a device to be fiddled and pleaded with for any hope of a warm shower. And rather than standing beneath a caressing stream cascading from a fixed but adjustable nozzle, you were left with a flexible metal tube to hose yourself off with. That was years before Ireland became much more racially diverse, and when my looks were a curiosity. B & B owners would usually politely ask what part of the world I was from.

In the back of my mind was the unsettling suspicion that some B & B owners might have feared my bath demeanour, me being an alleged native type. I wondered if at times I was half expected to exit the bath naked except for a towel wrapped around my head, my limbs streaked with soap bar squiggles, eyes transfixed from my first encounter with a mirror and tossing handfuls of toilet tissue to honour the God of Perpetual Water, an abundant deity which would by then have long overflowed the gleaming edges of its porcelain altar.

No matter how my morning ablutions turned out, I found that a full Irish breakfast can be especially enjoyable, although some folks think that such cuisine is wholly traditional to Ireland and recorded in the *Book of Kells*. Except for the tomato and black and white puddings and great Irish bacon, a full Irish breakfast was familiar enough. But I had trouble figuring out the takeaway, a literal phrase I somehow failed to take literally.

If in America you want to take away your food you can order from your car into a speaker, then drive up to a window to collect your tacos or chicken or burgers, however genetically altered those morsels may be. Yet optional fiberglass seating awaits inside any American takeaway. Eventually I caught on to which cafes in Dublin weren't takeaways, but for a while I was wandering into chair-less places, buying food, and then consuming it outdoors.

I enjoyed buying things so that I could accumulate solid-feeling Irish coins, back when large punt and 50p pieces made your pockets jingle. It was hefty money that clunked and thudded together, resonating prosperity, coinage big enough so that when you ran it sounded as if you had a wind chime down your pants. I spent quality time gnawing sausages by the street while jingling coins and watching cars whiz by going the wrong way.

In England I'd found that when you're offered tea it's usually only tea, and you won't be asked a second time. But by custom Irish teas are chances to break away with friends or family and gather your hands around a warm and cosy cup, frequently with enough buns, biscuits, sweets, or sandwiches around to make you feel that should a disaster occur you'll have ample carbohydrates and sugar to keep you going. To Indians such abundance is good hospitality, and in Ireland tea and snacks are often politely but insistently pressed upon you.

Someone once made the remark that Ireland would be a great place if it had a roof. That's not exactly true. Ireland has sunny weather, but maybe less frequently than, say, Puerto Rico. In Ireland rain can pile up, damp, wet, and oozing for days before the sun at last appears like a god of light but often briefly, as if hurrying off to another engagement. And everyone seems surprised at yet another soft or rainy day. It's like after 5,000 years the Celts in Ireland still don't want to admit that they are no longer living in Spain. What … rain again? Jesus.

You know it's summer in Ireland when the rain gets warmer

Hal Roach

I wasn't there when the Choctaw gave money to Famine Ireland, and was only being asked to represent the spirit of the donation. But the Irish have treated me well even when they don't know about the Famine link. Overall,

Irish society is nicer than most places in America seem to be, but my looks meant then, as now, that I was often mistaken for someone or something else. Like when Don and I were in Meath checking out a buffalo herd.

The herd's owner took us to his local and soon a woman in her twenties hit the door in heavy make-up and wearing a very short dress. She hurriedly sat down, panting from fast and fancy scurrying. An older guy approached me and asked if I thought she was dressed nice, and I said yeah, which was sort of true, though I was suspicious. Did rural Ireland have pimps? But I'd just done a radio interview. Maybe they recognise me from the radio, I thought improbably.

'G'wan tell her she's a nice dresser,' the old guy insisted. I went over obligingly and said, ''Scuse me, you're a nice dresser,' and the woman smiled as if she'd won some sort of prize. 'Thanks a million, John,' the guy remarked, and then I understood. They thought I was John Rocha, a Chinese fashion designer from Dublin. 'Do you have a card, John?' the guy pressed. So I gave him my friend Emer's number and she soon began getting late night calls from the woman about being a fashion model. I wasn't trying to be evasive. I just didn't know what to do.

Around this time I was rescued by the well known Frankie Gavin. I took the bus down from Derry to Galway, where Don had arranged for me to catch a ride to Dublin. Late in the afternoon the man who was supposed to give me a ride showed up. But he and his wife had just had a huge fight, and after making rambling remarks about how ultimately everyone is alone in a cruel uncaring universe, the man wandered off. I then found out that the businesses in Galway wouldn't accept pound sterling. Suddenly I too was feeling alone.

So I sat on my bag by a bridge, watched the sun sink and, with real intent, muttered my first Irish exclamation. 'Jesus Christ,' I mumbled. I remembered I had a few coins in my bag, Irish money, and wondered who I could call. I'd met Frankie Gavin earlier in Dublin and still had his number. Frankie came right away and took me to his house, which turned out to be an American-style southern mansion. He and his family were very gracious considering they hardly knew me, and after staying with them for a couple of days I made it back to Dublin.

In Dublin I was almost stabbed by an ice cream cone, a strange event which somehow made the *Irish Times*. I was talking with my family in a phone kiosk on O'Connell Street when these two guys began banging on the glass door. They wanted me to hurry up. I ignored them to a point, and finally I poked my head out to tell them to go away. One of them tried to force their way in, and we struggled. He was holding an ice cream cone, and began trying to jab me in the face with it. I grabbed his wrist as if he were holding a knife.

> I doubt whether the world holds for anyone a more soul-stirring surprise than the first adventure with ice cream.
>
> *Heywood Broun*

I shoved the guy backwards, and he and his friend ran off. In its own way, the incident was sort of dramatic, that is if you in any way want to consider that an ice cream cone could be a threat. As I recall, the ice cream was an angry strawberry colour. Over the next while I would bounce back and forth to and from Ireland, Oklahoma, and a dance troupe gig in Florida. After my second trip to Ireland ended, my tribal employment ended as well.

Then I was back in Ireland that November for a painting residency in County Clare. It was for the December show that began at the American Embassy in Dublin, went to Derry and then came back to Dublin. After returning home from Ireland for the third time I finally told my father about my Irish experiences. I thought since he'd been around the world with the US military he'd appreciate my travel stories. He frowned, listening silently.

Permitted To Land In Ireland

6 November / 5 December 1995

His only remark was that if I died in Ireland no one could afford to attend the funeral. OK I get it, I thought. If I die I'm on my own. My older aunts didn't comment at all when I told them I'd been to Ireland, and I think it was because they didn't believe me. To them, Oklahoma City was a foreign country and I'm not sure if their world view ever included the Atlantic Ocean. So I settled in and painted through the cold winter months. Christmas came and went.

When March arrived Don called again, asking me to come to New York for St Patrick's Day, and to Derry again after that. He had another project in mind. Would I be interested? I said sure, and there we were at Iona College once more, and then there we were facing Fifth Avenue in New York from the steps of St Patrick's Cathedral as I witnessed my first St Paddy's Day parade, the largest in the known galaxy. It was there I almost met the cardinal.

Permitted To Land In Ireland

18 March 1996

When you're in the mood nothing beats a good Ulster fry. Sure, they call such a breakfast a heart attack on a plate, unquestionably it's not healthy, certainly even the breads are scorched in bubbling bacon lard, but if you recklessly fancy fried foods, then the Ulster fry is the greased pinnacle of lubricated culinary delight. Like running with the bulls in Pamplona, senseless risks can trigger scandalous pleasures. But be forewarned that an appetite for the succulent taste and beckoning sheen of liquid fat can be a slippery slope.

Quite naturally, the Ulster Scots excel at Ulster fries. Within such shining, sublime creations a disregard for mortality mingles with the pleasures of being mortal, a recurring symphony free of Calvinist guilt. I had my first Ulster fry in Derry, where Don had arranged another art residency for me, sponsored by a community development organisation. It was March of 1996, and I was assigned a flat on Pump Street inside the Derry Walls. I was to show my artwork at the Calgach Centre, then at a new office building which the Bogside Artists sometimes used.

It was also the time of the RUC, the Royal Ulster Constabulary, a mostly Ulster Scots police force, and of British army checkpoints. A military presence permeated the city. Coming into my front door one day I walked past two RUC men standing shock still like statues wearing bulletproof vests and with automatic rifles at the ready. More RUC men stood at the bottom of the escalator in the Foyleside Shopping Centre, and on weekends the army was out on patrol. My Derry residency was near the end of what has been called the Troubles.

Don is from Ulster, and many Ulster Scots there resented the Irish Famine commemorations. An Gorta Mór had far less impact on their population than it did on native Irish Catholics. The Ulster Protestant community prefers its own observances, foremost the Glorious Twelfth, the celebration of William of Orange's victory over Catholic forces in July of 1690. Fought near Drogheda, Co. Louth, the engagement reinforced Protestant and English rule.

> [T]he Battle of the Boyne, though relatively minor in military significance, was a landmark event in British affairs, as well as a continuing landmine in Irish history.
>
> *Derek Brown*, The Guardian, *12 July 2000*

Ulster Scots have been celebrating the battle for over 300 years, which is a bit long to still be cheering. The Orange Order is an all-Protestant organisation that forbids Catholic membership, and its many branches march defiantly through the Irish North on holidays like the Glorious Twelfth mainly to make the point that the six Ulster counties they occupy are still under Protestant and British control. Because triumphalism is what Orange Order parades are mainly about, holidays like the Glorious Twelfth often provoke sectarian conflict.

Overall, the European concept of time seems to have a lot to do with grudge carrying. For the western world, time is a linear progression of repetitive dates. Generally, the traditional Indian concept of time is cyclical. The time bus shows up according to its own sense of occasion, sort of like buses do in rural Mexico, maybe. Within an Indian concept of time and motion, renewal comes circling around in cycles like seasons, or a series of seasons.

I've been on a calendar, but I've never been on time.

Marilyn Monroe

Without repetitively preset annual calendar stops there are no sullen crowds of contentious dead from past events lining up on cue to jump on the time bus. This is partly why I had trouble getting excited over Andrew Jackson. He belongs to a different cycle of time. But if you reckon time to be a bright, straight line eternally connecting red-letter occasions, then the revolving present can become haunted, filled with agitated spirits.

The past is a foreign country: they do things differently there.

Lesley Poles Hartley

Fixed annual observances will continue for as long as there's a Santa Claus, anyway. However, some commemorations are so amazingly haunted, potentially conflictive, or otherwise provocative that they should always be left for outside experts to organise, folks who really know how to celebrate fixed dates, like Brazilian Carnaval people. If Carnaval people ever organised the Glorious Twelfth, the effect would be brilliant.

Colourful Cariocas would bop down the Garvaghy Road to syncopated rhythms, leading a festive parade to the local sambodromo. Instead of guys in bowl˝er hats trudging onward, the observance would be represented by sparkling sequins and radiant plumage. Parades wouldn't be rerouted, only rescheduled to coincide with Carmen Miranda's birthday. Floats and samba clubs would throng parade routes, and samba solidarity would prevail.

But I dunno … it could be that rogue mambo enthusiasts would mount a competing Tito Puente Day, or declare a conflicting Xavier Cugat Week, leading to ugly dance-offs between the mambo and samba communities. Maybe marathon baile-dansa clashes would escalate and then rage out of control, and the Parades Commission would again have its hands full. Perhaps fixed yearly conflicts are inevitable, but it might also come down to how you tend to want to see history; that is, the way in which you wish to reckon time.

Look at me and tell me if I don't have Brazil in every curve of my body.

Carmen Miranda

Those were good days inside the Derry Walls. I liked to stroll the ramparts and look out over the Bogside and Creggan, Free Derry Corner and St Eugene's Cathedral, to pace the broad stone width and length of it all, and there below to go into my flat on Pump Street and out again, and then around the Diamond, through Butcher's Gate, past the Gweedore Bar, down to Frankie Ramsey's hearing 'What about ye hi,' as music drifted out of pub doors and echoed off cobblestones.

But a dark undercurrent was also there during my times in Derry, like a *na losa falaya*, a long black being. I remember a police woman giving Don and I hard looks when we walked by her checkpoint. Shortly afterwards a delivery van stopped. From the back of the van, shots were fired, and the RUC woman fell wounded. *The Derry Journal* deplored the incident, reporting that the woman was a mother and a good community person.

Yet compelling evidence suggests that a covert 'shoot-on-sight' policy was in full effect for assumed members of the Provisional Irish Republican Army; the IRA. If you were only a suspected member of the IRA it was possible that security forces would kill you quick without benefit of arrest or trial. Strong evidence suggests as well that British army and RUC intelligence was being routinely shared with Loyalist death squads. And in some ways I would have been regarded as a person of interest by Crown security forces and the RUC.

Although I was only working on an art exhibit, my interaction and sympathies were with the nationalist Catholic community, and I observed obvious parallels between my people and Irish nationalists. In 1972 after twenty-six unarmed civil rights protesters were shot in Derry by the British army and fourteen of them died, the native Irish again rose up in armed defence against a British colonial regime that had preyed upon them for centuries. The Troubles was a guerilla war, a shadowy conflict that everyone in the North internalised and carried.

> This war did not spring up upon our land, this war was brought upon us by the children of the Great Father who came to take our land without a price, and who, in our land, do a great many evil things ... This war has come from robbery – from the stealing of our land.
>
> *Spotted Tail, Lakota*

You noticed the tension leaving when you crossed into the Republic. No more checkpoints, army roadblocks or soldiers with assault rifles looking under your car for bombs. A sigh, a strangeness lifted from your gut when you knew there would be no more surveillance cameras, listening posts, threats of being shot, jailed, or abducted either and that Gardaí certainly weren't armed or dangerous. You knew then that you were alright, you would be alright, and inside you smiled when you saw again that all the road signs were in Irish.

Permitted To Land In Ireland
17 December 1996/21 March 1997

The following March I was asked by RTÉ to be a guest on *The Blackbird and the Bell* and once more I found myself in Dublin. Then in July 1997 Don landed me another art residency, and again I went to Derry. I'd been asked to paint an outdoor mural on the side of the Creggan Neighbourhood Centre; the Corn Beef Tin. During that commission I began to examine my own political identity. Again, the army was on patrol and the RUC were everywhere, dressed in black with automatic weapons.

The first violent threat I received didn't come from the RUC, the British Army, or a Loyalist paramilitary. As I was being driven to the Corn Beef Tin for the first time I was asked, 'How would you like a bullet in the back of your head?' The question came from a Nationalist teenager sitting beside me in the back seat. The two older occupants of the front seat began laughing. I shot them all evil looks and decided that although it was probably a joke, if I saw a pistol or if the car suddenly sped up, I'd bail out the door.

> Democracy don't rule the world; You'd better get that in your head; This world is ruled by violence, But I guess that's better left unsaid.
>
> *Bob Dylan*

My mural's theme was peace, friendship, and solidarity; an image to coincide with the celebration of the 50th anniversary of the Creggan Estate, and I had to have the mural completed before the Creggan 50 Parade passed in front of the Tin. When Kitt came by I was up on a scaffold working on the mural. My friend Kitt is a well known photo artist from New York. 'Want to meet Martin McGuinness?' Kitt yelled up. 'What are you doing here?' I yelled down, surprised. 'Never mind, come on,' Kitt yelled back.

It turned out that he was in Ireland checking on property. I climbed down the scaffold, got in Kitt's car and we cruised the Bogside. Kitt had driven over from Belfast where he had been hanging out. 'You should meet Martin McGuinness,' he declared again. 'Oh yeah?' I said. 'Yeah,' Kitt answered, pointing. On the sidewalk by Sinn Féin headquarters was a sandy-haired man about my own age who had just managed a friendly wave when a kid came by on a bike and suddenly raised a straw to his mouth. Kitt knew the man, and started to wave back.

Then the kid on the bike shot the man on the sidewalk with a spit wad. And that was how I met the future Deputy First Minister of Northern Ireland. Instantly we became friends. I was struck with his easy-going humility, his interest in First Nations. I knew who he was. And I knew what some people were saying about Martin McGuinness, that he had a seat on the IRA's army council, that he was a terrorist and not an ordinary politician.

> The lilac creature lay silent and unmoving
> As the peaty water flowed over the last of the Mohicans
> Stones were the wigwam in a Donegal river
> For a decimated breed of free spirits.
> Tribes and shoals disappeared as we polluted and devoured
> With our greed and stupidity the homeland of the brave
>
> *'Breac Gheal' by Martin McGuinness*

My clear sense on that day was that I'd met a warrior who after Bloody Sunday had bravely accepted a leadership role to protect his people during an extremely dangerous time, and who was committed, even then, to seeking a fair and lasting peace. Martin gave me a poem he had written titled 'Breac Gheal' or 'Bright Trout' that draws on a metaphor that links the disappearance of the Irish trout to the decline of First Nations.

We shook hands and Kitt and I drove to Belfast, because for some reason Kitt wanted to have tea in the Europa Hotel, known as 'the most bombed hotel in Europe'. After we returned to Derry, I began noticing a shift in community attitudes about the mural. It was rumoured that I was getting paid ten times what my fee really was, and there were also questions as to why an Indian was picked to do the work instead of a local artist. Suddenly the Corned Beef Tin got word that Martin would be visiting. Tables were set up and tea cups and buns quickly appeared.

Community members began filing in and taking seats, waiting and wondering. Martin had driven over to inspect the art. He stood at the table and announced that he liked my mural. That was it. All speculation ended and there were no more rumours or offers to shoot me in the head. But I had fallen behind my painting schedule and I hurried to catch up. One day I walked down from the Creggan to the Derry Diamond for more paint. It was then I ran into the Apprentice Boys march.

> He has Van Gogh's ear for music.
>
> *Billy Wilder*

But I was still pushing a deadline; the Creggan 50 Parade was only days away, and by then I was painting until it was too dark to see. Finally, I completed the mural on parade day, and quickly took down the scaffolding just as the parade turned the corner towards the Tin. Then I rushed to catch the Dublin bus, missing the celebrations. Emer, a friend who was then living in Finglas, had insisted that I be at Tara in Co. Meath by sunset.

People from all over Ireland would be coming to Tara to see me, she said. If I didn't show up, everyone would be disappointed. I knew Tara was once the seat of the High Kings of Ireland. 'Why Tara?' I asked. 'Who were these people? Why do they want to see me?' But Emer was being mysterious. She and her boyfriend picked me up at the bus station in Dublin. We approached Tara in a rush just at sunset, let in after hours by the caretakers. I noticed what looked to be a high mound, taller than Nanih Waiya it seemed.

There were about thirty people on Tara standing in a circle and as we came closer I noticed everyone was dressed in capes and tunics and bits of armour. We ascended Tara and joined the circle. The people were smiling, but a little oddly, I thought. Then Emer's boyfriend invited Lugh, whom he called the god of light, to join us. I didn't know who Lugh was, and I was beginning to feel nervous. Why was everyone dressed strangely, I wondered.

Trumpets, harps, hollow-throated horns, pipers, timpanists, unwearied … fiddlers, gleemen, bone-players, and bagpipers, a rude crowd, noisy, profane, roaring and shouting.

Description of the Harvest Festival of Lugh in early Ireland

A golden goblet was passed around and everyone took a sip. I remembered visiting Emer where I had noticed her pentagram wind chimes and a sculpted coffin on her mantle with a skeleton in bat wings. And I recalled a photo in her hallway of some old guy holding a golden goblet and what looked to be a human leg bone. I'd thought that Emer and her boyfriend were merely being eccentric, or that maybe they really liked Halloween. Then it occurred to me that the people I was standing among were probably practicing pagans.

Were they after another leg bone? My leg bone? 'Let everyone who has gifts bring them forth,' Emer's boyfriend intoned. One by one, people left the circle and walked towards me. I began to feel better. If they were going to give me money they probably wouldn't want to sacrifice me, I reasoned. But the gifts turned out to be small stones and poems. Later, everyone sat around a patio and drank mead, a kind of ale made of fermented honey.

After a few more odd smiles I was driven back to Dublin. Since then I've taken pentagram wind chimes more seriously. Time passed with a few flights to Dublin here and there, and gradually I began to lose contact with Ireland. In 2005 I was staying near the Mississippi Choctaw reservations with my wife Maxine when we heard Hurricane Katrina was on its way up from New Orleans. Just in time, we booked into the Golden Moon Casino Hotel on the Pearl River reservation which had an electrical back-up system, and we watched as Katrina roared by our window.

The devastation central Mississippi experienced was milder than in New Orleans, but power, water, and petrol were out for the region. Trees had smashed through houses and people lined up at filling stations before daylight, jostling for position. Maxine began to put together a Katrina relief effort from our room for the Choctaw reservations. She emailed Don Mullan for assistance with fundraising, and I helped to shape the effort, naming it the Choctaw Hurricane Assistance and Relief Association, or CHARA, the Irish word for 'friend'.

> I also want to encourage anybody who was affected by Hurricane Corina to make sure their children are in school.
>
> *Laura Bush*

With Maxine, I formed an all-Choctaw board and asked Father Dave at St Therese's on the Pearl River Reservation to account for the donations. My friend Ken York raised half of our funds from Indian tribes while an RTÉ appeal in Dublin that Don had started brought in the other half. Hardest hit was Bogue Homma, the southernmost Mississippi Choctaw reservation, and almost all of the monies raised went to buy food for the community. No one had been killed at Bogue Homma but several houses and a church had been damaged.

Then in 2007 I was asked by Joe Murray to come to Ireland as an Afri Famine Walk leader in Mayo once again. Nearby, Rossport was battling a proposed Shell Oil refinery. Maxine and I were invited to a meeting in the parish hall where we saw farmers, fishermen, and schoolteachers, ordinary men and women who were resisting a high-pressure gas pipeline through dangerously unstable boglands and a refinery that could spew deadly toxins into the bay; a remote place where there were endangered species, including the people who live there.

> I accuse Shell and Chevron of practicing racism against the Ogoni people because they do in Ogoni what they do not do in other parts of the world where they prospect for oil. I accuse the oil companies of encouraging genocide against the Ogoni people …
>
> *Ken Saro-Wiwa;*
> *hanged by the Nigerian government for protests against Royal Dutch Shell*

181

On that day I heard how people weren't objecting to Shell Oil refining offshore, they didn't want an unsafe refinery in their community. It was a familiar sounding conflict. Large and powerful interests were in collusion. Local people had stories of the Gardaí harassing them, of Shell Oil hiring thugs to turn them away. When my turn to speak came, I promised that I would return with money to help, although I hadn't quite figured out how.

I caught a plane to the States, went to Mississippi, and asked about the CHARA funds. The hurricane emergency had passed and the monies were idle and dwindling, taxed every year. The all-Choctaw board allowed me to take the rest of the CHARA monies and give them to the Rossport resistance. I came back to Ireland with about eight grand, American. It wasn't a large contribution but worth about as much as the 1847 Choctaw Irish Famine donation would be now.

In 2009 Joe asked me to come to Mayo again to be a Famine walk leader. The conflict with Shell Oil had escalated. There was a growing solidarity camp, beatings of demonstrators, and many more police. Everywhere else many people seemed dismissive or embarrassed about what was happening at Rossport and about Ireland's minuscule share of huge oil profits, the result of high-level backroom deals.

How much is enough?

My father

It was around this time that I met my friend Peter from Dún Laoghaire, a filmmaker with a strange but unfeigned charm; his dog, Boo the Alsatian, once bit a lady in Dalkey, and after Peter's shy apology she not only forgave him but said he had a nice dog. When Peter told me he'd set up an American lecture tour sponsored by three Irish consulates, I reflexively agreed to take part. The other speakers were two prominent Irish American women. I was to discuss the Choctaw donation after *Remember Skibbereen*, a film I was in, had been shown.

The 2010 tour kicked off in Chicago and went to New York, Boston, and back to New York where we had been invited to Irish President Mary McAleese's official events. There was a lot of fancy running for trains, planes, and taxis, with some good restaurants along the way. In Chicago I told Peter about the Choctaw Snake Band. It was a dinner conversation and I didn't think Peter had paid much attention. But when we arrived in New York he began following me around with a camera. He wanted to make a Snake Band documentary, he said.

The next year Joe again asked me to be an Afri Walk leader in Mayo, and afterwards Peter and I began work on the documentary through the summer and into fall. Joe was wonderful as usual and he and his wife Mary Lou kept me busy with side projects. Don and I hooked up in Dublin, and after more than a decade he had plans again to do art exhibits. Through the years, Don's humanitarian projects have greatly increased his profile but he was, as always, modest.

Margaret Mullan is very gracious and hospitable, and when I'm sitting by the fireplace in the Mullan parlour I know for sure I'm back in Ireland. I've watched their children grow; bursts of stop-start images from quick visits through the years. Then Don asked me to write a memoir. Repeatedly. His boyhood hero was the legendary English goalkeeper Gordon Banks. After Bloody Sunday when English troops occupied Derry and many of his classmates were joining the IRA, Don found a common humanity in Gordon Banks through the transcendence of sports.

> We had lived through exceptional moments together; we faced what were for us epic choices about life and death, war and peace. At the same time, we lived in an era when sporting heroes were ordinary and unassuming people whose very modesty was the oxygen of dreams. And across the water, on a neighbouring island with whom we Irish had been in conflict for centuries, I had a hero who could fly. His name is Gordon Banks. From being a timid, fearful young boy, he taught me that impossible doesn't exist. Unknown to him, he helped save a young fan from making choices that had brought too much sorrow and sadness to Irish and British alike. Who knows? Perhaps it was his best save ever.
>
> Don Mullan, The Boy Who Wanted to Fly

You know how it is when you visit a place until you think you understand it a bit. And if you stay in a place you understand it better. But when you start to live in a place the strange slowly becomes familiar and the air and rain, dark and light, wash over you again and again to smooth you like a stone in a river you begin to know the name of. And if you look around with eyes renewed, you still sometimes blink and lose the view. There is an overarching storyline out there about all of us, and we rarely fit the narrative.

America has an Irish storyline that runs through films like *Darby O'Gill and the Little People* and *The Quiet Man*, and maybe through green beer on St Paddy's Day, and perhaps rivers with emerald waters. To these we can add harps and castles and old images of superstitious whiskey drinking redheads who loved to fight and dance jigs and blow up buildings but somehow ran out of potatoes and then foolishly starved, their last words being 'sure and begorrah'. In America if you don't fit the storyline, whoever you really are stays invisible.

In December of 2011 I sat down in Dublin with a well known Irish journalist. One of her first comments was that I could be South American. Hmmm, I thought. I forgot my feathers. She wanted to know my Indian name, since my given name was English. I pointed out that her name was also an English one, and not Irish. Describing my family, I said that they lived next to one another. She remarked that us Indians must like living close. 'Not necessarily,' I said, 'those houses are inherited properties that some now-forgotten white people originally built.'

She was concerned that many of my relatives lived in town, until I told her that I'd raised my family in a rural Indian community, which she felt better about. When I used the word 'phenotype' in a sentence she seemed disturbed, and it's true that most Indians I know wouldn't use 'phenotype' unless they were in a hot game of Scrabble. She was surprised when I said that while painting the Derry mural I felt shaky up on the scaffold. She thought Indians weren't afraid of heights. We're supposed to be building skyscrapers for New York City.

The lady journalist appeared genuine, and I saw she was struggling to see beyond film images and understand. It's an awkward process, asking about folks you don't really know. Most people don't often attempt it, including me, and I admired her for asking. But before our conversation started I'd already decided that I too would ask. My Irish storyline, my times in Ireland, my observations of seeing and wondering are sometimes based on comparisons between Ireland and First Nations. And those comparisons may not always work.

But I remember a beautiful island of thin cars and thin roads before the time of the Celtic Tiger; and then there were big fat Hummers on O'Connell Street and Dublin was an expensive city with building cranes, and dual carriageways leading to almost everywhere. There was a swift economic decline, and now the children of my friends have emigrated, another lost generation out of Ireland, and those big cars can be bought cheaply. The Celtic Tiger died, they say, run over by a Hummer somewhere out in Dublin 4. Maybe that's what happened.

> Yet, in reality, every lie that's been told to the Irish people over the past 50 years has been told on TV.
>
> *Liam Fay*, The Irish Times

Travelling on the surface of circumstance you wonder what really lies below. I'm on the Dart or on a train or in a car or on Bus Éireann to Derry or Cork or

Mayo or Donegal or Wicklow and I look around and see everything as I saw it before, but I know everything has changed. There is fast change and slow change and I think I understand that. But why, I ask, are the road signs in Irish but almost everyone still talks in English?

And why are the Six Counties thought to be another country by those in the Pale? And after the failings of the Church who or what do you believe in anymore, with your children emigrating as you struggle to pay off huge bank debts? And what about colonialist attitudes still embedded in Ireland? And what is Irish identity really? And where are Catholic–Protestant relations going? And what about the Orange Order? And yes, also, how are immigrants doing in the Republic?

What the hell are you talking about?

My father

It was while running around New York with Don that I first encountered Irish America. Thickly concentrated on the east coast, dwindling through the mid-west and then blooming full force again in Chicago, these Irish were different from the Scots–Irish in Oklahoma. Irish Americans were mostly Catholic, most of them readily identified with their Irish roots and heritage, and many seemed preoccupied with actually being Irish. On St Patrick's Day the bars in New York sell green beer.

> I came across Irish Americans when I was working in Irish bars in America. I hated the way they were presenting what was Irish; fake Irish. When I came across people who said they were Irish they had a certain image of being Irish that didn't fit us.
>
> *My friend Maeve, Co. Kerry, Ireland*

Not all Irish Americans crave green beer, probably only a few do. But what may be said of their practice of dyeing the Chicago River green on St Patrick's Day? There is a certain perceived group identity in Irish America which frequently doesn't translate well in Ireland, a country where no one would think of dyeing the Liffey green. Often the craving for an imagined land of thatched cottages and misty glens inspires Irish Americans to visit Ireland, where they routinely buy Aran jumpers, claim county origins and talk far too loudly on the Dart.

Maeve lives in rural Ireland, and says that after observing the Irish in America they seem to have more in common with rural Irish counties, as Irish Americans are 'sometimes a bit racist and a bit red-necky'. She thinks Irish American politics tend to follow local Irish patterns of backing a certain kind of favourite politician, the 'cute hoor' who is slick but effective. My friend Peter is from Dublin, and acknowledges the pride Ireland still takes in President Kennedy. Yet when he's asked whether Kennedy was Irish, Peter qualifies him as an Irish American.

> I don't see the relevance of Irish Americans to Irish culture, apart from financing arms, and their first generation sending back money. They've really sentimentalised Ireland but have no idea of what it's like on the ground. Nor do they want to know. They're not Irish anymore, they're Americans.
>
> *My friend Brendan from Dalkey*

I noticed similarities in cravings between displaced urban Indians and those segments of Irish America who, with nostalgia and stereotype, attempt to defy the Great American Wilderness of Isolation, a generic place without heart or hearth. There's a willful otherness among Indian Country urbanites, a similar longing for homeland that I also sensed in some of the American descendants of an emigrant's Ireland that no longer exists, and perhaps never did.

> Against the dark background of this contemporary civilisation of well being, even the arts tend to mingle, to lose their identity.
>
> *Eugenio Montale*

Such longing has power. We all want to somehow go home again and we would all like, in some ways at least, to be rare and fascinating creatures, if only to ourselves. In Irish America these themes often intertwine, as they do among other groups whose cultural umbilical cords have been severed by mass emigrations. Often among the American Irish, distended memories of an ancestral homeland are inevitably replaced with identity imagining, reinventing 'Auld Éireann' even as modern Ireland tries to disengage from its colonial past.

A Toronto radio show host originally from Galway pointed out to me that Irish immigrants, unlike those of colour, are invisible in most English-speaking countries where the majority of the population is white. 'It's the same reason St Patrick's Day is only big in English-speaking countries,' he said, 'because those are the places Irish people emigrated to.' Maybe if you're part of an otherwise invisible group you may feel the need to dress up, in green maybe, especially on St Paddy's Day, wear a tall leprechaun hat and then dye a river green. Maybe.

Or maybe not. While I was living in Dublin in 2012 I watched the St Paddy's Day parade on television. The crowds were peppered with people inexplicably wearing Irish caricature head-gear; green shamrock antennae and leprechaun hats planted above fake orange beards. On Grafton Street in Dublin the next day, people were still strolling around smeared in green paint and wearing tricolour fright wigs. They look so ... Irish American, I thought, feeling slightly disappointed.

Most Irish Americans have more practical notions about group identity which fit well within a nation where the American Dream always trumps cultural origins. There are 37 million Irish Americans and their above average median income easily evokes an all-American profile. Still, for many, Irish American identity remains a paradox, a cargo cult of mainstream invisibility longing for a communal hearth. Yet, precisely from such longing, a mythology has emerged which allows the Irish in America to continue as a distinct people. Green beer, anyone?

I watched Therese grow up in quick visits, like stills from a home movie. The daughter of friends, she was eight when we met and now she is twenty four. Therese was raised in Dublin 12, and went to Trinity College. And Therese has emigrated. I see that in Indian America. The American government once convinced many Indian families to move to faraway cities for jobs. The programme was called Relocation, and now there is a diaspora, a hemorrhaging that constantly flows out of Indian communities. 'And so Therese,' I asked. 'What about Irish emigration?'

Approximately half of my friends have emigrated in the past four years – that's nearly forty! Quite an epidemic! All aged twenty-four to thirty. More planning to after university ... I think about my family all the time, nearly every second of the day. London is a great city but it can be very lonely at times. I miss them mostly on a Sunday, I always imagine them coming home from Mass, sitting down to dinner.

I know they miss me too and they are great at keeping in touch. I don't like them to know how much I miss them because I'd never want them to be worried. I miss physical contact with them so much, sitting down with my mam for a cup of tea, watching films with them, messing with my brother and sister and going for walks with my dad. I miss us all squeezed into the car, driving and laughing together. They are such a huge part of my life and it was a very difficult decision to leave something like that behind ...

I feel like I didn't have that much choice. I could have stayed doing jobs that didn't allow me to use my education ... I mostly, however, feel confused. I was the Celtic Tiger Generation. We were encouraged to think outside the box which is perhaps why I chose to take a less skill-based degree like drama ... We were told to educate ourselves as much as possible ...

Dreams are not something I invest in too much – so I don't get hurt ... We're working hard, not getting a lot in return ... I think that I'm mostly in shock about what happened to our country. It was one extremity to another and I think that has been difficult to handle for my generation. We are going around pretty dazed because we were raised with a mindset of affluent opportunity …

I feel the one thing our Famine ancestors would be disappointed in is that we became overwhelmed by having unnecessary things which contributed hugely to our downfall. We gained independence in one way, but lost it in another as we became dependent on projecting an image of ourselves across the world that didn't actually exist …

The other day I looked out my window in London and saw a crane busy at work in the skyline. It had been so long since I noticed one. It reminded me of the Celtic Tiger days when all we saw were nothing but cranes building an imaginary economy. I'll return when I feel we've learned and moved on. I'll return when we build a stable future for generations to come as opposed to empty penthouses.

My friend Therese, now in London

Cranes and empty penthouses. It's enough of an image. All the world it seems, is emigrating. Today in Ireland the person who waits on you is often from Latvia, or Poland, or Croatia or a dozen other countries, and sometimes they learn to speak English with a Cork or Donegal or Galway accent. But in Dublin you'll hear them routinely say 'sorry' like everyone else. It's a word used as a phrase that seems to mean 'pardon me'.

But does it really? I once observed a man absently walk into the back of a phone kiosk and say 'sorry'. A bystander who observed the accident was sorry, too. Don feels the word is used subliminally to apologise for ones existence, a remnant of colonialism, while Peter thinks saying 'sorry' really does mean 'pardon me'. The remnant of colonialism idea interested me. My people don't say sorry, but too often we act as if we are. So does saying sorry have deeper meaning?

There are two origins for use of the phrase 'sorry'. You had to show deference to the landlord, because they could be very cruel. And an inconvenient truth that Irish nationalism tends to overlook is that many landlords were Irish Catholics. And the Catholic Church demanded material obedience to the establishment, psychological obedience to the Church.

This combination has formed a quickness to say 'sorry' but if an Irish person does you a wrong, they'll not be as quick to say they're sorry because it means they're culpable, and also because the Irish don't have an absolute sense of honour. It's not in our nature to behave honourably, going back to Hugh O'Neill and his 'disassembly' (to analyse and then rationalise). We've lost our centre and lost our truth. The example would be Irish politicians today.

We don't do verbal confrontation and we don't do verbal truth.

My friend Brendan, from Dalkey

Culture is the water in which language swims. As in Choctaw, a timid 'sorry' doesn't exist in the Irish language. But speaking Choctaw doesn't make you Choctaw, unless you see the world through tribal eyes. Missionaries became fluent Choctaw speakers, but only so they could blind us to our own way of seeing. In Mississippi, the Choctaw have always seen more clearly. And the Mississippi Choctaw reservations may in some ways be like Irish *gaeltacht* areas, places where original language never died.

After Ireland gained free state status, Irish was proclaimed the official state language. For decades it has been taught in schools. You would think it's again the language of the street corner but that's not true. So I wondered, why not? And if a free nation of millions no longer speaks its mother tongue with fluency, what might that mean for much smaller nations like mine who still try to see the world through our original languages?

> Language is the biggie. Language was driven out of us systematically over a couple of centuries. The British media dehumanised the Irish, portraying us as something between ape and man, like black people who were also made out to be monkeys and apes, made to speak the Queen's English.
>
> Since we've gotten our independence the Irish government has also tried to systematically beat the language back into us. I think you can beat language out of someone but I don't think you can beat it back into them. We were made to study Irish for forty minutes to an hour a day, five days a week, for twelve years, but no one I know speaks a damn word of Irish. People don't have an interest in it.
>
> Our largest commercial neighbour is the UK. Everything we listened to since the fifties and sixties was English. People bought into the soap operas on television, and those standards are sort of the death knell for culture. Once you lose the language, you lose the greater part of your culture. We have here the *gaeltacht* areas where language remained on the same land for hundreds of years. People had a stronger relationship with the language.
>
> When the Irish go to the EU they go cap in hand, the rest of the EU speak their languages. Our government has a subservient attitude that seems to have popped out more so recently, but going back to being subservient to the British Empire, it was 'impress the bully'.
>
> What you see in a classroom you can see in a country. You remember that from school, how to placate a bully.
>
> *My friend Eoghan, from Dún Laoghaire*

Irish is my friend Róisín's first language. Róisín is from Galway and after learning English when she was five she went through a long period of being ashamed of the Irish language. 'The reasons why many Irish people still have issues with becoming fluent Irish speakers are complicated,' she says. 'Irish is a gentle, emotional language that was taught forcibly to make up for its decline during British rule.' Róisín points out that Irish, therefore, became the language of revolution.

Associated with the nationalism of the 1916 Easter Rising and the civil war which followed, the Irish language came to represent, for some, an internecine conflict which was never quite resolved. Róisín says that while English is spoken from the mouth, Irish is spoken emotively, from somewhere in the back of the head. English speakers say 'I am sad' while the same sentence in Irish translates to 'sadness is upon me'. 'Watch the body language of television news readers speaking Irish,' Róisín says. 'It's noticeably different from English-speaking news readers.'

English is the conduit of popular culture, of what is considered cool and trendy. I asked Róisín if an overwhelming number of native English speakers in Ireland means that Ireland sees the world more through the eyes of its former oppressor. 'Definitely yes,' Róisín says, 'and some Irish kids are picking up American television accents as well.' Yet, Róisín also observes that the native Irish world view is not only carried by Irish speakers, but by many whose English-based dialects have concepts, contexts, and expressions that are much more Irish than English.

In Derry, interest in Gaeilge, the Irish language, seems strong. Motives there might be different; speaking Irish involves Nationalist pride. There's a movement in the North to make Ulster Scots an official language. Although Ulster Scots is English based, I think it should be officially recognised not as a language but as a *heritage dialect* because within its sounds lives an original Lowland Scots world view. And most standard English speakers find Ulster Scots very hard to follow.

The British army and the old RUC are gone now from the streets of Derry. There's a Peace Bridge that I walked over to the Waterside on, and much of the old tension seems to have diminished. My friend Martin McGuinness is now Deputy First Minister for Northern Ireland and very involved in the peace process with both communities. It's not hard to see changes in the North. But I also saw something happen during the 2011 Irish presidential race in Dublin that made me wonder.

It was during the final presidential debate in Dublin. A woman asked Martin McGuinness how he could represent the Irish Republic when he was from another country, meaning the Six Counties. Her remarks were made while Mary McAleese was still the sitting Irish president. Her Excellency is from

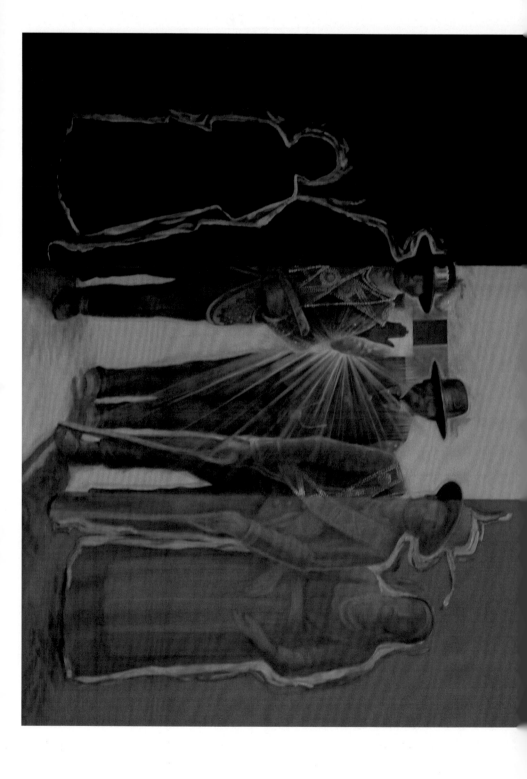

Belfast, part of the Six Counties. It was an expression of an attitude that I've run into often in the South, the Irish Republic, which is; those people aren't Irish like we are. So I asked someone in Sinn Féin, Martin's political party, about that.

> We can't generalise. We in the North very definitely have similar views as Republicans in the South. But you can't separate politics from culture. Even though Nationalists in the North were subjected to vicious colonialism, it didn't have the same effect as in the South. Yet even parish-to-parish, pre-Famine to post-Famine there were differences. Maybe industrialisation in the Six Counties helped Ulster survive. Post-partition did colour attitudes in the South. Dana (Scallon) commented that Nationalists looking south didn't see the border, but people looking north did see the border.
>
> There was almost guilt in the South, although a huge Republican sentiment also. Fianna Fáil had lip service sentiments, becoming a safe form of Republicanism. How can anyone be surprised if people in the South didn't want to be part of the North after thirty years of war? People became 'sneaking regarders' of the IRA; they didn't want to pay the awful price of Irish unity.
>
> It's why everyone in the South supported the peace process. People in the South didn't go North – they were afraid. Afraid to have change, to deal with Unionists if there is a United Ireland.
>
> *Rita O'Hare, Sinn Féin*

Joe Murray made the observation in front of a church building that the Papal flag was flying at the same height as the Irish tricolour, visual proof of a singular identity in the Irish South made of equal parts Catholicism and nationalism. Joe also noted how militarily unaggressive the Republic became after centuries of conflict against British rule due to the strict neutrality of the de Valera government, a foreign policy legacy that is now changing.

As of 2011, eighty-seven per cent of the Irish south remains Catholic, but attendance at Mass has fallen dramatically. In Dublin, fewer than one in five Catholics are in church on any given Sunday. Irish Rigorism, a strict interpretation of Catholic doctrine, was weakened by the secular weight of the Celtic Tiger, but there have been widespread church sex scandals as well which have undermined religious faith in the Republic overall. Still, in the Republic the Catholic Church maintains primary control over public schooling.

During much of this writing I stayed with the Holy Ghost Fathers in Dublin, and at St Patrick's Missionary College in Wicklow. I lived among older missionary priests retired from years of service spent in poor and often dangerous countries. In their company I felt a strong but kind and gentle spirit, generous and encouraging. Some read and pray in languages they learned during the years they were away. They've returned to the same buildings many knew when they were young seminarians. But Ireland is a far different country now.

And the Choctaw–Protestant missionary onslaught has either lost momentum or fulfilled its objective to transform, for aside from facilitating funerals it has led flocks into a Jonestown Koolaid kind of consumerism, the perpetual bottom line of mainstream America. Tribal casinos, and a multitude of less obvious transitional omens now cast huge shadows across Indian Country. Here and there, disaffected Choctaws lunge for the spiritual traditions of other First Nations, even as some Choctaws remain within the ancient circle of their own tribal spirituality.

One version of that spirituality describes a Creator spinning into motion a great circle made of *aiyokchaya* or life force. The motion of the great circle creates time. One half of the circle, the left half, is spirit, and the other half of the circle is the world of flesh. Because the circle moves as cycles of time, spirit is constantly flowing into flesh through the portal of birth, the mid-point at the bottom of the circle, while flesh is constantly flowing into spirit through the portal of death, the mid-point at the top of the circle.

We may also think of the great circle as a thread made of life force running through the cosmos with all things, including ourselves, as beads upon the necklace of creation. A blade of grass, a drop of water, a mountain, a fox, a person, a star, an insect; all are beads in a wonderful design strung together by life force. To keep the great circle flowing well, four progressive conditions must be present; balance, order, harmony and finally, peace.

Balance is always the beginning condition and it creates order, for if things are in balance they are orderly. Order then creates harmony, for if things are in order, harmony follows. And in its turn, harmony creates peace. What happens when a process begins with imbalance? Disorder follows, then disharmony, leading to chaos. Not surprisingly, *alikchi* or Choctaw medicine people are preoccupied with renewing balance upon the great circle and within the cosmic design.

Thinking of the neo-paganism I once encountered on Tara, are there more genuinely surviving elements of a pre-Christian Irish spirituality? Where is the post-Celtic Tiger church? What ongoing effects might centuries of Christianity still have? And what were the causes and effects of Church sex scandals? Everywhere you can feel the presence of what went before, and which may be resurfacing in other forms. So I asked a Dominican priest about all that.

Irish Catholics suffered a huge shock in 1992 when they learned Bishop Eamon Casey fathered a child twenty years earlier and had also misused diocesan funds. Most people were behaving honourably in sexual life and handling money honourably. They found that a highly popular bishop had behaved disappointingly in both areas. Then child abuse by clergy came into the public arena.

At first the shock was very great that a minister of the gospel would abuse a child, which was deepened by how Church leaders had dealt with the abusing clergy, sending them to counselling and then when they were successfully counselled, transferring them to another parish. Since 1996 the policy is that all allegations are reported to civil authorities and it is left to police to investigate. In the meantime the accused priest is taken out of the ministry.

We know from general reports that child abuse is in all aspects of society and all professions. We also know that a priest is in a position of trust and if he breaks that trust there is properly a greater sense of outrage than when someone else offends. A celibate who hasn't integrated his own sense of masculinity is immature in a way that other men his age are not, and that could make them dangerous. A study has indicated that offending clergy are not always paedophiles matching the psychiatric definition, and what's happening can be an 'abuse of power' relationship. We still have a lot to learn.

The spiritual configuration of society has changed greatly, with a noticeable drop in church attendance. Some areas have fallen below ten per cent. Surprisingly, surveys show there is still a high degree of trust in the local pastor but not in Church leadership. There is also the fact that far more lay people are studying theology now than when the seminaries were full, which suggests a deep hunger for spirituality, and that the people haven't written the gospel of the Church off completely. The challenge for the Church is to recognise that the tried and true ways are not working, and to find the way of acting and speaking that will address people's real needs.

What's different about Irish Catholicism is in the first place when Christianity came to Ireland it didn't generate martyrs or raise conflict with local religious culture. It was able to Christen local religious sites and practices. So you have Croagh Patrick, Lough Derg, and holy wells ... there are traces of the gospel in Irish life and they're quite strongly there, even among people who aren't practicing regularly. I'm thinking of commitment to the Third World. Although that commitment is often thought to be related to folk memories of the Famine, sociologists say it is also related to the experiences of having neighbours or family members as missionaries overseas ...

Fr Bernard Treacy, Dublin

Sometimes distant fires are easier seen than flames nearby. Rossport is a small rural community that encircles a bay. A few scattered farms dot the seven-mile inlet and the sea beyond is dotted too, with fishing boats. At Rossport there are a couple of B & Bs and McGrath's Pub, open by about nine most nights. Slanting up the foot of a towering hill are graveyards and down the road, a parish hall and a church. The nearest commercial centre is Belmullet, a few miles away. Like so many places of beauty along the Mayo coast, the landscape has a lyrical sense of isolation.

That isolation has been shattered. A new remoteness has swept across the Erris Peninsula; a palpable feeling of living under siege. Betty, a local resident, talked to her neighbours and found 'a strong sense of isolation, of feeling cut off, not being understood and of being ignored'. She shared some of their comments during a community address in 2012 at the Rossport Parish Hall. I was at the meeting, and afterwards I asked Betty for her copy of her neighbour's quotes:

'When I go and check on my cattle at night, torches light up and shine in my face.'

'I wake up in the middle of the night because a jeep full of private army personnel has landed on my car park.'

'I go to my local church and find the car park is full of paddy wagons and patrol cars. When I ask why they are here, I'm told that's none of my business.'

'When my wife hangs out the washing she realises she is being filmed.'

'My stomach is in knots. My blood pressure is too high.'

'I need to visit my elderly client. A policeman insists on driving me there in my own car.'

'Strangers come here and know everything about me while I will never even know who they are.'

'There is division amongst school children and amongst their parents.'

'I come home at night and the boss of the security firm pulls away from my driveway.'

'Private security men direct the local traffic.'

'I close my curtains so the constant glare from the floodlights does not get in.'

'I have to keep the radio on all the time to blank out the noise from the machinery.'

'My family wants me to move away because they fear for my safety.'

'Sometimes I feel like crumbling under the raw sense of loss.'

> *Quotations compiled by my friend Betty;*
> *Rossport, Co. Mayo*

A massive project involving a gas well to be located in an earthquake zone, a high pressure pipeline slated for a landslide zone, and a refinery built on a bog that may be sinking has been allowed to proceed. Willie Corduff is a middle-aged farmer and one of the 'Rossport 5'; local men who were jailed in 2005 following a peaceful environmental protest against Shell Oil. The incident sparked international media attention and engaged the Irish people. Willie was awarded the prestigious Goldman Environmental Prize in 2007 for his part in the protest campaign.

On 23 April 2009, Willie Corduff reported being beaten by Shell security; bruises so deep they weren't visible to hospital staff for days. He had non-violently occupied machinery inside the Shell compound and was assaulted in the dead of night. Witnesses observed masked security men mingling freely with police while waiting for an ambulance to arrive. The severity of the beating, along with the lack of immediate signs of injury, fuelled local speculation that perhaps the intent had been to skillfully induce cardiac arrest, giving the appearance of death from natural causes.

In the spring of 2012, I talked with Willie Corduff and his wife, Mary, about the conflict. We sat at their kitchen table. Outside, fields were turning blue and hills loomed like shadows. It was rural Ireland; cows and sheep, no evening traffic, bay waters shining smooth and faintly luminous. But from across the slender bay and through the kitchen window came an unnatural brightness. Over at the Shell installation rows of sharp yellow lights burned holes through the cool and dusk.

> Willie: When Shell came out we protested because they didn't have authority to be there, they had an illegal injunction. We stopped them peacefully. That protest brought us [the Rossport 5] to the High Court and they jailed us for ninety-four days for stopping Shell's work. It was probably Shell's way of doing business with local communities.
>
> Mary: Prior to that we had made submissions about the refinery site and exhausted the processes. We were unknown, no media would take our stories, just a few families submitted our objections from day one against the refining site … after the jailing the government had to deal with the community …
>
> Willie: After the 2006 police baton charge at Ballinaboy, the government handed it over to the Gardaí then. From 2006 to now, the police in the hundreds have come in. The jailing really sparked it off. National and international media came on our side and Shell and the government started losing the battle. During the whole campaign the jailing of the five men was the best thing they could have done, although it's hard to say that … whatever little bit of support Shell had, they completely lost it …
>
> Mary: A condition was attached [to the project] that Shell would have to spend so much in the community so they're looking for applications for footpaths and gateways, lighting, stone walls, little scholarships, little school activities,

sending Mayo County Council to talk to the kids about safety when you're dealing with a high-pressure pipeline running right through this community – we feel we're safe with cement footpaths and gates and picnic areas a few metres away from the pipeline – pathetic kinds of things. Shell is trying to buy their way back.

Willie: Our biggest fear is that we have nobody to protect us. I've seen what the State has done since 2006. There's no way we can monitor Shell … the Ogoni people said the first thing the multi-nationals do is bribe the government. After that they can do whatever they like.

Mary: The bruises from Willie's beating were so deep it took days for them to come to the surface. It was a very skilled beating; it just wasn't an ordinary beating. As soon as it happened my brother gave a statement to the Guards and the Guards handed him a summons accusing him of a previous assault … the Guards knew he was Willie's only key witness so they tried to criminalise him.

Willie: They're going to have something against you if you do speak out.

Mary: The media has gotten tired of our story, they want new news every day of the week and our story is an old story. But that still doesn't mean that there isn't opposition; there is. Shell claims that road for themselves and the Guard protects it for them. It's the main road to get to the church and three graveyards. It's been a busy road for the community for generations but now Shell are claiming it as its own road. Along that route, it's some people's emergency exit and there are times when you're impeded from getting out or blocked from getting in.

Willie: Shell is not on schedule; they're almost ten years behind.

Mary: They're way behind because it's an experimental project. Shell never had a Plan B. It's nothing to do with the protest. It has to do with bad planning … our priority always was about health and safety; our community. Our argument could be the next county or the next country's argument. It can happen anywhere. Lots of parts of the world can look back and see what Shell has done to them … I walk into the kitchen and they're there – Shell; the protests. The water carries the sound. We've complained about lights and noise and to no avail. Can we live with the noise when they start tunnelling …

First Nations also face powerful forces intent on exploiting lands and resources. Similarities are easy to see. The Corrib Gas Field is worth an estimated 9.5 billion euro. But one hundred per cent of Shell tax write-offs for all exploration and development costs deducted from a minimal twenty-five per cent royalty fee means that Ireland's revenues from any profits Shell declares could be as low as seven per cent. (*Irish Oil and Gas* [Blog], William Hederman, 3 July 2011) Meanwhile, a non-violent community campaign to simply require Shell to refine at sea continues to be forcefully opposed by the Irish State.

You know, I have a theory about Charlie Haughey. If you give him enough rope, he'll hang you.

Leo Enright, referring to a former Taoiseach (prime minister) of Ireland

There are, of course, older conflicts alive in Ireland, and although religious differences in the Republic remain relatively minimal, they can take an occasional jarring turn. After Katie Taylor won her gold medal for boxing at the 2012 London Olympics she began publicly thanking Jesus, a cultural anomaly for an Irish sports figure. Her Jesus-praising surprised both the Irish media and fans with Catholic-based sensibilities who don't normally profess their faith at secular events.

They [the media] tell us that Katie is a 'simple' and 'humble' girl. Allow me to translate: 'Katie is a great girl when it comes to the boxing. We wish she were more like us and did not have her head stuffed with this simple-minded stuff about Jesus, but in the circumstances we are prepared to overlook this eccentricity.

'Normally we would insist she keep her religious beliefs to herself, but we are tolerant people and, since she is the most successful Irish sportswoman for aeons, will not make an issue of it. Please understand, though, that in our endorsement of her there is no approval of the delusions which she, in her simplicity, insists upon purveying.'

John Waters writing in The Irish Times

Katie Taylor is Pentecostal. In largely Protestant America, athletes publicly thanking Jesus is routine stuff, and Pentecostalism is one of several 'charismatic' faiths that loom like giant neon crosses over the Bible Belt. In the Irish Republic, Protestantism is still mostly confined to the more demure Church of Ireland. In the Irish Republic, Protestantism and Catholicism benignly co-exist … or do they?

What of Protestant concerns not readily apparent in a mostly Catholic country? And what about how Protestantism picks up speed in the Irish North, resolutely marching towards an always fateful crossroads of religion and politics? I asked my friend Andy about all that. Andy is from County Cavan, along the border with Northern Ireland. Although his father is a member of The Royal Black Preceptory, which in many ways acts as an inner circle for the Orange Order lodges, Andy has lived in Dublin since he was seventeen.

The ultra-Protestant Church of Ireland community I came out of had strict Sabbath rules and was closer to evangelical Protestantism, reflecting the culture of a community cut off by partition from their natural hinterland. The political Unionists of Donegal, Cavan, and Monaghan exist in a region where that identity makes no sense. It's a curious kind of border identity that is seen as alien within the Irish Republic. The people were betrayed by partition; Northern Ireland was created as an artificial province, and three counties of Protestants were dropped for political expediency.

They live a curious kind of twilight existence, observing rituals that really don't fit where they have found themselves. They are more hardline than Dublin Protestants, their standard image of Southern Protestants is that they are fairly wealthy and fairly liberal, whereas rural Protestants in the border counties are neither rich nor liberal overall. My parents are closer to the small farmers in Fermanagh than they are to the Protestants in Dublin's Monkstown.

Church of Ireland membership is something of an anomaly. Border Protestants are disillusioned with the liberalism of the Church of Ireland, seen as being not sufficiently hardline or pure; ceasing to be 'real Protestant'. Had my parents lived in the North they might well have switched to more radical Protestant sects but that option wasn't really available in the Republic. Church of Ireland membership in border areas is more retro, my parents are more ideologically close to Free Presbyterianism.

The Protestant community in the South did feel itself to be a community under siege and not accepted as equal citizens. The identity of the Irish State is defined in very Catholic terms, its cultural identity sees the nation as homogeneously Catholic. It's a nation that Protestants in border areas don't really want to belong to. The single most practical consideration in the South after partition has been trying to make sure your children stay Protestant.

The Protestant community in the Republic always felt their numbers would be submerged and they were; their numbers have fallen steadily because of the symbolic construction of the Irish State. For example, the playing of the Angelus on RTÉ state broadcasting reflects a Catholic state. Intermarriage is a second threat. More Protestants will marry Catholics and the vast majority of times the children will be brought up as Catholic due at least partly to the *Ne Temere* policy of the Catholic Church.

Discrimination against Protestants in the Republic parallels discrimination against Catholics in Northern Ireland, but it's a matter of limited degree. Protestant discrimination in the South has been largely cultural, not in employment, housing, or right to vote, whereas in all these areas Catholic Nationalists in Northern Ireland were discriminated against, and they also suffered the violence of the state.

The Orange Order is designed to make people identify with their own repression and their elites, but they get certain benefits. Because it was a Protestant state in the North, Protestants were materially bound to the state through the ideology of Orangeism, used as a glue to hold Northern Protestants together, created and maintained precisely to prevent class politics. It was a way of binding the working class and farmers, your identity as a Protestant being much more important than vocation.

The function of the Orange Order was always to insist upon a cleavage between those who believe in the right thing and those who do not. Maintaining this identity is crucial, accomplished through a huge degree of militarism. The real threat is that the Protestant working class will turn on its elites, therefore, the threat of 'popery' is used to keep poor Protestants in line by designating Catholics as an enemy; using the threat of an external enemy to forge a common identity.

It's a model that hasn't fit so well over the last decade, and Northern Protestant elites; the farming aristocracy, the official Unionist party, merchants, had ceased to be a particularly useful instrument for British policy by the 1960s. Northern Protestants do have a real identity; religious beliefs, linguistic terms and more. Every identity invents and reinvents itself. To say something like 'Ulster Scots isn't a real language', is to miss the point – Irish Nationalism also reinvented itself in terms of the Gaelic revival.

Nationalists are right that, as a language, Ulster Scots is a utilitarian cultural construct, just as Ireland constructed a post-partition state. But if you're a Dubliner struggling to pay bills or have lost a job, ending partition is irrelevant; it has nothing to do with your situation.

My friend Andy Storey, Co. Cavan

First Nations can empathise with a community feeling submerged, and of being given a social image that never quite fits. But are native Catholics and Protestants both feeling a bit submerged from the flood of immigrants coming into the country? I can remember when the Republic of Ireland was almost a monoculture and I was the only *fear dubh* on O'Connell Street. These are different times, and my friend Gerry sometimes feels a bit submerged.

He says that many of the newcomers haven't learned a familiar sense of Irish civility yet, especially noticeable when they take your money in shops or restaurants. Immigrants can sometimes seem brusque by Irish standards, he thinks, and I've sometimes observed that myself. Peter believes that's because many of the immigrants are working at low-end jobs in a bad economy. 'Would you be as cheerful,' he asks, 'if you were in a minimal service job and under pressure?'

My friend Carl says that Irish people are generally accepting of new residents unless they steal, physically harm others, or scam the public welfare system. He offers an example. In 2010, Iceland spewed clouds of volcanic ash into the atmosphere, shutting down Irish airports. Suddenly, thousands of welfare cheques went unclaimed. It turned out that 'welfare tourists' – immigrants still living in other countries – were catching cheap flights into Ireland each month to pick up jobseeker allowances and flying home again at a regular rate.

As I walked back to the car, I chatted with an Englishman, who confirmed that, indeed, sheep are dropping into the oceans around Ireland at a regular rate.

Margeret Lynn McLean, 'Insights on Ireland'

Regardless, I'm not the only *fear dubh* on O'Connell Street anymore. Now there are many ebony and earth-coloured people waiting in the crowds at the lights or striding past the shops and cafes all with a brisk Dublin gait, and even the ivory coloured people sometimes have foreign accents. A lot of these folks are residents now. So have the newcomers found the 'Ireland of a Thousand Welcomes', or at least a number close enough to Bord Fáilte standards?

You'd like Denny. Originally from California, he was pulled in by the expanding Irish economy. Although the Celtic Tiger has since died, Denny is still around; genial, greying and burly; looking American and prosperous with his coat and tie and leatherette folder. Denny relates to Ireland mainly through Dublin which he admires as an international city, one that's 'always looking outwards'. Denny is no American tourist. He never acts like he's visiting a zoo, nor does he make annoying ethnocentric comparisons about the size of Irish cars, buildings, or appliances.

Nor does he wear a plastic horned helmet and scream down on cue at people from the top deck of a Dublin viking tour bus. An architect by profession, when life was sleek and fat Denny morphed into a successful Dublin real estate developer. Although some of Denny's associates still drive Mercedes they now meet in hotel lobbies instead of nice restaurants to talk business deals. But the money isn't there anymore. Swimming against a dark tide of elusive projects and diminished capital, these days Denny the Immigrant often flounders.

No one is illegal.

Graffiti seen from a number 150 bus, Ardee Street, Dublin

Yet there are darker waters than the Liffey that Denny could be struggling in. Ireland is a country where American flags hang from posh hotels. American music and programming saturate state television and radio. And white American businessmen like Denny who live abroad are still more liable to have access to the champagne and lobster end of any local food chain. Sometimes colour makes a difference but, in fairness, sometimes it doesn't. Once, near the top of Dawson Street in Dublin, I ran into a Butler descendant, Lady Who-zit or something.

With sweeping gestures and an Anglo–Irish accent, Who-zit announced herself to be on her way to the RDS horse show. When I mentioned my extremely distant Butler ties, Lady Who-zit wrinkled her nose and declared that I was the wrong colour. Then she flounced off, seeking new nadirs. Not so for Barack O'Bama, who has been zoogered into Irishman acceptability. I was in Dublin when he whizzed by to check on his ancestral Irish digs. Moneygall will never be the same.

> It was the kind of scene dreams are made of.
>
> Dreams a tiny village community had dared to believe for four years ever since they learned of how the world's most powerful man came from within their midst.
>
> Moneygall's finest hour-and-a-half was realised around 3 p.m. last Monday when US President Barack Obama touched down in his ancestral home village.
>
> Spirited from St Flannan's GAA field over to the Cloughjordan side of the village via a specially constructed road and cavalcade of armoured jeeps, the President and First Lady Michelle Obama stoked scenes of frenzied excitement when they emerged on Main Street …
>
> 'The day Obama came home to Moneygall', Nenagh Guardian, 28 May 2011

The media said the President drank his first Guinness on Air Force One en route to Ireland. I wonder if his encounter with the Blonde in the Black Dress was from a can, or if Air Force One had a proper keg stashed, along with some extra craic. No matter; your man's visit stoked even more Bord Fáilte points in Denny's favour, which encourages Denny not to emigrate back onto First Nations lands again, but to stay in his ancestral European hood instead. Think he could start a trend?

Abdul and I met at an art show in Dalkey during Christmas 2011, and he was excited; he'd just found out that he'd be getting Irish citizenship. Abdul had once been a soldier in the Northern Alliance, fighting the Taliban. In 1996 Abdul, his wife, and two small children fled from Afghanistan to Ireland as asylum seekers. Abdul says that for them it's been an Ireland of 900 Welcomes, close enough to Bord Fáilte standards. Post-Celtic Tiger, Abdul is doing well; he owns a successful Dublin-based business that supplies cuisine items to ethnic restaurants.

> I have a business in Ireland, that's why I became a citizen. It was for economic reasons. I employ twenty people from different parts of the world, almost all of them immigrants. I've had no problems as an immigrant. No one's ever discriminated against me or my family. I've had no problem being a Muslim in Ireland. I now consider myself Irish, not Afghan.
>
> My two youngest children were born in Ireland, and all my children are much more Irish than Afghan. Every other year they go to Afghanistan and learn from the culture there … we didn't have a lot of money when we came here but

now we're much better off. If the situation gets settled in Afghanistan I'd spend more time there … people were being killed where we were. We saw a lot of war, and we just couldn't stay.

I've seen the Irish economy develop a lot. At least people had credit before the economy got difficult, but if things continue the way they are going now, I think life will be easier again … as a businessman I'm against people coming to Ireland to take advantage of the welfare system. Attitudes towards immigrants haven't changed since I first came, they are still treated well … if I were away for a long time I would miss the people of Ireland the most; they're so nice.

Abdul, Dublin City Centre

Travelling on the surface of circumstance I was given snapshot images of Ireland, a few ways of seeing among numberless others. Each image widens my vision of people and places I've come to know a bit, one glance at a time. And what I see and feel is a great wind, like the one that scattered my people once, swept over Ireland, and so renewal sometimes seems slow. Gerry says that Ireland is a dreamy land and a dreamy culture and sometimes you get lost in dreams and sometimes you get found, and maybe that's true.

Because you also see and feel old and beautiful cycles returning through new generations. They come in sounds; music, language. You feel them when the land touches you or where earth, sky, and water meet. Still in Ireland are the Shining Ones, and there are abiding spirits deep within an endless green that colours the life force of everyone who walks upon it. Outside my window clouds are rolling in. Soon it will be morning here in Dublin.

Otto Von Wieghorst: Goot day, Chimmie!

Jimi Hendrix: I can feel time flowing backward, Otto.

Otto: Vass?

Jimi: Pretend not to notice man, but we're being written into the past again.

Otto: Or maybe it iss the voice uff time returning und returning.

Jimi: That's a repetitive statement, man.

Joe the Contrary: Goodbye, guys!

Otto: Vass?

Joe the Contrary: I belong to an armed Plains Indian warrior society called the Contrarys. We do everything backward. When we say, 'goodbye, guys!' we really mean, 'how's it going?'

Jimi: Hey Joe, where you going with that gun in your hand?

Joe: Well I'm going down to shoot my old lady, you know I caught her messing around with another man … 'not'.

Jimi: See Otto, Joe really is a contrary …

Otto: Are you two taking zee same drugs?

Joe: Goodbye, guys!

Jimi: That's a repetitive statement, man.

Otto: Or maybe it iss the voice uff time returning und returning.

Jimi: Pretend not to notice man, but we're being written into the past again.

Otto: Vass?

Jimi: I can feel time flowing backward, Otto.

Otto Von Wieghorst: Goot day, Chimmie!

Some days I've never felt more alive than when I've been in Ireland. Other days, I've felt like one of my mother's ghosts. Family ghosts, what would they say to us? What were we given that was lost on our way to somewhere else? In our own cycle of time even the ghosts walk faster. We glance behind us and there are all the changes; multi-national oil refineries, building cranes, tribal casinos. And I hear my father asking, 'how much is enough?' Maybe we don't know anymore. We do know there will be other renewals.

But later I'll take the 15A. Don and I are going to a film premiere, and he wants me to meet Seamus Heaney. We'll move through Rathgar, Rathmines, then get off by Dame Street. The 15A. Sometime I'll look back, as we all do, moving fast into a tomorrow somewhere else. Tonight I'm in Ireland, and tomorrow is a bus stop away.

****

That's my story, or at least parts of it. I didn't tell you everything; half-forgotten moments, further lapses of judgement, secret confidences or darker complaints I wouldn't want to burden a friend with. But maybe you saw more of me than you expected, or wanted to. I know you saw other people through my somewhat clouded eyes, those who my thoughts still hold. And I hope you saw part of my heart; the good part maybe.

So may the god of little monkeys who play checkers watch over you, and give you happy dreams.